Chick Lit

The Stylistics of Cappuccino Fiction

Advances in Stylistics

Series Editor: Dan McIntyre, University of Huddersfield, UK

Titles in the Series:

Oppositions and Ideology in News Discourse
Matt Davies

I. A. Richards and the Rise of Cognitive Stylistics
David West

Style in the Renaissance
Patricia Canning

Pedagogical Stylistics
Michael Burke, Szilvia Csábi, Lara Week and Judit Zerkowitz

Stylistics and Shakespeare's Language
Mireille Ravassat

Corpus Stylistics in Principles and Practice
Yufang Ho

D. H. Lawrence and Narrative Viewpoint
Violeta Sotirova

Discourse of Italian Cinema and Beyond
Roberta Piazza

Opposition in Discourse
Lesley Jeffries

Chick Lit

The Stylistics of Cappuccino Fiction

Rocío Montoro

Advances in Stylistics

BLOOMSBURY
NEW DELHI • LONDON • OXFORD • NEW YORK • SYDNEY

First published in India 2018
First published 2012
Paperback edition First published 2013

Bloomsbury Academic India
An imprint of Bloomsbury Publishing Plc
BLOOMSBURY, Bloomsbury Academic India and the Diana logo are trademarks of Bloomsbury Publishing Plc

This edition published with permission from Bloomsbury Publishing Plc,
50 Bedford Square, London, WC1B3DP, UK

British Library Cataloguing-in-Publication Data
A catalogue record for this book is available from the British Library.

Library of Congress Cataloging-in-Publication Data
Montoro, Rocío.
Chick lit: stylistics of cappuccino fiction/Rocío Montoro.
p. cm. -- (Advances in stylistics) Includes bibliographical references and index.
ISBN 978-1-84706-479-0 (alk. paper) -- ISBN 978-1-4411-8727-7 (ebook pdf: alk. paper) -- ISBN 978-1-4411-9717-7 (ebookepub: alk. paper) 1. Chick lit--Authorship. I. Title.
PN3377.5.C45M66 2012 808.3'85--dc23
2011046624

ISBN 978 93 88002 25 7
10 9 8 7 6 5
For sale in the Indian subcontinent only

Bloomsbury Publishing India Pvt. Ltd
Second Floor, Building No. 4
DDA Complex LSC, Pocket C – 6 & 7
Vasant Kunj, New Delhi 110070
www.bloomsbury.com

Typeset by Fakenham Prepress Solutions, Fakenham, Norfolk NR21 8NN
Printed and bound in India by Replika Press Pvt. Ltd.

To M. Araque, for that support which is not so much seen or heard but felt

Contents

Acknowledgements

Besides the pleasure of seeing the physical result of your toil over a period of years, publishing a book also gives you the opportunity to humbly acknowledge how many other people are also a part of the pages of your monograph. I would like to thank first the series editor, Dan McIntyre, for his immense patience and support over the time during which the project was taking shape. Eszter McIntyre deserves double credit for helping with the distribution of my questionnaire and providing the most welcoming 'hotel' during my research visits to the UK. Two other people helped me circulate the questionnaire far more widely than I could have done on my own, so for that I would like to thank Holly Ungerbuehler and Dawn Matthews. My two 'scanning fairies', Rocío Bonoso and Pilar Expósito, spared me the tedious scanning chores and provided beautifully turned-out material ready for use. Finally, I thank the publishers Pan Macmillan, London, for allowing me to reproduce the cover of the first edition of Helen Fielding's *Bridget Jones's Diary*, Copyright © 1996 Helen Fielding.

Chapter 1

Introduction

1.1 What is Chick Lit?

This study investigates the distinguishing features of the genre commonly known as Chick Lit which, for the reasons initially sketched in this introduction and developed in the rest of the book, I will also occasionally refer to by my own coined term, *Cappuccino Fiction.* My approach is primarily informed by the discipline of stylistics, understood as the interface of language and literature in its broadest sense. To this purpose, Chick Lit is here examined in relation to the linguistic features that embody and project the narrative, sociological and feminist issues, among others, that jointly typify this genre. I also emphasize that a stylistic approach is especially successful at shedding light on this genre's features, and on how it has set itself apart from related novelistic forms, in a way that has not yet been addressed by scholars investigating Chick Lit from the various perspectives afforded by literary criticism. Furthermore, a stylistics of Chick Lit can also help to underscore that the genre needs to be understood in its context of production and reception, as readerly matters are also considered, so my focus here intends to be interdisciplinary and holistic. In sum, this book aims to inform equally about the genre itself and about stylistics as a discipline.

Providing a comprehensive definition of a particular genre, however, tends to be, if not a totally contentious matter, certainly a rather complex one in relation to which stylistic, narrative or linguistic elements need to be assessed and which other components must be left out of this default definition. This unsurprisingly is also the case when trying to provide the series of guidelines that both embody the main features of Chick Lit as a narrative genre in its own right and equally allow enough room for manoeuvre in relation to how these novelistic forms are growing and being reinvented. The considerable scholarly effort already devoted to formulating such a comprehensive definition (Ferriss and Young, 2006: Gormley, 2009; Knowles, 2004a; Traister, 2005) attests to this complexity. In a special issue of *Working Papers on the Web,* for instance, Gormley (2009) has recently put forward what appears to be a particularly thorough account of the genre. She considers Chick Lit an expression of contemporary popular fiction which,

> by the end of the 1990s [...] had become established to describe novels written by women, (largely) for women, depicting the life, loves, trials and

> tribulations of their predominantly young, single, urban, female protagonists. As Joanne Knowles (2004a: 2) writes, whilst plotlines are variable, chick lit can be internally defined by the structure of a female central character 'seeking personal fulfilment in a romance-consumer-comedic vein'. Furthermore, as Rosalind Gill and Elena Herdieckerhoff (2006: 488) point out, by the end of the last decade of the twentieth century, the genre of chick lit was also identifiable by the establishment of 'clearly marked jacket designs'. Indeed, chick lit's bold, pink or pastel-coloured covers with cursive fonts and line drawings of handbags or shoes seem ubiquitous, at least in the U.K., gracing the shelves of bookstores, supermarkets, railway station and airport shops.
>
> (Gormley, 2009)

Gormley's definition is exhaustive and comprises what could be considered the major 'pillars' of the genre. The first characterizing trait refers to the gender of both the prototypical author and the reader, as Chick Lit is generally acknowledged to be primarily written 'by women and (largely) for women' (Gormley, 2009). It certainly seems to be the case that the target consumers that authors (and publishers) generally have in mind for Chick Lit are female, despite the fact that when ascertaining the actual demographics of a particular readership the publishing industry would tend to avoid the total exclusion of any population group, in this case male readers.[1] Gender specification also applies in relation to the authors themselves. A quick scan of some of the prototypical representatives and best-selling authors of Chick Lit, for instance, reveals names such as Helen Fielding, Jenny Colgan and Sophie Kinsella, among countless others. The true identity of these female writers, however, is not always immediately transparent as even those authors identified as female occasionally write under an, albeit also female, pseudonym, such as Sophie Kinsella whose real name is Madeleine Wickham. In addition and most interestingly, there are also some male authors who have recently started publishing books with a female readership as target audience but who have done so by using a female *nom de plume*, such as Chris Dyer (real name Christopher Santos) author of *Wanderlust: A Novel of Sex and Sensibility* (2003) and *The Loves of a D-Girl: A Novel of Sex, Lies and Script Development* (2005), and Alex Coleman, real name Damien Owens, who in 2008 published *The Bright Side.* Although both names, *Chris* and *Alex,* seem to have been purposefully chosen as sufficiently ambiguous so that the gender of the writer is left unresolved, the fact that these two authors' works adhere, for the most part, to some of the basic tenets of Chick Lit forms would, at least in principle, determine that most readers might not even question the identity of these authors as female. Having said that, the overwhelming majority of Chick Lit writers and readers is female.

For the description of the second foundational component of Chick Lit, Gormley (2009) relies on Knowles's assessment concerning the prototypical characterization of the genre's protagonist who is, as is the case for writers and readers of the genre, primarily identified by being female; additionally, she is also defined as a very specific type of woman who is 'seeking fulfilment in a romance-consumer-comedic vein' (Knowles, 2004a: 2). The stereotypical Chick Lit protagonist would, therefore, be interested in happily resolving her quest for a prince charming, in the context of a consumer society which not only invites but even urges these protagonists to overspend, all of it framed as comedy which tends to make light of some of the rather 'serious' themes developed in some of these works.

The third major characteristic of the genre flagged up by Gormley (2009), this time echoing work by Gill and Herdieckerhoff (2006), is the type of 'clearly marked jacket designs' (Gill and Herdieckerhoff, 2006: 488) that are virtually always exploited as the first point of contact between readers and works. Colour, typographical design, layout and images of objects reminiscent of the consumer culture these characters are immersed in are semiotic resources other than the writing itself that, nonetheless, have ended up forming an integral part of the prototypical image of Chick Lit as a genre; in fact, it could be argued that these semiotic resources now stereotypically characterize these novels to such an extent that the reader will identify and clearly distinguish books belonging in this genre even before she has had a chance to familiarize herself with the narrative.

The 'eureka moment', therefore, occurred when authors and the industry in general identified all of these components and the final generic formula on which most Chick Lit novels are based was successfully put together: author, reader and protagonist are female, with the latter living in a markedly consumerist society in which she thrives; additionally, the original Chick Lit novels tend to prefer a woman who is white, middle-class, heterosexual, young and single. This woman also has some idealistic romantic aspirations and beliefs which often give rise to comedic moments; comedy, in turn, is further exploited as a means to disguise this protagonist's shortcomings and some of her many flaws as well as to downplay the general vicissitudes of her life. Finally, the physical packaging of these novels uniformly links the genre in the way particular semiotic resources are exploited. As explained below, this formula has by now been subjected to quite a few reworkings, so much so that some of the most recent offshoots might only have some generic aspects in common with the original, the clearest of them being the fact that these novels are, by and large, still written by women and for women.

A further aspect that scholars, critics and even journalists tend to discuss in relation to Chick Lit is the exorbitant sales and subsequent profitable figures emerging from the genre as an industry. As Gormley (2009) states:

> In 2002 chick lit sales in the U.S. grossed 71 million dollars and by 2005, the *Wall Street Journal* quoted figures predicting that sales of chick lit in America that year would total around $137 million (Ferriss and Young, 2006; Trachtenberg, 2005). [...] Sales figures for individual chick lit authors equally attest to the popularity of chick lit; for example, whilst the 'average'

> novel sells approximately 5000 copies (Chambers, 2004), in 2005 Marian Keyes was placed in the top five of UK *The Bookseller's Top 100,* with her novel *The Other Side of the Story* (2004) having sold 488,508 copies during 2005, and in *The Bookseller's Top 100* for 2007, Marian Keyes reached third place, with her novel *Anybody Out There?* (2006) having sold 585,026 copies (Stone, 2008; see also Pérez-Serrano, this issue).
>
> (Gormley, 2009)

Some people, however, have challenged whether this financial success will be tenable for very much longer or even whether it still, in fact, applies, as the demise of the genre has been repeatedly announced (Thomas, 2002).[2] Only the perspective afforded by time will provide an answer to the question of whether Chick Lit as a genre has already peaked and is in decline, or whether we are simply witnessing a reinvention of the original formula.

1.2 A Brief History of Chick Lit

A brief history of Chick Lit needs to consider where the origins of the term itself might lie. Although there is no agreement concerning who coined the term or where it was first used, there are a couple of convincing claims that most scholars tend to accept. Yardley (2006), for instance, suggests that Chick Lit as a label followed that of 'city girls books' (2006: 3); the latter label was given to a particular line of novels published by Harlequin as they were being written under an umbrella set of common characteristics which differed from the prototypical romances generally appearing in Harlequin publications (see below for more on the commonalities, overlaps and dissimilarities between these two forms). Mazza (2006), however, maintains that the way the term was originally conceived stands in stark contrast with the way it has been subsequently employed and generally embraced. According to Mazza (2006: 18), Chick Lit was chosen as part of the title for an edited collection published by herself and Jeffrey DeShell (Mazza and DeShell, 1995); the main aim of that collection, Mazza explains, was to bring together writings by contemporary women that reflected the different way in which females were reacting to previous feminist tenets, as these principles of the past simply did not apply to the contextual circumstances of the time any longer. The result was a collection of short stories which were

> [...] simultaneously courageous and playful; frank and wry; honest, intelligent, sophisticated, libidinous, unapologetic, and overwhelmingly emancipated. Liberated from *what*? The grim anger that feminists had told us ought to be our pragmatic stance in life. [...] Liberated to *do* what? To admit we're part of the problem. How empowering could it be to be *part* of the problem instead of just a victim of it? I can't remember the titles we

> rejected, but the one we ultimately chose encompassed all of the above: *Chick-Lit: Postfeminist Fiction.*
>
> (Mazza, 2006: 18)

The main justification behind that label, Mazza continues, was to highlight a primarily sardonic intent by choosing precisely a term that had traditionally been used to describe women derisively. The ironic consequence of that choice, however, was that the label was eventually used to refer to forms of writing that reflect virtually the opposite concerns to those the original collection, *Chick-Lit: Postfeminist Fiction* (1995), intended to portray and celebrate:

> This was the ironic intention of our title: not to embrace an old frivolous or coquettish image of women but to take responsibility for our part in the damaging, lingering stereotype. [...] What we couldn't anticipate was that less than ten years later our tag would be greasing the commercial book industry machine. [...] Somehow chick lit had morphed into books flaunting pink, aqua, and lime covers featuring cartoon figures of long-legged women wearing stiletto heels.
>
> (Mazza, 2006: 18)

Mazza goes on to explain that an article first published in the *New Yorker* (Wolcott, 1996), subsequently followed by some reviews of their collection (Royle, 1996), somehow encoded the 'new' take on Chick Lit which encompassed all that is now accepted as representing the prototypical format of the genre. Mazza concludes by stating that the label, as it is used nowadays, abandoned the post-feminist claims proposed in their collection; this assertion, however, is contested by current scholars (as discussed in Chapter 4) as post-feminist issues are still addressed, although perhaps in ways distinct from those originally suggested in *Chick-Lit: Postfeminist Fiction.*

There appears to be more agreement in relation to which novel sparked off this trend as well as the 'nationality' of that initial work. Most studies (Ferriss and Young, 2006; Gill and Herdieckerhoff, 2006; Gormley, 2009; Modleski, 2008; Yardley, 2006) trace the origins of the genre back to the publication of *Bridget Jones's Diary* (1996) by British author Helen Fielding:[3]

> In the beginning, there was Bridget. That's not entirely true – there were Chick Lit books in circulation in England for some time before anyone realized a trend was starting – but by all accounts, the Chick Lit wave started with a British invasion, spearheaded by one plucky young 'singleton' by the name of Bridget Jones.
>
> (Yardley, 2006: 6)

Nowadays, Fielding's novel tends to be acknowledged as the first embodiment of the prototypical features of the genre, which does not imply that there were no predecessors or even contemporaneous publications. For instance,

Yardley (2006: 7) calls Marian Keyes the 'godmother of Chick Lit' and claims that *Watermelon* (1996) was already creating considerable interest in Ireland by the time *Bridget Jones's Diary* appeared in Britain. Mazza (2006: 25, quoting Laura Miller [2004] from the *New York Times Book Review*; see also Modleski, 2008: xxvi) goes further back in time and suggests that Erica Jong's *Fear of Flying* (1973) already contained some of the elements we now find in prototypical Chick Lit novels, such as the confessional style, the flawed young woman and the comedy component. Even further back in time, of course, most scholars name the influential role of Jane Austen's novels, especially on Helen Fielding's work. Although the part played by these predecessors needs to be rightfully acknowledged, the genre's precursors now appear to be only tangentially related to Chick Lit, primarily because these novels have tended to be seen in isolation and not as part of a specific narrative genus.

One immediate and recurrent effect of the consolidation of these novels as a narrative genre in its own right has been the amount of negative, sometimes plainly derogatory publicity that the genre has received. Most famously, Beryl Bainbridge dismisses such novels as 'froth':

> 'It is a froth sort of thing. What is the point in writing a whole novel about it?' she asked BBC Radio 4's *Today* programme during a discussion between women writers. 'As people spend so little time reading, it is a pity they perhaps can't read something a bit deeper, a bit more profound, something with a bit of bite to it.'
>
> (Bainbridge, 2001; see also Ezard, 2001)

Doris Lessing (2001; see also Ezard, 2001) similarly expresses her disappointment with the genre:

> Literary grandee Doris Lessing agreed with Bainbridge's verdict on chick lit, asking why women write such 'instantly forgettable' books. 'It's a pity that so many young women are writing like that. I wonder if they are just writing like this because they think they are going to get published,' she said.
>
> 'It would be better, perhaps, if they wrote books about their lives as they really saw them and not these helpless girls, drunken, worrying about their weight and so on.'
>
> (Lessing, 2001)

Conversely, the genre has also spurred plenty of sympathy, not simply from its practitioners but from other established and respected authors, among them Jeanette Winterson who, in 2001, was quoted as follows:

> 'I am unashamedly high art,' she said. 'There is such a thing and we need it in our lives. But I also like entertainment. Chick lit? No problem. *Bridget Jones's Diary*? Love it, just great. I feel completely easy with all that.'
>
> (Winterson, quoted in Allen, 2001)

Nevertheless, most instances of the defence or, at least, of the recognition of some of the merits of the genre have appeared in reviews and articles in the press (Evans, 2009; Jones, 2008) and in some scholarly work (Konchar Farr, 2009). What seems apparent from all of this debate is that Chick Lit novels are still sparking as much controversy now as when they first appeared on the publishing scene.

1.3 Chick Lit, Romance and Romantic Fiction

Chick Lit is sometimes seen as a revamped version, a rebranding, or (for some) simply a renaming, of other more traditional forms of popular writing, namely romance or romantic fiction. These terms are not always used synonymously either, so providing a clear-cut definition of where the boundaries for each 'sub-genre' lie (if, indeed, romance and romantic fiction are to be understood as such) could be seen as a contestable matter. For instance, the origins of the term 'romance' remain lodged in narratives detailing heroic tales and sagas, on the one hand, while also referring to stories of a particularly marked sentimental nature, on the other. It is the latter meaning that Chick Lit is associated with. As is the case with Chick Lit proper, some scholars have taken issue with this form of popular fiction, more often than not in an attempt to debase its worth or merits. As Hollows states, 'Many literary critics regarded romantic fiction as the ultimate example of the trivial and dangerous fantasies which characterised a mass culture produced for mindless, passive consumers' (Hollows, 2000: 68; see also Dixon, 1999, and Selinger, 2007[4]). But despite the negative assessment of the genre made by some, its popularity has not waned and some studies (particularly feminist) that initially viewed these works in a derogatory light have subsequently re-evaluated their positions:

> The chapters which make up this book [...] represent an enquiry into why romance retains such a hold in the postmodern world. Neither intellectual nor political scepticism seems to save anyone – feminists included – from succumbing to its snares. We may (as individuals, as communities, as nations) no longer believe in love, but we still fall for it. [...] [This book] goes some way to explaining why romance is unlikely to go away.
>
> (Pearce and Stacey, 1995: 12)

What follows is an attempt to understand whether romance and romantic fiction are indeed sub-genres that need to be acknowledged as clear and distinct from Chick Lit, or whether their commonalities simply turn the latter into a 'rewrite of the romance' (Gill and Herdieckerhoff, 2006) whichever way that concept is, in turn, to be understood.

Paizis's *Love and the Novel: The Poetics and Politics of Romantic Fiction* (1998a), for example, illustrates the way in which scholarly work tentatively attempts to explain the distinction between romance and romantic fiction outlined above:

> The terms romantic fiction and romance can mean many things, both diachronically and synchronically; […] Here I use the terms in their narrow sense, to mean those contemporary love stories published in series and known in the trade as category romances or simply romances. These books are so known because they privilege a standardised format, length and appearance rather than sell themselves as 'individual' or 'unique' books. At present, they are published most famously by Mills & Boon in Britain and by Harlequin and Silhouette in North America.
>
> (Paizis, 1998a: 182)

Paizis (1998a) underscores a series of features that most analysts agree on as being illustrative of the romance/romantic fiction genre. On the one hand, a diachronic consideration of the term 'romance', strictly speaking, stretches as far back as Grecian times (Regis, 2003) and refers to narratives that contain heroic, fantastical or supernatural deeds, sagas and tales. This sense of the romance, however, is mostly discarded in the way modern romantic fiction is conceptualized and, hence, any possible interconnections between romance and Chick Lit leave out, for the most part, these references to the heroic tales of the past in favour of distinct contemporary components. Paizis (1998a) focuses, instead, on 'the narrow sense' of the terms romance and romantic fiction whereby he analyses contemporary novels that primarily pursue the satisfactory and happy development of a romantic relationship. Paizis (1998a) further emphasizes the fact that these works are to be confined to appear as part of a series and to follow a pre-established format. The fact that Paizis initially uses the label 'romantic fiction' in the title of his book, but subsequently employs 'romance' and 'romantic fiction' indistinctively to refer to the same type of novels, seems symptomatic of the lack of clarification regarding what actually distinguishes these forms; in fact, it could be said that Paizis either simply merges the two categories under just one, or perhaps misnames some of the references to romance or romantic fiction respectively.

The Romance Writers of America association, on the other hand, stays clear of providing a clear-cut definition that could dissipate any doubts concerning the boundaries of each form, and focuses, instead, on identifying which components a 'romance novel' is known to include:

> Two basic elements comprise every romance novel: a central love story and an emotionally-satisfying and optimistic ending.
>
> A Central Love Story – In a romance novel, the main plot centers around two individuals falling in love and struggling to make the relationship work. […]
>
> An Emotionally-Satisfying and Optimistic Ending – Romance novels are based on the idea of an innate emotional justice – the notion that good people in the world are rewarded and evil people are punished […]
>
> Once the central love story and optimistic-ending criteria are met, a romance novel can be set anywhere and involve any number of plot

elements. These settings and distinctions of plot create specific subgenres within romance fiction.

(Romance Writers of America, http://www.rwanational.org/cs/the_romance_genre)

For as long as the love story, acting as the backbone of the narrative, results in the satisfactory emotional resolution of whatever complications arise in the plot, it seems the objectives of the romance novel are met, for its two main components have been successfully included. A further aspect that tends to be investigated by those interested in romance and romantic fiction concerns the possible variants and categories that the genre has evolved into. The Romantic Novelists Association, for instance, appears to be rather accommodating in this respect:

> Romantic fiction is the cross-genre genre. In the UK it appears under a variety of publishers' labels including general fiction, women's fiction, historical, romantic comedy, chick lit, sagas – even spooky – as well as romance. [...] It embraces Jilly Cooper's 900 pages as well as the 187 Harlequin Mills & Boon category romances which are published every month; multi-generational sagas and Regency romps; deeply serious meditations on life and flippant twenty-somethings' metropolitan shenanigans. The engine of romantic fiction is love and relationships. The bodywork is infinitely variable.
>
> (Romantic Novelists' Association, http://www.rna-uk.org/index.php?page=romanticfiction)

If such an assessment is valid, the only compulsory component in romantic fiction is, once more, the existence of a love connection between some of the characters in the story, that is, the structural feature that defines the genre appears to be solely plot-based. Were 'plot' to be accepted as the defining constituent, though, I would argue that the classification above presents some confusing facts regarding the possible labelling of the different narrative variants also mentioned in this definition. For instance, despite the fact that romantic fiction, romance and even Chick Lit all deal with the similar unravelling of a romantic relationship, the above quotation names the three forms as separate but, nonetheless, still somehow part of this 'cross-genre genre' called romantic fiction; as a definition and taxonomical classification of its different forms, it seems to me, this is rather convoluted. Furthermore, if romance, romantic fiction and Chick Lit are to be understood as related but distinct categories, the above quotation fails to explain what such similarities and distinctions entail.

The Romance Writers of America also provide a taxonomy for these novels, but they select book-length and publication-regularity as the basis for their distinction:

> There are two formats for romance fiction:
>
> Series or 'category' romances – shorter romances that are released in

> order and by month, with a series number on each title. These books are most commonly published by Harlequin/Silhouette.
>
> Single-title romances – longer romances released individually and not as part of a numbered series.
>
> (Romance Writers of America, http://www.rwanational.org/cs/the_romance_genre)

This new component in the categorization of romantic fiction suggests that plot-based features do not solely provide the basis for a comprehensive definition, as decisions concerning the books' publication – as part of a series, or as an individual volume – can also determine the grouping of novels under one label or another. Regis (2003), finally, echoes some of the assessments above but additionally pinpoints some specifics related to the prototypical structure of the novels:

> The romance novel is a work of prose fiction that tells the story of the courtship and betrothal of one or more heroines. All romance novels contain eight narrative elements: *a definition of society*, always corrupt, that the romance novel will reform; the *meeting* between the heroine and hero; an account of their *attraction* for each other; the *barrier* between them; the *point of ritual death*; the *recognition* that fells the barrier; the *declaration* of heroine and hero that they love each other; and their *betrothal*.
>
> (Regis, 2003: 14)

Regis's identification of the eight components that necessarily compose the archetypal romance still appears to rely heavily, if not solely, on the narrative structure of these works following a particular pattern. Regis also traces the origins of romance back to canonical works such as Samuel Richardson's *Pamela* (1740), Jane Austen's *Pride and Prejudice* (1813), Charlotte Brontë's *Jane Eyre* (1847) and E. M. Foster's *A Room with a View* (1908), which would bring to the fore the diachronic understanding of the term highlighted above by Paizis (1998a; see also Dixon, 1999). In relation to Chick Lit, some scholars have pointed out the obvious influence of historical romance understood in a strict diachronic sense, as certain aspects of the characteristic nineteenth-century romance novel are still evoked:

> So, while *Bridget Jones* is punctuated by 'ladette' episodes in which Bridget, Shazzer and Jude get spectacularly and publicly drunk, the narrative follows the old romance-plot of *Pride and Prejudice* with great fidelity.
>
> (Hanson, 2004: 18)

Therefore, attempting to provide a definition of exactly what the terms romance and romantic fiction refer to, and trying to suggest a plausible taxonomy of their variants, as well as their connection to Chick Lit, is a complex matter. To avoid this terminological confusion, I will be using the terms romance and romantic fiction indistinctively in this introductory chapter, irrespective of whether I am referring to the serial forms prototypically published by Harlequin and Mills and Boon or to individual works such as those of Georgette Heyer, Mary Stewart, Janet Dailey, Jayne Ann Krentz or Nora Roberts (Regis, 2003: 107), for instance. Chapter 4, nonetheless, takes on this challenge again to investigate the differences and commonalities between these otherwise closely-linked popular fiction realizations; the focus in that chapter is mainly linguistic, which is a perspective that scholarly work has somehow neglected (for exceptions see Ryder, 1999, and Wareing, 1994). In this introduction, I aim my attention primarily at Chick Lit so I look for those non-linguistic aspects of agreement with, as well as separation from, romances to see whether Chick Lit can be set apart as a popular fiction variant in its own right.

As far as the similarities between romances and Chick Lit go, the most immediately obvious meeting point is the gender of authors and readers, as both forms are still being written fundamentally by females for females. Since this tenet is understood as a given, scholars sometimes neglect to summon it as the basic preliminary that sets these two forms apart from other realizations of popular fiction such as sci-fi, thrillers or crime fiction.[5] Furthermore, the prototypical feminine nature of both the producers and the consumers of the genre most importantly implies a stereotypical feminization of the themes, topics and ideals presented in the novels, for which romantic fiction, in particular, has been accused of simply perpetuating some firmly established old patriarchal values (Dixon, 1999: 3; see also Radway, 1991). Second, both formats also share the 'mass culture' gene, as they are primarily produced and marketed as popular fiction, so saleability is of utmost relevance. In third place, and most significantly, romantic fiction and Chick Lit partake of the fact that romantic resolutions are, for the most part, a key ingredient in relation to plot structure. Those novels in which a positive romantic dénouement is not achieved are rare. Finally, Chick Lit would seem to have more in common with those romantic fiction realizations that stand as individual novels, for, despite some volumes appearing as part of trilogies (Sophie Kinsella's work, for instance), Chick Lit writers tend to publish their work as standalone books and not constrained by the demands of a particular series.

Scholars have been more involved, however, in discussing what sets Chick Lit apart from romantic forms. Gill and Herdieckerhoff (2006), for instance, focus on the way feminist concerns have evolved, if at all, from romantic forms to prototypical Chick Lit writing:

> Specifically, we ask whether and in what ways chick lit might be said to be 'rewriting' the romance by breaking with conventional formulae. Do chick lit novels offer new versions of heterosexual partnerships? How different are their constructions of femininity and masculinity from those of 'traditional' popular romances such as those published by Harlequin or Mills and Boon?

> How, if at all, are they positioned in relation to feminist ideas and concerns through their expression of a postfeminist sensibility?
>
> (Gill and Herdieckerhoff, 2006: 489)

The specific connections between Chick Lit, feminism and post-feminism are developed further in Chapter 4. For now, I would emphasize that Chick Lit has succeeded in demarcating itself from the traditional romances in more than one way. First of all, it seems that the urban setting that has been primarily selected to geographically anchor (at least in prototypical examples of) Chick Lit differs from the preferred setting for romances. The latter opt for locations that range from the exotic to the pure mundane, whereas metropolitan localities offer the Chick Lit protagonist the stage on which most of her mishaps take place. Second, characterization is also distinctly differentiated in romantic fiction and Chick Lit. Chick Lit characters, as will be elaborated in the book, tend to mock the various situations they find themselves immersed in, their obsessions with weight issues and their general appearance; their general take on life, thus, differs from that of the prototypical heroines of romance novels. It appears that, where the latter heroine is portrayed as either an independent and strong-minded character, or simply as one who wants to survive the vicissitudes of life, the Chick Lit protagonist, instead, tends to make light of the misadventures and misfortunes coming her way. An immediate consequence of this new take on characterization is the humorous tone of the genre as a whole. Third, the book covers that so characteristically typify Chick Lit have, as early examples of the genre show, set these novels apart from their romantic predecessors, as a multimodal analysis demonstrates in Chapter 2. Finally, and most importantly, there are some linguistic features, especially in relation to transitivity markers and speech and thought presentation indicators, that specifically distinguish Chick Lit from its sister genres but which tend to be largely overlooked by most analysts discussing either form. As stated above, this book is as much about attempting a definition of a particular narrative form as about the tools that stylistics, as a discipline, makes use of and which can fill some lacunae left by previous non-linguistic analyses of the genre.

1.4 Chick Lit Offshoots

Despite the charges brought against Chick Lit concerning the sameness, repetitiveness and recurrent invariability of the works produced by Chick Lit authors, the market is witnessing the emergence of some by-products that display varying degrees of adherence to the prototypical formula described above. Some of these offshoots are, I would argue, only tangentially related to the core components of Chick Lit, such as the recently emerged Christian Lit or Church Lit; Ferriss and Young (2006: 6), in fact, wonder whether perhaps 'the genre's emphasis on consumerism and sexual escapades necessarily clash with Christian values', but the answer to this question is that, apparently, they do not. Yardley (2006) identifies the following branching-outs emerging from the original Chick Lit formula: '1) Chick Lit Mystery and Tart Noir; 2) Rise of the Antiheroine; 3) Small towns, Chick Lit style; 4) Mommy Lit; 5) Lady Lit or Hen Lit; 6) Widow Lit; 7) Bride Lit; 8) Full-figured Chick Lit; 9) Young Adult Chick Lit; 10) Lad Lit; 11) Paranormal Chick Lit; 12) Ethnic Chick Lit; 13) Christian Chick Lit; 14) Chick Lit Nonfiction' (Yardley, 2006: ch. 4). Ferriss and Young similarly consider that 'in the decade since *Bridget Jones*, it [Chick Lit] has crossed the divides of generation, ethnicity, nationality and even gender' (2006: 5) They, in turn, name 'hen lit' (or 'matron lit' or 'lady lit'), 'chick lit jr.', 'mommy lit', 'Ethnick lit' (including subgenres such as 'Sistah lit' and 'Chica lit'), the Indonesian 'sastra wangi' (or 'fragrant literature'), 'Hungarian chick lit', 'Christian chick lit' or 'church lit', 'lad lit' (or 'dick lit'), 'bride lit' (or 'wedding fic', or even 'Bridezilla' novels), and finally 'Southern fried chick lit' (Ferriss and Young, 2006: 5–7.) Because of such a multifarious assortment of forms, I would argue that the actual connections of some of these varieties with the archetypal Chick Lit novel could be, at least, questioned. For instance, whereas Bride Lit and Mommy Lit could be seen as the logical progression for the twenty- and thirty-something heroines of the 1990s who are now 'grown-ups' and trying to juggle a different set of responsibilities, others such as Widow Lit would appear to address issues that might be too far apart from the core concerns initially established by the original Chick Lit works of the 1990s. Furthermore, both taxonomies identify a gender crossover with writers such as Nick Hornby, Scott Mebus and Kyle Smith (Ferriss and Young, 2006: 5) being at the forefront of what has come to be known as Lad Lit. In relation to this gender crossover, I would like to distinguish novelists such as the three mentioned here by Ferris and Young, and others such as Chris Dyer (real name Christopher Santos), Alex Coleman (real name Damien Owens), Patrick Sanchez, Matt Dunn and Mike Gayle. The latter group's novelistic production differs from that of Hornby or Mebus in more ways than one: first of all, some of these male writers publish under a *nom de plume* which is, if not unequivocally female, certainly ambiguous (Chris and Alex), but they otherwise abide by the fundamental requirements of the genre, such as, for instance, the obligatory female protagonist; Chris Dyer's *Wanderlust* (2003), moreover, 'borrows' the confessional style of *Bridget Jones's Diary* although upgraded and transformed into email use instead. Other works, such as Patrick Sanchez's *Girlfriends* (2001), fully embrace the Chick Lit mantra inasmuch as it incorporates twenty-something female protagonists looking for the perfect job, apartment and man. Finally, other authors such as Mark Mason (*The Catch*, 2004) or Matt Dunn (*Ex-girlfriends United*, 2008) prefer to transpose some of the more common concerns of Chick Lit to a world in which the main character is male. As a group, the last set of authors certainly appears to show some commonalities with Chick Lit writing but I would seriously hesitate to bring the work of Nick Hornby, for instance, into this same category.[6] In sum, the apparent gender crossover highlighted by Yardley (2006) and Ferriss and Young (2006) giving rise to the Lad Lit variant seems to project a rather loose category which might not satisfy the demands of the most orthodox Chick Lit readers.

In this book, the decisive issue to consider in relation to the sometimes rather disparate variants presented by some taxonomies of the genre is that of prototypicality. I would argue that, on the one hand, these many branching-outs help to show the healthy status of the genre; but also, the various categories need to be placed in a continuum of prototypicality, with some retaining the original concerns of the novels of the 1990s whilst others simply maintain the bare minimum connection to those. My work mainly looks at those examples that are closest to the core components of the genre, as, I would argue, they still form the bulk of the whole genre production and they embody the original and prototypical definition of what Chick Lit entails.

Finally, it is worth recalling that most Chick Lit works have been published in English, which highlights the dominance of the UK and USA markets for the genre. However, Chick Lit has recently started to flourish in other languages too (see reference to Hungarian Lit above). Donadio (2006; see also Smith, 2008), in what she calls 'the chick-lit pandemic', states that the once English-focused novels have transcended the language barrier and are now being written in a variety of other languages: Katya Metelitsa's *Diary of Louise Lozhkin/ Dnevnik Luizy Lozhkinoy* (2008) published in Russian; Kajsa Ingemarsson's *Small Yellow Lemons/Små Citroner Gula* (2004) in Swedish; or Liz Tuccillo's *Como Ser Solteira* (2008) in Portuguese. Indian Chick Lit, although being published in English, is also emerging, as, for instance, Swati Kaushal's (2004) *Piece of Cake* and Rupa Gulab's (2005) *Girl Alone.*

1.5 The Stylistics of Chick Lit: Structure of the Book

This book provides an analysis of Chick Lit that is directly informed by the discipline of stylistics. I argue that the considerable number of studies of the genre published so far have somehow neglected to look at the stylistic aspects that can shed light on how Chick Lit's successful format has come into effect. To address this lack, I employ some of the frameworks and models that stylisticians commonly use to try to account for the way meaning, understood in its broadest sense, is created in texts. The methodologies I take advantage of are also manifold and adapted to the investigative endeavour I embark upon in each chapter. I thus apply multimodal stylistics principles, quantitative and qualitative approaches, corpus stylistics as well as some more traditional manual analyses, among others. My final aim is to provide a thorough account of the linguistic and stylistic features of the genre to complement the already existing ample body of scholarly work that has looked at Chick Lit with a critical but non-linguistic eye.

Some further clarification concerning the subtitle of this monograph is required here, as I have elsewhere (Montoro, 2003; 2007) substituted the label *Cappuccino Fiction* for the most widely used term Chick Lit. I argue that this alternative label neatly embodies some of the core characteristics of the genre such as, for instance, the 'feel-good' factor typically evoked in these novels. Chick Lit readers seem to yearn for a sense of satisfying contentment at the moment of novel-closure and this is always associated with the happy ending and congenial resolution that they have come to expect in the works. This happy resolution of the novels begets the comforting feeling that readers pine for so that they are left with a 'sweet taste', as if they had just enjoyed a cup of their favourite cappuccino. Furthermore, the label also conjures up images of a kind of aspirational lifestyle among the females of the genre, symptomatic of a kind of middle class existence which also encodes certain urbanite and consumerist values of the society these females live in and which is so often depicted in the novels. And, obviously, the label also makes reference to the very many appraisals of these works as mere 'froth' (see p. 6) because of the apparent inconsequentiality and, perhaps, insubstantiality of some of the novels. Especially because of this last aspect, this label might suggest that I am judging the genre derogatorily, which by no means is my intention, especially, as will be discussed in Chapter 5, in light of the analysis of real readers' responses to the novels. Thus, when I use my own coined label Cappuccino Fiction in the rest of the book I do so mainly in order to emphasize the 'feel-good' factor that the novels are so clearly characterized by; also I use it to bring to the fore the contemporary life of Chick Lit urbanites, but I stay away from any possible biased and pejorative consideration concerning the literary merit of the genre.

Chick Lit: The Stylistics of Cappuccino Fiction sets off by considering in Chapter 2 the first point of contact that readers have with the novels, the book covers. Following principles from Systemic Functional Linguistics and applying them to the non-verbal aspects of texts, I consider how multimodal stylistics can help identify the way some of the peculiar features of Chick Lit are realized non-verbally. I look at a series of novels and, by analysing semiotic resources such as the colour, typography and general layout of the book covers, I conclude that these semiotic resources are especially successful at encoding meaning for the genre as a whole rather than for individual works. This is further proven by the fact that some of the significations associated with the multimodal exploitation of the semiotic resources prototypically used in Chick Lit books are now being used to project similar meanings in what Yardley (2006: 25) calls 'Chick Lit non-fiction'.

In Chapter 3, the focus shifts to characterization concerns. I attempt to find out who the 'chick' in Chick Lit is, for which a two-fold theoretical perspective is used. The first half of the chapter is informed by theories from cognitive psychology, especially those of social cognition, because they can help explain how readers literally flesh out the traits of characters – that is, I focus on how texts trigger character impression formation in readers' minds. In the second half, I contrast the findings that a socio-cognitive analysis throws with a corpus stylistics analysis of the actual language used in the novels. I analyse a corpus of novels and, by paying special attention to certain semantic categories, I study whether the conclusions concerning a characterization of Chick Lit females drawn from a socio-cognitive analysis find some kind of correlation in the linguistic make-up of the novels.

Chapter 4 attempts to contextualize further some aspects previously discussed in Chapters 1 and 3, so I delve into the connection between Chick Lit and feminism, on the one hand, and the status of Chick Lit as a genre, independent and separate from cognate forms of popular fiction such as romances, on the other. My objective in Chapter 4 is to view these concerns in light of two of the frameworks more characteristically employed in stylistics: a transitivity analysis, and a speech and thought presentation analysis. I abandon the computational slant of Chapter 3 and, later, of Chapter 5, in favour of what Ronald Carter calls 'steam stylistics' (quoted in Gavins, 2005: 405). I adopt a manual analysis of a number of samples from six different novels and conclude that the combination of models I propose bears fruitful results with regard to the categorization of Chick Lit as a distinct genre; also, the way Chick Lit distinctively exploits certain thought presentation patterns is used to illustrate and clarify the somewhat controversial connection Chick Lit-feminism.

Finally, Chapter 5 brings to a close the discussion of the genre by paying attention to the otherwise essential component of the reading act: the reader. I discuss that my interest is with real readers, so I do not delve into theoretical notions such as the ideal or implied reader. Instead, I analyse the responses of Chick Lit readers from two methodological perspectives: on the one hand, I look at a series of theories of emotion to consider how they can help explain the strong affective reaction to the genre experienced by the Chick Lit readership. Second, I also analyse the way Chick Lit readers evaluate the genre, not necessarily always in positive terms. In order to pursue these two objectives, my methodology, as has been the norm in the whole monograph, is two-fold and, thus, oscillates from being primarily qualitative in the first half of the chapter, to being mainly quantitative in the second. The qualitative slant is justified by the analysis of a questionnaire that I use to assess how theories of emotion can shed light on Chick Lit readers' responses to the genre. The quantitative stance emerges from the computational analysis of a series of online blogs and book-club forums in which real readers discuss, analyse, appraise and rate their favourite novels.

Chapter 2

The Packaging

2.1 The 'Packaging'

Never judge a book by its cover ... or so the saying goes. Instead, in this chapter I argue that Chick Lit book covers do indeed need to be, not so much 'judged', but analysed and studied as meaning-making components in their own right. To this aim, I implement a multimodal stylistics analysis of a number of prototypical Chick Lit book covers in the way proposed by scholars such as Kress (2010), Kress and van Leeuwen (2001, 2006), Nørgaard (2009, 2010a, 2010b, 2010c), and van Leeuwen (2005a, 2005b), among others. The chapter concludes by suggesting that stylistic analyses of literary texts can benefit from, and should perhaps pay more heed to, the way in which the stylistic characteristics of a work or, as is the case here, a specific genre, might in fact already emerge and materialize in the way the book cover has been semiotically realized. Although a univocal and default correspondence between the semiotic resources employed in book covers and specific meanings cannot be established, and although this meaning resonance might only indirectly manifest in other literary genres, I argue that there is a much more immediate correspondence between Chick Lit book covers and the significations they project. This means that the semiotic resources employed in these novels are especially successful at encoding meaning for the genre as a whole rather than for individual works. Crucially, these resources also need to be considered in relation to the way they are being exploited in formats other than the original literary context they were initially employed for; thus, non-fiction books have started to exploit colour, layout and typographical techniques to evoke the kind of values that Chick Lit book covers are meant to embody, such as female identity, consumerism or body issues. It can be argued, therefore, that the particular combination of semiotic resources used in the genre has struck a chord with readers and publishers alike and that these benefits are being reaped for purposes other than the purely literary (that is, for marketing or sales).

In this chapter I start by providing an introduction of the pivotal concepts that grease the multimodality machine. Although multimodality as a discipline is now well established, and multimodal stylistics (Nørgaard, 2010b), in particular, is quickly emerging as a strong discipline, most studies of Chick Lit have so far failed to take into account the role of multimodal aspects in a comprehensive and methodical way. Work on the genre tends to limit itself to simply highlighting the fact that pastel colours, pictures of stiletto heels, mobile phones or shopping bags customarily characterize a prototypical Chick Lit cover and make these novels instantly recognizable.[1] I propose, instead, to analyse systematically why those book covers are so conspicuously distinguishable and associated with the genre, for which the framework proposed by Kress and van Leeuwen (1996, 2001, 2002, 2006), among others, presents clear methodological advantages. To this aim, I look at a corpus of 10 novels[2] and consider how semiotic resources such as, for instance, colour, typography and general layout (Machin, 2010) are exploited. This is followed by a case study of the novel that most prototypically illustrates the genre, *Bridget Jones's Diary* (Helen Fielding, 1996). These two complementary analyses help shed light on the way semiotic resources other than the written medium, that is, the non-verbal components of the genre's packaging, also define and characterize Chick Lit. Second, I argue that the kind of signification conveyed occurs as the result of a combination of semiotic principles, including those of discursive import and distribution (discussed below); that is, meaning operates at levels higher than the book cover itself, which also helps explain how the values projected by the novels' packaging are being transposed onto books dealing with, for instance, finance, or body issues. The magic formula characteristically typifying the genre has, thus, been established. The following is a summary of the main concepts discussed by multimodal scholars and an analysis of how multimodal principles are exploited in Chick Lit book covers.

2.2 Multimodality Principles

Multimodality stems from the premise that communication needs to be understood as an act that comprises a series of semiotic modes. For instance, Kress and van Leeuwen (2006), on the one hand, and Baldry and Thibault (2005), on the other, highlight the fact that monomodal communication is fallacious as even the most stereotypical cases of printed verbal forms (the prototypical novel, for instance) can potentially encode a variety of meanings via resources such as the weight (Machin, 2010: 94), slope (Machin, 2010: 97–8) or curvature (Machin, 2010: 99) of the particular typographical variant employed in each case. Semiotics and multimodality are, in fact, two related disciplines that nowadays tend to be discriminated in terms of how the various principles are applied:

> Whereas earlier semiotic traditions tended to look at individual signs and their simple, direct meanings in terms of what they connote or symbolise […] a multimodal approach considers the way that signs are used in combination.
>
> (Machin, 2010: ix)

Machin (2010: ix) argues that, whereas semiotic approaches to the study of signs could be likened to how meaning is created by the lexicon of a given language, multimodality veers instead towards the kind of meaning analysed in sentence and discourse grammars, that is, multimodal approaches consider meaning projection in the syntagmatic axis whereas earlier practices focused more on the meaning of individual signs. In practice, however, multimodality still borrows terminology, principles and basic tenets originally discussed in semiotics as they clearly befit multimodal objectives. Baldry and Thibault (2005) further expand on how multimodality is concerned with 'lexico-grammatical' aspects of communication, that is, with the selection from a paradigm and subsequent combination of signs, in what they term the 'resource integration principle':

> The resource integration principle views a semiotic resource as something used for the purposes of making meaning [...] . Multimodal texts integrate selections from different semiotic resources to their principles of organisation [...] . These resources are not simply juxtaposed as separate modes of meaning making but are combined and integrated to form a complex whole which cannot be reduced to, or explained in terms of the mere sum of its separate parts.
>
> (Baldry andThibault, 2005: 18)

The emphasis on multimodal analyses of texts, therefore, lies in accepting the complex and intricate nature of how signs signify both on their own and in relation to those with which they interact.

Multimodal stylistics has recently emerged as a further response to the claims and tenets discussed in multimodal approaches:

> Multimodal stylistics is a very recent development in stylistics [...] . By bringing together literary studies, linguistics and multimodal semiotics, multimodal stylisticians wish to develop a framework for the analysis of modes like typography, layout, colour and visual images – and of the interaction of these modes – which matches and combines with the systematic detailed analysis that characterises more traditional stylistic approaches to wording.
>
> (Nørgaard, 2010b: 63–4)

Multimodal stylistics favours a rather encompassing outlook in the way it aims at embracing, on the one hand, linguistic frameworks (prototypically employed in stylistic analyses) and literary studies in relation to the verbal mode, in combination with the study of semiotic resources as described by multimodal analysts, on the other. In order to account for how such claims of exhaustiveness can actually be applicable to the analysis of the genre that occupies me here, some clarification concerning which are the main tenets, concepts and principles discussed by multimodal scholars[3] is required.

Multimodal approaches to the analysis of communication are based on the assumption that, by putting together a series of semiotic resources, we are capable of conveying certain meanings. Multimodality, van Leeuwen states, is 'the combination of different semiotic modes – for example, language and music – in a communicative artefact or event' (van Leeuwen, 2005a: 281). Multimodal principles, therefore, should be able to account for how quite a wide spectrum of communicative interactions[4] comes into effect. Multimodality scholars argue that such a comprehensive view on aspects of communication is possible via the examination of the way in which semiotic modes become realized by semiotic resources, which van Leeuwen defines as:

> The actions and artefacts we use to communicate, whether they are produced physiologically – with our vocal apparatus; with the muscles we use to create facial expressions and gestures, etc. – or by means of technologies – with pen, ink and paper; with computer hardware and software; with fabric, scissors and sewing machines, etc. Traditionally they were called 'signs'.
>
> (van Leeuwen, 2005a: 3)

Semioticians and multimodal analysts alike concur in underscoring the central role of these resources as meaning creators, but the latter especially emphasize that meaning relies heavily on contextualization too (see Baldry and Thibault's resource integration principle above). Context and the way it determines the meaning projected by the various semiotic resources, as will be explained later, particularly resonates in the analyses I implement in this chapter as defining the characteristics of a narrative genre requires that it is understood in relation to the very specific social, financial, or marketing circumstances in which it occurs.

A second clarification concerning the models employed here is the fact that this chapter is directly informed by the frameworks proposed in Systemic Functional Linguistics (SFL),[5] as illustrated in the work of Kress (2010), Kress and van Leeuwen (1996, 2001, 2002, 2006), Machin (2010) and O'Halloran (2004), for instance. These multimodal scholars, among others, have attempted to transpose paradigms originally thought out to account for the way language works to resources other than the verbal. One such fundamental principle in SFL is that of the three metafunctions of language, originally formulated by Halliday (1966, 1967, 1968; Halliday and Matthiessen, 2004): the ideational,[6] interpersonal and textual metafunctions, each one in turn realized by a series of grammatical systems. The ideational metafunction is concerned with how experience is inlaid in language; the interpersonal explores the relationship between interlocutors in an act of communication; and the textual deals with the structural aspects of word organization. These metafunctions are realized by the lexico-grammatical structures of a given language and, therefore, help the analyst to account for how these systems linguistically shape meanings in any text. The ideational metafunction is analysed in terms of transitivity patterns that explain the processes, participants and circumstances that verbally encode a particular experience. Interpersonal meaning is projected via the concepts of mood and modality: the former notion is linguistically marked by speech functions as they illustrate the type of relationship existing between different interlocutors; modality is, in turn, concerned with the way in which speakers verbally characterize their commitment to the truth value of what is being said. Finally, theme structures and cohesion provide the basis for explaining how textual organization is achieved and how the previous two metafunctions are actually materialized in texts; in sum, theme structures and cohesion aid in explaining how the text is held together as a unit. The three metafunctions are regularly revisited below in relation to the way they translate (if indeed they can be transposed) to non-verbal semiotic resources.

Most multimodal analysts highlight the influence that the work of Kress and van Leeuwen (1996, 2006) has had in assessing the way in which semiotic modes other than the written can be approached using principles originally formulated for the study of language, such as the three metafunctions above, for instance. *Reading Images: The Grammar of Visual Design* (Kress and van Leeuwen, 1996, 2006) is still singled out as the most influential study of (mainly) visual communication via the application of SFL paradigms and taxonomies to signs other than the verbal and written. Their work has subsequently undergone substantial modifications and reworkings; for instance, in *Multimodal Discourse. The Modes and Media of Contemporary Communication* (2001), Kress and van Leeuwen expand on the way multimodality needs to be conceptualized:

> We move towards a view of multimodality in which common semiotic principles operate in and across different modes, and in which it is therefore quite possible for music to encode action, or images to encode emotion [...] . We want to create a theory of semiotics appropriate to contemporary semiotic practice.
>
> (Kress and van Leeuwen, 2001: 2)

The main development in their new view on multimodality lies in the fact that multimodal analyses, if they are to be at all successful, need to be far more malleable and fluid in their understanding of how different semiotic modes and the resources that realize them actually interact. To supply the lack that Kress and van Leeuwen acknowledge in their initial 1996 monograph, they propose to consider the issue of meaning creation in multimodal texts as emanating from 'multiple articulations' called 'strata' (Kress and van Leeuwen, 2001: 4): 'discourse', 'design', 'production' and 'distribution'. Discourses are 'socially situated forms of knowledge about (aspects of) reality' (2001: 20). Designs are 'conceptualisations of the form of semiotic products and events' (2001: 21). Production is 'the articulation in material form of semiotic products or events, whether in the form of a prototype [...] or in its final form' (2001: 21). Finally, distribution 'refers to the technical "re-coding" of semiotic products and events, for purposes of recording [...] and/or distribution' (2001: 21). The new reorganization of layers suggested by Kress and van Leeuwen, however, is not without its problems either. For instance, Nørgaard claims that these four strata of meaning creation are 'less clear when it comes to the question of how to handle the complexity of meaning making at the four different strata' (2010b: 65). Nonetheless, she clarifies that the 'recognition that semiosis takes place at different levels of the communication process makes discourse, design, production and distribution useful analytical concepts to "think with"' (2010b: 65). As Nørgaard claims here, I also consider that Kress and van Leeuwen (2001) have tapped into some core principles concerning the way multimodality needs to be conceived. I am especially interested in the role of the production and distribution strata, for they can shed light on how the semiotic resources prototypically characterizing Chick Lit book covers are being used to create meanings in discourses other than the original literary work. In this respect, it is worth revisiting these two strata and considering their significance in relation to this genre.

Production aspects, Kress and van Leeuwen explain, refer 'to the organisation of the expression, to the actual material articulation of the semiotic event or the actual material production of the semiotic artefact' (2001: 6). Production, therefore, should be viewed as the way the various semiotic resources are felicitously combined to encode particular meanings. The boundaries between production and design (that is, the stratum that generally comes into play before production), however, are not always clear-cut; in fact, bearing in mind Kress and van Leeuwen's insistence on the fluidity with which semiosis is to be seen as working at different levels of communication, the various strata, perhaps, should be understood as lying in a continuum rather than as discrete categories. For instance, Kress and van Leeuwen acknowledge that 'sometimes design and production [...] are hard to separate. Improvising musicians, for instance, both design and perform their music' (2001: 7). As far as the distribution stratum is concerned, they contend that any particular combination of realized semiotic resources needs to be eventually 'delivered'. For instance, 'musical performers may need the technicians who record the music on tape and disc for preservation and distribution' (2001: 7). Crucially, they also maintain that even this later stratum should be viewed as semiotic in its own right and, consequently, as potentially capable of adding new meaning:

> Distribution technologies are generally not intended as production technologies, but as *re*-production technologies, and are therefore not meant to produce meaning themselves. However, they soon begin to acquire a semiotic potential of their own and even unwanted 'noise' sources such as the scratches and discolorations of old film prints may become signifiers in their own right.
>
> (Kress and van Leeuwen, 2001: 21)

For instance, they illustrate the clear ability of distribution technologies to add further signification with the example of music recordings aimed at the home listener: according to Kress and van Leeuwen, having access to acoustically flawless and faithful copies of live shows in the comfort of the audience's own home is, semiotically, a completely different experience to being able to attend an actual orchestral performance in a music hall. This final stratum is, consequently, also capable of projecting new signification that needs to be equally acknowledged.

Re-evaluating the multimodal semiosis of book covers in terms of the four strata is especially fruitful in the case of Chick Lit, as the semiotic resources employed in individual works take on further meanings once they are considered as part of a whole genre. The kind of meaning that the production and, especially the distribution stratum, have added to the genre, not to individual works, can be seen in the fact the typical signifiers found in Chick Lit book covers have been incorporated into what Yardley calls 'Chick Lit Nonfiction' (2006: 25):

> If it can be marketed to women with Chick Lit trappings, it *will* be marketed to women with Chick Lit trappings. Case in point: [...] the bright magenta hardcover of *Cooking for Mr. Latte,* which is both memoir and cookbook combined [...] . There are also a slew of how-to books aimed at the Chick Lit reader [...] . The fact that the marketing and voice of Chick Lit has spilled over from the fiction aisles is the ultimate proof that Chick Lit is not a series of stock elements, but an attitude.
>
> (Yardley, 2006: 25–6)

I concur with Yardley's assessment concerning the way in which some of the prototypical meanings associated with the semiotic resources used in the book covers (and by extension with the wording proper of the novels) seem to have been borrowed for use on the covers of non-fictional publications. These non-fiction books are, nonetheless, still primarily aimed at a female readership and have been largely written by female authors too. So, in this respect, they still partake of two of the basic characteristics of Chick Lit (see Chapter 1 for a preliminary definition of this genre). Other than these commonalities, instances of Chick Lit non-fiction seem also to evoke the genre's 'attitude', mentioned above by Yardley. Thus, the mindset, approach to life or general behaviour of Chick Lit protagonists is summoned up in non-fictional formats. Chick Lit non-fiction tends to be thematically organized, with one particularly successful sub-genre being that of publications devoted to providing financial advice for females. Curiously, the titles chosen for these works could be said to display a certain derogatory and derisive attitude towards females' ability to deal with high-brow matters of the type discussed in these works. They are marketed, instead, as a type of dumbed-down version of financial advice manuals that seems to be, after all, the only accessible way in which a prototypical Chick Lit reader would be able to comprehend such complex issues. Examples include Jill Keto's *Don't Get Caught with your Skirt Down: A Practical Girl's Recession Guide* (2008), Catey Hill's *Shoo, Jimmy Choo!: The Modern Girl's*

Guide to Spending Less and Saving More (2010), Susan Hirsman's *Does This Make my Assets Look Fat?: A Woman's Guide to Finding Financial Empowerment and Success* (2010), or Manisha Thakor and Sharon Kedar's *On My Own Two Feet: A Modern Girl's Guide to Personal Finance* (2007). A second major group into which these monographs are classified is that of self-help manuals specifically dealing with diet dilemmas, clearly another of the prototypical issues associated with the genre. For instance, Melissa Clark and Robin Aronson's *The Skinny: How to Fit into your Little Black Dress Forever* (2006), the highly successful Rory Freedman and Kim Barnouin's *Skinny Bitch. A No-Nonsense, Tough-Love Guide for Savvy Girls who Want to Stop Eating Crap and Start Looking Fabulous!* (2005) (as well as all its sequels), or Kami Gray's *The Denim Diet: 16 Simple Habits to Get you into your Dream Pair of Jeans* (2009). It could be claimed that distribution technologies – in the case of Chick Lit, the publishing industry, for instance – have played a significant part in the way signifiers from a particular literary discourse are being reutilized; that is, the non-fictional market, by absorbing characteristics of fictional accounts, has contributed to the addition of certain meanings to those non-fictional books. These meanings generally include references to a particular type of female reader, to their competence (or lack of it) in relation to financial matters, or to their being focused on receiving help, all of which appears to play down the actual subject matter of these publications, that is, financial information or diet advice.

Some of the semiotic resources that have helped filter these meanings through from one discourse into another are the use of colour (especially pastel shades), the amount and type of illustrations and drawings, and the typographic variant employed. For instance, as will be discussed in Section 2.3.1 below, two of the distinctive features of typographical variants are 'slope' (Machin, 2010: 97) and 'curvature' (2010: 99). Machin (following van Leeuwen, 2006) argues that letterforms that tilt, slant and emphasise roundness, instead of standing in an upright stance, tend to give the impression of a more personal style because they become reminiscent of handwriting. The financial-help book covers, as much as those of the diet manuals mentioned above, tend to favour curved variants, consequently creating a kind of inviting, friendly, nearly intimate connection between the interlocutors of this particular communicative event, the book writer and the readership. The personal flavour imbued in curved letterforms is complemented by the way the semiotic resource of colour is used; in fact, this becomes yet further proof of how the distribution stratum has semiotic potential of its own and, therefore, is capable of projecting new meanings. Moreover, it is not just any colour, but especially *pink*,[7] that seems to have transcended the pages of prototypical Chick Lit novels onto the packaging of other non-Chick Lit works. Such a leap is interestingly assessed by Russell Williams (2010) who, in an article written in *The Guardian Online* ('Pink book covers make me see red'), complains about the excessive presence of pink: 'the bloated pinkness of the whole thing brings me back to the vexed question of why publishers like to candy-coat books for girls.'[8] Her complaints in relation to the use of this colour are prompted by the way the rose-tinted book covers of the teen-fiction market have appropriated, almost without a fail, not just the hue itself but also certain values and attitudes identified as pertaining in Chick Lit proper:

> Last week I strove to overcome the prejudice [...] and bit the rosy bullet, seizing three books of undeniable pinkness from the library's teenage-fiction shelves. [...] Caroline Plaisted's *10 Things to Do before you're 16* featured a relentless round of half-arsed beauty treatments, boob-plumping bras and hobbling in heels – as feminism gave a last, faint, despairing squeal and died.
>
> (Russell Williams, 2010)

The issue of how feminist values are presented in Chick Lit will be discussed in much more detail in Chapters 3 and 4. For now, suffice it to say that, even from a lay person's perspective, that is, from the viewpoint provided by a non-specialist on the analysis of multimodality as Russell Williams's would be, semiotic resources are being assessed as potential meaning-creators, in this case as specifically embodying values of the original discourse with which they are mostly associated, that is, the prototypical Chick Lit fiction.

The applicability of some tenets from SFL, such as the three metafunctions, as well as the four strata at which multimodal texts work, are just some of the principles discussed in multimodal analyses of communication, with many more also at work. One such core notion, admittedly related to the strata just discussed, is the concept of 'experiential meaning potential':

> The idea that signifiers have a meaning potential deriving from what it is we do when we produce them, and from our ability to turn action into knowledge, to extend our practical experience metaphorically, and to grasp similar extensions made by others.
>
> (Kress and van Leeuwen, 2001: 10)

Kress and van Leeuwen illustrate this with the example of 'breathiness': our understanding of this concept as a sign directly emanates from our experience of the situations in which it occurs (being out of breath, or rapid breathing because of excitement). Should we encounter such quality in songs, for instance, we will draw on previous experiences to ascribe a particular meaning to this sign (sensuality, for instance). Machin (2010), whose work is directly informed by that of Kress and van Leeuwen and hence by an SFL perspective, also discusses the 'meaning potential' of signs:

> Rather than saying what the sign means or connotes, we say it has meaning potential. This potential is realised only in the sign's use through grammar. In this case, since we move away from simple sign ⇒ meaning, there is a greater meaning potential. This offers the possibility of more complex, subtle and precise meanings.
>
> (Machin, 2010: 161)

My own analyses are concerned with this notion in a way that encompasses the experiential nature suggested by Kress and van Leeuwen alongside the emphasis on contextual signification highlighted by Machin. Hence, signs do not simply become realized in particular contexts (consider the transposition of various signs onto Chick Lit non-fiction discussed above) and prompted by previous experiences of such signs; they also project specific meanings only when combined in a particular syntagmatic relationship. The many cartoon-like pictures of mobile phones or women's silhouettes sketched on Chick Lit book covers, for instance, do not project meanings associated with individual Chick Lit works any longer but as part of the whole discourse that is this narrative genre.

In this respect, and to close off this introductory presentation of the main principles underlining a multimodal analysis of texts, Nørgaard's (2009) discussion of the concepts of connotation, metaphor and discursive import is, finally, also pertinent to a discussion of Chick Lit book covers. Nørgaard, who focuses specifically on typography as a meaning-making semiotic resource, echoes van Leeuwen (2005b), who describes typography alongside two semiotic principles, those of connotation and metaphor:

> I use the term connotation in a specific sense [...]. Connotations come about through the 'import' of signs into a specific domain where they have hitherto not formed part of the accepted, conventional repertoire. Their meanings are then formed by the associations that exist, within the domain *into* which the signs are imported, with the domain *from* which they are imported.
>
> (van Leeuwen, 2005b: 139)

In a similar fashion to how this concept is conceived of in relation to verbal signs, non-verbal, multimodal markers can also acquire distinctive signification based on the environment into which that sign is imported. Connotative meaning, thus, embodies more than the original sense prototypically assigned as part of the 'accepted, conventional repertoire' (van Leeuwen, 2005b: 139) of any sign. The acquired extra meanings are, thus, intricately linked to contextual factors. Van Leeuwen goes on to add that there is a second principle at work in the way typographical meaning is projected – the principle of metaphor:

> Not all typefaces can be understood on the basis of connotation, because it is not always possible to 'place' typefaces, to understand them on the basis of 'where we have seen them before', 'where they come from'. In that case another semiotic principle can nevertheless provide meaning, the principle of metaphor, or, more precisely, of the metaphoric potential of specific features of letterforms.
>
> (van Leeuwen, 2005b: 140)

According to this second tenet, the transposition into environments other than the originating one in which any sign would be created does not necessarily always explain how meaning is created. It is, instead, the typical understanding of one particular sign in terms of another (the prototypical definition of metaphor) that would explain how typography encodes further signification. Despite the usefulness of these two principles, Nørgaard (2009) is right in highlighting certain shortcomings and possible misconceptions regarding the way these two principles work:

> I shall [...] argue for a slightly different approach to the categorisation of typographical meaning [...]. Since connotation is a very broad principle which is at play in many contexts – amongst others as an important inherent feature of metaphor – Van Leeuwen's alternative term of 'discursive import' appears to be a more apt and precise term for capturing the kind of meaning that is at play when typographic signs are imported into a context where they did not previously belong.
>
> (Nørgaard, 2009: 147)

I find Nørgaard's rationale behind a recategorization of van Leeuwen's principles into that of discursive import particularly sound and especially fitting when analysing multimodal signs in the context of literary discourses, such as is the case here. She goes on to state that 'in a literary context, Van Leeuwen's choice of "connotation" and "metaphor" as coordinate principles of meaning-making may seem particularly confusing' (2009: 147), as these two notions are already heavily loaded with specific meanings for linguists and literary critics. This is not to mention the fact that the terms 'connotation' and 'metaphor' are particularly associated to verbal signs. It would appear, thus, that the notion of discursive import can encompass fully the way in which the semiosis of typography can be accounted for and can also avoid possible terminological misunderstandings. Although both van Leeuwen and Nørgaard limit the application of the notion of discursive import to the discussion of typographical variants, I propose to push the boundaries of operation of this principle to include further semiotic resources. The semiosis of multimodal signs, after all, is based, first and foremost, on the lexico-grammatical potentiality of signs; so the intricate nature of how these signs, initially, signify and, subsequently, combine with others for further signification needs to comprise the transposition of meaning defined by the concept of discursive import too.

To sum up, this section has introduced some of the preliminary notions with which multimodal scholars function and which allow them to account for the complexities of multimodal texts: the resource integration principle; semiotic resources; the three metafunctions; the four strata of signification (discourse, design, production and distribution); (experiential) meaning potential; and discursive import. The rest of the chapter attempts a practical application of multimodal principles to Chick Lit book covers, first by focusing on typography and the use of colour in a representative corpus of novels, and then by describing in detail the book jacket of *Bridget Jones's Diary* (Helen Fielding,

1996), for which further theoretical definitions, such as the notion of modality, will be summoned up.

2.3 The Corpus[9] of Novels

In the spirit that characterizes stylistic approaches to the study of literary texts, this section presents a systematic analysis of some multimodal realizations in 10 Chick Lit novels, chosen according to the prototypicality guidelines described in the introduction. These are: Elizabeth Noble's *Alphabet Weekends,* Liza Palmer's *Conversations with the Fat Girl,* Bernadette Strachan's *Diamonds and Daisies,* Adele Parks's *Game Over,* Paige Toon's *Lucy in the Sky,* Imogen Edwards-Jones's *My Canapé Hell,* Maggie Alderson's *Pants on Fire,* Lauren Weisberger's *The Devil Wears Prada,* Sarah Tucker's *The Last Year of Being Single,* and Sophie Kinsella's *The Undomestic Goddess.*[10] My aim is two-fold: on the one hand, I am interested in testing, in a methodical way, whether the claims made by multimodal scholars can, indeed, shed light on the general characterization of this particular narrative genre. On the other, I am concerned with how these tools can actually be combined with other, more traditionally stylistic, analyses, as performed in the chapters that follow. In sum, I focus on assessing to what extent multimodal stylistics may have been neglected as an effective and convincing way of considering meaning-creation in texts.

The way I propose to evaluate meaning-making using multimodal tools is by looking at two main semiotic resources: colour and typography. Because of the repeated acknowledgement by many scholars (Gill and Herdieckerhoff, 2006; Gormley, 2009; Modleski, 2008) regarding the ubiquitous presence of pastel colours on the covers of these novels, the choice of the former semiotic resource might not be unanticipated. Typography, on the other hand, has received far less attention as a potential core projector of the kind of values associated with this genre. It is this lack that I propose to address here, so I set off with a multimodal consideration of typographical variants and continue with the use of colour.

2.3.1 Typography

When discussing typography as a semiotic resource, Nørgaard's (2010a) clarification concerning what semiotic components of the verbal mode typography illustrates merits discussion. She refers to Halliday's (1994; Halliday and Matthiessen, 2004) distinction between the notion of 'typography' and that of 'wording' as both are realized by the same markers, namely written/printed words, but each signifies in a clearly distinct way. Nørgaard (2010a: 436) argues that 'even printed verbal language is multimodal, since it consists of a visual side, that is, typography, as well as […] "wording"', which she goes on to explain is 'the combination of the lexis and grammar of verbal language' (2010a: 447). As already mentioned, the combination of the lexical and grammatical axes is at the core of how Systemic Functional Linguistics describes the functioning of a language:

> There is another level of organization in language to which both the sound system and the writing system are related, namely the level of *wording*, or 'lexicogrammar'.
>
> (Halliday and Matthiessen, 2004: 7; italics mine)

This section focuses on the former notion, typography, defined as the 'visual side' of words; that is, I am concerned with the materiality of words as shapes on the page. A further reminder required at this stage is where typography's capability for meaning creation lies:

> We have to remember that the meaning in such a typographic profile is only meaning potential that will be actualized when the letterforms are (1) combined with other features (colour, dimensionality, texture, etc.) and (2) used in a specific context.
>
> (Machin, 2010: 93)

Establishing a univocal, one-to-one relationship between signs and specific meanings would be a flawed and, for the most part, unsubstantiated enterprise, as meanings arise out of contextualization and can only be assigned to typographical features once these have been contextually considered and in tandem with further semiotic resources (cf. Baldry and Thibault's resource integration principle (2005: 18) discussed above). Typographical variants' potentiality for meaning-projection based on contextualization and combination, moreover, also applies to other semiotic resources, and will be summoned up again when colour is analysed.

Van Leeuwen's (2006) inventory of typographic meaning potential is the taxonomy mostly preferred by other multimodal scholars working within the SFL paradigm, for it encompasses quite an array of features in relation to the materiality of letterforms on the page. Crucially, van Leeuwen's inventory feeds off the notion of 'distinctive features' (2006: 147), first proposed by Jakobson and Halle (1956), to describe the characteristic components of phonemes. Following this, phonemes are not to be seen as 'the minimal, not further analysable units of speech, but as "bundles of features", different combinations of "distinctive features" such as "voicedness", "frontality", "openness" and so on' (van Leeuwen, 2006: 147). Van Leeuwen proposes to view typographical variants in the same light, so that these distinctive features are to be understood, first, as inherently defining, that is, they can be used to make typographical variants apart. Second, though, each formal feature should equally be viewed as capable of signifying, because they form part of 'bundles' and function when mixed with others. The resulting list is a collection of what van Leeuwen calls the 'distinctive features of typography', that are 'weight', 'expansion', 'slope', 'curvature', 'connectivity', 'orientation' and 'regularity'.

On top of these, van Leeuwen also discusses 'flourishes', although he states that they are, 'strictly speaking, not necessary for telling them apart' (2006: 151), and hence non-distinctive. This would indicate that, although their role is not to distinguish one variant from another, they are still capable of adding further signification. In the case of Chick Lit, however, these flourishes seem to have been customarily used and exploited, so they are also included in my description of book covers. It is important to highlight that van Leeuwen's inventory is by no means discriminatory of further additions, nor does he claim it to be so. In fact, following Lupton (2004), for instance, Machin also highlights line spacing and alignment as efficient meaning-projectors, whereas Nørgaard (2009: 145) considers colour a semiotic resource that might also need inclusion in van Leeuwen's list of distinctive features. Starting with the first of these distinctive features, 'weight', it is generally defined as having to do with:

> [...] how bold or 'heavy' a typeface appears. This can be the difference between bold and regular versions, for example between this and **this**. This is not about oppositions but a continuum going from maximally bold to maximally lighter. Increased weight is often used to increase salience.
>
> (Machin,[11] 2010: 94)

Nørgaard (2009: 145), following Felici (2003: 41–2), suggests that boldness might be better defined in relation to 'lightness' than 'regular-ness',[12] with the latter placed alongside the continuum also mentioned by Machin, rather than at the opposite end of the scale. In fact, I would suggest that most of the features identified in van Leeuwen's inventory should be considered as realizations of a certain value within a particular range (whether that is thickness, boldness or slant, etc.) rather than as discrete categories. Such a statement, however, does not invalidate these features' discriminatory values. What it does underscore is their 'ranging' potentiality and nature, with the most prototypically heavy (or sloping, curved, connected) forms, for instance, being on one end of the scale, while the most prototypically narrow would be located on the other.[13]

In relation to weight and, by extension, to the rest of the distinctive features, however, there is one aspect which perhaps has not been sufficiently underscored or, rather, only tangentially highlighted, in the initial taxonomy proposed by van Leeuwen. If we consider the main tenets of the resource integration principle (Baldry and Thibault, 2005: 18), on the one hand, and the emphasis on contextualization highlighted by SFL scholars, on the other, it should ensue that the weight of any letterform should also necessarily be measured in relation to the weight of those surrounding letterforms alongside which it occurs. In the case of book covers, such a ratio between the various weights of the letterforms on the book jacket plays a decisively significant role because, in order to be maximally communicatively efficient, they need to project meanings in a more 'compressed' form than would apply in the case of the wording of the novel proper.[14] Issues such as the weight of the wording of the title itself as displayed next to the weight of the name of the author, for instance, must necessarily be borne in mind. Salience is the most immediate meaning (albeit not the only one) ascribed to the use of increased weight, so a heavier font for the name of a novel's author should indicate some special salience if lighter letterforms are used for the title. Such increased explicitness might be explained because of a special emphasis being placed on that particular author rather than on the novel itself. One such example can be found in the novelistic production of the best-selling writer Dan Brown, whose book covers opt for a rather heavy, particularly prominent, typeface for the name of the author; in fact, such prominence seems to have been emphasized as his worldwide success has consolidated. As far as Chick Lit is concerned, a rather similar case is that of Sophie Kinsella, whose name has progressively increased both in size and heaviness (when considered in relation to the books' titles) as her success has grown.[15] Thus, to Nørgaard's suggestion (2009: 145) above concerning the existence of a continuum ranging from maximum 'lightness' to maximum 'boldness' should be added the fact that such lightness or boldness arises out of contextualization so that any evaluation of weight must be considered in relation to the weight of the surrounding letter shapes. One specific heavy form such as **arial black**, for instance, might appear less so if standing next to **Gill Sans Ultra Bold** than if placed near a paragraph set in arial narrow. Boldness or regular-ness are not self-contained categories, and the meaning potential of what appears to be a heavy letterform is only to be decided alongside the heaviness (or lack of it) of the letterforms standing next to it or in the immediate environment.

My corpus throws some interesting results in this respect (see Appendix 1 for a summary of the typographical features of each novel). For instance, all of the 10 novels opt for variants which favour a certain heaviness in their letter-shapes, with *Pants on Fire* and *Diamonds and Daisies* carrying the most weight (also enhanced by further features, as discussed below). The wording of the first of these novels is realized by the following:

> Pants on Fire
> 'A witty modern romance … much more than a *Bridget Jones's Diary*' *Vogue*
> maggie alderson[16]

The letterforms of the title (three words) are the component carrying the most weight, especially the final word; some critical appraisal on Alderson's work ensues with the name of the author finally tailgating. The three sections into which the wording of this book jacket is divided abide by the mentioned preference for bold typefaces, although the relative weight-ratio arising out of contextualization underscores the title itself as the boldest component; admittedly, this prominence is also aided by the bigger font size used. The most immediate meaning customarily associated with heavy forms is salience, but this signification requires some extra fine-tuning, as meaning projection within an SFL paradigm, one needs to remember, is always framed within the three communicative metafunctions which explain how signifiers operate. The ideational metafunction, for instance, is 'the function of constructing representations of what is going on in the world (and in our minds)' (van Leeuwen, 2006: 142). In a social semiotic framework, justifying the use of font-heaviness simply out of salience might be insufficient and could present a slightly reductionist perspective on the actual signification. On the contrary, the literal 'boldness' of the typefaces on the book cover ideationally projects a sense of 'adventurousness' in the novel. *Pants on Fire* relates the story of Georgia Abbott, a journalist who moves to Australia to work in a fashion magazine. The reason for her move, moreover, is central to the novel's plot and prototypically reminiscent of Chick Lit concerns, as Abbott decides to leave after learning about her fiancé's infidelity, with further relationship complications and tribulations ensuing. The boldness of the fonts on the cover, consequently, seems to highlight a certain daring attitude on the part of the protagonist, who is also presented as playful and fun. Such a conclusion is backed up by what can be considered realizations of the textual metafunction which, van Leeuwen states, 'allows us to marshal individual representations-cum-interactions into coherent texts and communicative events, [...] in images through the systems of composition, framing and salience' (2006: 142). Textually, the general layout of the book cover dons a light violet and lilac background featuring a woman who is wearing rather short, bright pink hot-pants. She is depicted as seeming to walk along a city street, with a bottle of what appears to be champagne in one hand and a bright fuchsia cowboy hat in the other. Van Leeuwen's reminder that 'other, co-present signifying elements will narrow down the meaning potential and the values invoked, and make them more specific' (2006: 148) is a tenet at work here, since it is these signifiers that confirm the ideational meaning of adventurousness, freedom and general ludic attitude on the part of the protagonist. The composition of the image on the page not only mirrors the signification projected by the lettering, but also supports the fact that typographical boldness is used to embody fun and casualness. Moreover, such meanings become further supported by the informal nature of the way in which the name of the writer is displayed because, although it is set in a font which still belongs at the heavy end of the weight scale, it has otherwise ignored some basic orthographical conventions such as using capitals for the initial letter of the name and surname of the author. The totality of signifiers, thus, endorses the same ideational value of playfulness, frolicsomeness, perhaps even frivolity, and certainly fun.

Conversations with the Fat Girl is the novel standing at the opposite end of the weight continuum, as the wording in the title uses, comparatively speaking, the lightest font in the corpus. Having said that, the principle of relative weight-ratio is also at play here; so whereas the title uses a heavier font than the wording assigned to the critical appraisal, also on the cover, the name of the author is set in the boldest letterforms. Interestingly, the typographical characteristics of this book cover could be used to dismantle any possibility of univocal and, mainly, simplistic conclusions drawn on the meaning potential of typographical variants. Despite the obvious reference to the physical appearance of the novel's female protagonist, there is no excessive 'thickness' or 'heaviness' in the typeface used for the title. As pointed out, *Conversations with the Fat Girl* opts for the lightest font in the corpus. What the typographical variant employed here does underscore, instead, are traits related to slope and curvature, as further elaborated below.

The second distinctive feature in van Leeuwen's inventory is 'expansion', defined by Machin as follows:

> Typefaces may be condensed or spread out. This is the continuum between maximally narrow and maximally expanded. [...] The metaphoric association of this feature draws on our experience of space. Highly condensed typefaces take up little space. This can have the meaning that they are precise, economical, humble even. Wide typefaces take up space. They spread themselves around confidently, even arrogantly. But depending on the context this meaning can be reversed. Narrow typefaces might seem cramped, restricted or crowded.
>
> (Machin, 2010: 96)

Expansion is concerned with how much area on the page a typographical variant does actually take up. The Chick Lit novels selected for study opt for distended typefaces with very little chance for blanks or 'unused' space on the page area. In fact, the textual metafunction of the corpus can be said to be generally realized by the book jackets being rather crammed, with very few voids. Three novels are especially prominent in making use of expansive typographical forms: *Alphabet Weekends, Lucy in the Sky* and *Game Over.* Once more, the meaning potential of this value needs assessing in relation to, and in combination with, many others, so it does not arise solely out of expansion. In *Alphabet Weekends,* for instance, the wording is made out of four different sections: a pre-title statement, the title, the name of the author, and some blurb from the publisher. The component stretching the most is the title itself, as it literally seems to unroll and unravel past the boundaries of the front page and onto the back cover. The picture of a flying kite explains such expansion: the letterforms of the title are made out of the kite's line and it is our experiential knowledge regarding the considerable length that kites' lines tend to have that aids such extended style. A similar case can be found on the book jacket of *Lucy in the Sky,* the vapour trail left by a flying plane being the connecting component this time. On this occasion, the end of the rather pronounced loop of the first letter in the title pours over the book spine and the extremely long descender of the final letter curls and twists in the shape of a heart before being connected to the picture of a plane as if the whole title was being formed out of its trail in the sky. There is, therefore, a rather marked sense of expansion. The expansion of the letterforms on both covers rather graphically conjures up images linked to the idea of flying, but ideationally it also evokes freedom and adventure: *Alphabet Weekends,* for instance, narrates the story of

Nathalie and Tom who, despite having been long-time friends, embark on a quest for romance when Natalie's boyfriend leaves her. Their quest involves spending 26 weekends together and attempting 26 different activities, each of which must start with one different letter of the alphabet. *Lucy in the Sky,* on the other hand, sets off by placing the main protagonist, Lucy, on a plane on her way to her best friends' wedding in Australia; when they are about to take off, an incoming text message lets her in on the fact that her boyfriend has cheated on her. What was going to be a pleasurable time spent with her friends turns into a sour experience. Needless to say, both books prototypically conform to the happy ending expected of Chick Lit novels so expansion also communicates a sense of positive resolution in addition to those notions of freedom and adventure. *Game Over,*[17] finally, also exploits expansion rather profitably, although the meaning potential of this distinctive feature is realized in a different way to those above. Despite the fact that the title has only two words, they virtually occupy more than the top and bottom thirds of the whole page, with the name of the author and some editorial information sandwiched in the middle. Van Leeuwen states that wide typefaces 'spread themselves around, using space as if it is in unlimited supply' (2006: 148); they can be said to make an 'arrogant' use of space, which *Game Over* just appears to do. In *Game Over,* Cas Perry is a TV producer not interested in romantic liaisons; she is, instead, a career-focused female who is not afraid of exploiting and enjoying her sexuality in a rather forward way. Her unseemly behaviour comes to a halt when she produces a new TV programme and simultaneously meets a man who will change her negative attitude towards love for ever. Ideationally, this protagonist is portrayed as one of the most brazen, outrageous, sometimes even impudent characters of my corpus by far, and the expansion of the title typeface seems to signify just that. It is the focus on her career that turns her into such a cold and distant female, one who is able to use men simply for sex, as she is not interested in love. These meanings will be revisited below when discussing angularity, but suffice it to say now that, significantly, this ideational representation is generally more associated with male than female characters. Also, and most importantly, love is finally the rescuing factor for her. Finally, on the opposite end of the expansion scale is *My Canapé Hell* which, comparatively speaking, is more economical with space than the rest of the novels.

The next distinctive feature in the inventory is 'slope' whose meaning potential appears to project particularly well a specific signification associated with Chick Lit. Machin defines it as:

> [T]he difference between type that is more like handwriting and print-like typefaces. The meaning potential is between writing and printing. In the first case we have the personal, the informal, the handcrafted, the organic. [...] Slope can also mean dynamic and full of energy, mainly when used with straight lines. [...] In the case of the use of print style, we have the impersonal, the important the technical, the new, the mass produced.
>
> (Machin, 2010: 97–8)

Slope mainly separates the handwritten from the printed. Sloping variants can be said to look the closest to what they would have done should a human hand have actually written them, so the principle of discursive import is of special importance when considering the meaning potential of sloping variants. As described above, discursive import is used 'for capturing the kind of meaning that is at play when typographic signs are imported into a context where they did not previously belong' (Nørgaard, 2009: 147) and such meaning seems especially to underscore the humanist side of typography. In my corpus, only one novel has used a non-script-like typeface, *My Canapé Hell*; *Pants on Fire* also eschews excessive slant but does not employ full print-like traits either. The rest, albeit to a different extent, all opt for some features reminiscent of cursive fonts. Furthermore, I would argue that sloping variants (together with curvature and connectivity, described next), are capable of projecting, perhaps in a more explicit way than other distinctive features, one of the core, defining meanings associated with Chick Lit as a genre. I am here alluding to significations which underscore the 'personal', more specifically, to any aspect that could connote feelings of intimacy, closeness and affection. It follows that this 'personal' meaning should also involve a sense of the 'organic' rather than the 'mechanical', for the various accounts and stories in the novels decidedly appeal to emotions and feelings rather than impersonal facts. The most significant instance of a sloping and script-like typeface in the corpus is that of the title of *The Last Year of Being Single*. In this novel, Sarah Giles is torn between two men, her boyfriend Paul and her lover John (Wayne!). Whereas the former provides stability and security, the latter symbolizes passion, adventure and thrills. This novel prototypically focuses on heterosexual relationships with a special emphasis on the sexual component of such liaisons. The typeface used for the title itself differs from that used for the editorial information on Sarah Tucker, the author, at the very top of the page (using a rather small font), and that employed for the name of the author herself. However, the three components concur in highlighting issues of intimacy and the personal aspects of the story by emphasizing the slope of the fonts, although, admittedly, the editorial information and the author's name heavily rely on curvature too. The title is reminiscent of handwriting, especially as far as the diacritics on top of the two instances of the letter 'i' are concerned; they are so pronounced that they look like the orthographical marks used to indicate stress in some languages rather than the dot on the 'i' used in written English. Because a stress diacritic is not customarily used in English, its presence would suggest penmanship, that is, a specific preference on the part of the 'human hand' presumably writing those words. Intimacy and the personal are, consequently, two notions projected by the typographical characteristics of this novel. Yet, it is important to remember that romantic liaisons, relationships and matters of the heart, as the main manifestations of the 'personal', lie at the core of the genre. The meaning potential of sloping variants should, thus, be considered alongside other non-typographical but crucially important aspects which can also encode a concern for the private and intimate. These are especially realized in the diary format and the first-person narration which are so clearly linked to the confessional style of Chick Lit. *The Last Year of Being Single* successfully combines the cursive font reminiscent of handwriting with the diary format where it is possible to follow diachronically the development of the protagonist's feelings. Contextualization, therefore, once more confirms that the meaning potential of any semiotic resource is best analysed in relation to other (verbal as well as non-verbal) markers.

Sloping variants must also be viewed in light of the three metafunctions van Leeuwen discusses following Halliday (van Leeuwen, 2006: 143). The textual and ideational metafunctions have already been addressed previously, and so they can be summoned up once again in relation to slope. Textually, *The Last Year of Being Single* is structured to forgo blank spaces although it is not the most over-crammed or saturated book cover in the corpus. The three components of the wording still take up roughly the top 50 percent of the page area, with the bottom featuring the picture of an attractive female who is standing at a crossroads signposting, as opposite directions, the names of the two men in her life. Whereas the focus on the personal brought about by the sloping variant of the title indicates the way the ideational metafunction is at work, the interpersonal metafunction needs consideration too, for the slant in the font could also point to the existence of a definite intimation between the 'writing hand' of the title and the receiver in this act of communication, the reader. The script-like nature of the title could be viewed as an invitation addressed to the female reader to participate in what is presented as the intimate thoughts and experiences of the writer rather than as a distant account of facts. Needless to say, this meaning potential is not exclusive to Chick Lit, but it does seem especially recurrent in this genre. Although the combination of cursive fonts on the book cover and the diary format is not mandatory, nor is it indeed found in all novels (not all Chick Lit works are written as a kind of personal journal), it can be said that the interpersonal function is especially underscored when this specific non-verbal semiotic resource is coupled with the verbal expression of a first-person narrator.

The fourth distinctive feature in van Leeuwen's inventory is 'curvature' which, especially for the purposes of this chapter, is to be investigated alongside slope:

> Typefaces can be highly angular or have a lot of curvature. [...] The significance of these may be based on experiential and cultural associations with essentially round or angular objects. Roundness can come to signify 'smooth', 'soft', 'gentle', 'natural', 'organic', 'subjective', 'emotional', 'maternal'. Roundness might also mean fluidity and ease. In contrast, angularity tends to be associated with 'harsh', 'technical', 'masculine', 'abrasive', objectivity, rationality and so on.
>
> (Machin, 2010: 99)

The meaning potential of the contrast between curved and angular lines is given particular emphasis in my corpus. Besides, sound conclusions can be drawn from considering the role of curved and angular forms alongside other distinctive features such as sloping, for instance, for this assessment will be based on an analysis of more than one discerning parameter. Two distinct camps can be acknowledged in my selection: on the one hand, there are three novels whose titles display a preference for the angular: *Pants on Fire*, *My Canapé Hell* and *Game Over*. The rest show an overwhelming partiality towards curved features, albeit manifested differently in each case. *Alphabet Weekends* and *Lucy in the Sky*, for instance, have already been discussed in relation to expansion, but the distended nature of these two novels' titles is best explicated in combination with curvature. Two helpful concepts generally used in typography are those of 'ascenders' and 'descenders'. An ascender is the part of a letter which rises above the so-called 'mean line', that is, the imaginary line which sets the highest point of small letters; ascenders, therefore, would rise above such a line, as do the strokes of the letters 'd'and 't'. Descenders, on the other hand, fall below the so-called 'base line', the imaginary line on which all letters are meant to rest; the letters 'q' and 'p' have descenders. *Alphabet Weekends* and especially *Lucy in the Sky* owe some of their expansiveness to the rather pronounced curvature of both the ascenders and descenders. Pairing up these two distinctive features reinforces the meaning potential of freedom and adventure previously identified, but it also seems to signify fluidity and ease, especially if ease is likened to playfulness. *The Devil Wears Prada* provides further instances of manifest curvature, with both ascenders and descenders employed in the title too. The meaning potential of curvature here is based, to a great extent, on cultural knowledge, for the hook of the final letter of the word 'Prada' is twirled up to mimic the stereotypical representation of what would be the devil's tail, also ending in a pointed arrow. The reference to the devil, apart from appearing in the title, comes clear in the novel's plot: the main character Andrea Sachs has to endure the outrageous demands that her boss Miranda Priestly, the 'devil', makes of her. Priestly is the editor of a fashion magazine and Andrea works as her junior assistant. The job virtually ruins Andrea's life, her relationship and friendships, until she realizes that her family and friends are more important than her job and eventually quits. Curvature here does not conjure up the same sense of freedom, adventure and ease that *Alphabet Weekends* and *Lucy in the Sky* seemed to evoke. On the contrary, the rounded loops of the ascender in the letter 'l', and the outward curve of the left stroke of the letter 'w', are over-exaggerated in a way that suggests 'sensuality' rather than 'gentleness'. It is true that this meaning does not arise on its own but in combination with a few angular strokes set up in stark contrast with the rest of the rounded forms: the pointed arrow at the end of the hook of the letter 'a', on the one hand, and two small horn-like strokes on top of the capital 'D', both reminiscent of devil-like characteristics, on the other. The tempting sensuality evoked by the curved forms of the title would conform to the alluring sense of danger sometimes associated with evilness and the devil; that signification would illustrate rather well the kind of love–hate relationship that Andrea Sachs has with her job and her boss. More stereotypical angular lines than these two small instances in *The Devil Wears Prada* are used in the three novels mentioned above, of which *Game Over* is, again, worthy of discussion. By looking at the expansion aspects of this novel's title, I was able to illustrate that the protagonist is ideationally presented as brazen, outrageous, certainly rather forward. Perhaps a reminder of the protagonist's female gender also merits mentioning here especially because I am proposing to evaluate the expansion of the title in tandem with the angularity of its letterforms. According to Machin, angularity 'tends to be associated with "harsh", "technical", "masculine", "abrasive", objectivity, rationality and so on' (Machin, 2010: 99). Of all of these traits, the commonplace, perhaps even clichéd, association between angularity and masculinity seems to stand out; in fact, *Game Over* has been chosen because it fits within a prototypical characterization as Chick Lit fiction and hence is not related to masculine concerns. One incontrovertible proof that *Game Over* falls well within the boundaries of Chick Lit is the happy romantic resolution at the end. Therefore, the avoidance of rounded and curved strokes, prototypically associated with femininity, supports the same sense of arrogance, self-assurance and audacity ideationally projected by expansive and distended forms and which, despite being generally linked with maleness, is here embodying the characteristics of a female protagonist. Needless to say, these traits change towards the end of the novel once Cas Perry discovers the meaning of 'true love', as if romantic and social order needed to be restored.

The next distinctive feature, 'connectivity', is said to describe whether:

> [...] [i]n typefaces, letters can be connected to each other or can be separated by space. This can mean that they are joined up as in handwriting or that they have features meaning that they almost touch each other. Or letters can be clearly separate and self-contained. [...] Connectivity is, again, associated with handwriting and therefore shares much of its meaning potential with 'slope'.
>
> (Machin, 2010: 100)

Once more the meaning potential of this feature is directly related to the representation of forms that look closest to handwriting. Consequently, most of the conclusions reached above in relation to slope, as suggested here by Machin, but also in connection with curvature, can be summoned up again. Those book covers in which slope and curvature are prominent also underscore connectivity: *Alphabet Weekends, Conversations with the Fat Girl, Diamonds and Daisies, Lucy in the Sky, The Devil Wears Prada, The Last Year of Being Single* and *The Undomestic Goddess.* I am focusing on two in the list because they successfully employ two typographical traits not mentioned so far: *Diamonds and Daisies* and *The Undomestic Goddess.* Both underscore most of the significations projected by the group of novels that embody a sense of the personal, the intimate, the emotive and the playful. *Diamonds and Daisies*, for instance, uses a bold typeface, which also expands amply over the top of the page; although it does not use an especially cursive typeface, the letterforms cannot be said to be particularly upright either. Curvature is, nonetheless, the most defining characteristic of the title as the bulging parts of the two capital letters 'D' are over-exaggerated. Curvature is, however, also prominent because of entasis, defined by van Leeuwen as the 'difference in thickness and thinness within letters' (van Leeuwen, 2005a: 28). This is a term borrowed from architecture where it refers to the curvature given to the shaft of a column to correct the optical illusion of concavity. Entasis, thus, is exploited to highlight the curved components of some of the letters and therefore to make them appear closer to the next one, although not necessarily always touching. *The Undomestic Goddess* also benefits from the use of entasis although, on this occasion, it is the straight strokes of the letters 'd', rather than the bulging parts, that are thickened in the word 'goddess'. Furthermore, this latter title is characterized because, although the letterforms are not actually touching, they have hooked feet and protruding loops that extend towards the next letter. Both entasis and the use of hooked feet and protruding loops would indicate that fluidity rather than self-containment is preferred, and such fluidity and togetherness would also be reminiscent of the personal rather than the factual.

The sixth distinctive feature identified by van Leeuwen, 'orientation', cannot be said to shed as much light on the meaning potential of typography as those above and the next two do. Orientation has to do with:

> [...] [h]ow tall or flat a typeface appears. Letters can be stretched vertically or can be flattened. [...] The meaning potential of horizontality and verticality could be based on our own experience of up and down, high and low, and gravity and walking upright. Up can mean 'lofty', 'high-status', 'lightness', 'aspiration', 'emotionally up', 'walking tall', elegant – although the slimness of this horizontal orientation could mean instability or even pompousness. In contrast, horizontal orientation could mean 'emotionally down', 'heaviness', 'stasis', but also stability or down-to-earth.
>
> (Machin, 2010: 101)

There are quite a few examples of ascenders and descenders in some of the book jackets, as already discussed, so horizontality is not characteristically defining in my corpus. *My Canapé Hell* can be said to be the most horizontally-oriented title, although it is true that such focus on the 'x-axis' is mainly the consequence of the 'regularity' aspects also favoured here, so it seems more appropriate to consider these two features side by side. Regularity can be defined as follows:

> Many typefaces have deliberate irregularities or an apparently random distribution of specific features. Regularity and irregularity have their metaphorical potential. Irregularity can mean creative or artistic or spontaneous or chaotic, out of control. [...] Regularity, in contrast, can mean conformity, restraint, order.
>
> (Machin, 2010: 101–2)

Of the 10 novels in the corpus, *My Canapé Hell* is the only one that opts for a rather constrained, regular format, while the overwhelming majority display some kind of irregularity instead. Irregularity can be realized by quite an array of specific characteristics, ranging from some 'deliberate irregularities' to an 'apparently random distribution of specific features' (Machin, 2010: 101). For instance, with the exception of *My Canapé Hell*, the letterforms of the rest of the titles avoid resting on the base line. Some of them, such as *Conversations with the Fat Girl*, move up from that imaginary mark as if someone had 'written' these words and had actually failed to stay on the line. Others, such as *Alphabet Weekends*, wave up and down in a way that reminds us of the flowing motion of the kite's line flying in the wind. A third group, illustrated by *Diamonds and Daisies* and *Pants on Fire*, do not seem to rest on anything at all since their base line is totally random. A further way of indicating irregularity is realized by the different font size (*Diamonds and Daisies* and *The Undomestic Goddess*) and different weight of the various words in the title (*The Undomestic Goddess*). On other occasions, it is the mixture of capital and small letters (*Diamonds and Daisies* and *Conversations with the Fat Girl*), or even the use of a different colour for each letter in the title (*Pants on Fire*) that create irregularity. In sum, if there is one prolifically used distinctive feature in the corpus, it can be said to be this particular one. As stated above, *My Canapé Hell* stands out because it favours regular features, which might be related to the relevance assigned to 'order' in the novel. Abigail Long is a journalist who finds herself living the life of celebrities and having to attend plenty of parties and events. What starts as the opportunity of a lifetime, turns sour as she eventually finds herself having to go into rehab to address her addictions. The novel ends with Abigail coming out of the clinic with her health totally restored and, as it could not be any other way, also having found true love. The emphasis of the novel, thus, is on finding some kind of mental, physical and emotional balance and stability, which the more restrained, regular features of the title on the cover also appear to evoke. The rest of the books in the corpus, on the other hand, purposefully eschew regularity which can signify creativity, artistry, spontaneity or even chaos. Because of the emphasis on the personal, by now repeatedly mentioned and amply justified, it can be argued that spontaneity is at the core of the meaning potential of the irregular features preferred in these novels. Furthermore, spontaneity should also be understood in terms of fun and playfulness, so, despite the 'chaotic' appearance of some of the titles, this apparent anarchy can be explained away by the genre's concern with the ludic aspects of the plots. Rather than seeing such irregular forms as a negative feature, they seem to be embraced as projecting the prototypically carefree spirit associated with the females in the genre.

The final aspect of typography dealt with in this section is that of 'flourishes', which van Leeuwen catalogues as a 'non-distinctive feature' for they are, 'strictly speaking, not necessary for telling them [typographical variants] apart' (2006: 150). This category includes quite an array of embellishments and adornments that typographical variants can take on:

> Typography has developed a wide range of flourishes and additions which also carry meaning potential. One common flourish is the serif which is the flat bit at the top of the letter or the 'feet' at the bottom. [...] The absence of any kind of flourish is also important.
>
> (Machin, 2010: 102)

The frequency with which some features that could be categorized as flourishes occur in my corpus and the obvious meaning potential they bring with them might raise some questions regarding the non-distinctiveness which van Leeuwen assigns to them. Nørgaard (2009), for instance, proposes that the list of distinctive features should incorporate the semiotic resource of 'colour', an aspect not contemplated in the original classification:

> A feature that could well be added to the list [...] is that of 'colour' [...] . However, the inclusion of colour automatically opens up for the inclusion of further choices such as 'colour saturation', 'colour modulation', 'hue', and so on (cf. Kress & Van Leeuwen 2002) and complicates the system, as would the inclusion of features like 'surface' (glossy ↔ matt) and 'edging' (straight ↔ blurred or shadows ↔ no shadows).
>
> (Nørgaard, 2009: 145–6)

Opening up the list of features initially devised by van Leeuwen might disturb the cohesiveness and functionality of the original inventory but, as has been referred to on several occasions in this chapter, van Leeuwen never claimed that such an inventory was exhaustive or discriminatory of further additions. Moreover, the claims made by Nørgaard apply mainly to those multimodal novels that eschew the prototypical monochromatic black for their printed matter and incorporate different-coloured inks which are capable of projecting various meanings. Similarly, my claims regarding the significance of some of the flourishes used in my corpus pertain only to the Chick Lit novels in my selection and, by extension, to the genre as a whole. That is, the flourishes I describe here might not be so meaning-loaded or might project different significations in other genres and in different contexts.

Colour, which is discussed in much more detail in the next section, has, nevertheless, a relevant role to play in relation to the distinctive features of typography. Only three of the novels use white ink in their cover lettering, while the rest opt instead for some variations combining monochromatic and polychromatic letterforms; either way, the lettering of the title always stands out from and contrasts with the cover's background. Most interesting, though, are some other features that new typesetting and printing technologies allow book covers to use. Two of these characteristics are to do with the raising (embossing) and etching (engraving) of letterforms on the page. To clarify, embossing creates a surface that is raised to the touch whereas engraving leaves a sunken impression on the surface of the page. The former technique appears rather frequently, as six of the novels make use of it; one uses etching for the title and three more abstain from either alternative and opt for a flat surface. Embossing is further embellished by applying satin and glossy finishes to the raised forms. As a result, Chick Lit covers appear highly polished, elaborate and carefully put together, to the extent that the many added flourishes seem to confirm and underscore the significations evoked by typography proper. For instance, *Pants on Fire* is characterized by each of the letters in the title using a different shade within the range of reds and fuchsias, all of them embossed and with a particularly glossy finish which strongly reflects light. In addition, the hot pants the woman on the cover is wearing are cleverly adorned with a small heart also within the same range of red and featuring the same kind of gloss used for the title; another heart is used instead of a dot for the letter 'i' in the word 'fire'. Textually, therefore, the final layout and general composition of the page are characteristically cohesive, for the semiotic resources of typography and colour become the lexicon which successfully combines in a very specific grammar. The meaning potential of fun and playfulness, therefore, can be confirmed once more. *Lucy in the Sky* also gives prominence to embossed letters but embossing extends too to the picture of the flying plane. The embossed lettering, on this occasion, might also be described as indexical of the plane and the general idea of flying, for the letterforms are made out of the trail the plane has left in the sky. Both the lettering and the drawing of the plane are also embossed in a kind of glossy ink. To complete the elaborateness of this cover, embossing is teamed with engraving, also used for the book jacket of *Diamond and Daisies*, in both cases mainly in the pictures of multicolour and golden stars respectively. The general effect of some of these techniques on the final composition of the covers could be described as being somewhat cartoon-like, certainly not factual or intent on representing reality. These are aspects especially related to the interpersonal metafunction and, more precisely, in relation to the system of modality that primarily realizes it. Since modality is fully developed below in Section 2.4.1, I redirect the reader to that section for further details on how modality is illustrated in Chick Lit.

Some other tools that modern printing allows typographical variants to utilize are, for instance, foil stamping or raised colour, both used in *My Canapé Hell*. Foil stamping endows the lettering with a sophisticated, metallic finish whereas raised full colour presents a similar effect to the touch as embossing does but, additionally, incorporates a variety of colour shades. *My Canapé Hell* uses the former for the title which bestows some sophistication to the simplicity and order with which these letterforms are presented, and raised colour is chosen for the images of caviar canapés and cocktail and wine glasses, alongside stars in a variety of colours. In sum, the flourishes that technological advances allow typographical variants to enjoy, afford further creativity and variation and seem to play a crucial role in the semiotic meaning potential assigned to Chick Lit book covers.

To conclude this section, we should remember that the meaning potential described in relation to all the typographical aspects in the novels rises out of contextualization and that a certain genre expectation is also at play for the conclusions that can be drawn concerning the use of these and any other semiotic resources. What follows is a similar attempt at discerning how the semiotic resource of colour is employed in the novels, especially as Chick Lit critics and scholars have recurrently highlighted the genre's focus on this semiotic resource.

2.3.2 Colour

In order to explain the meaning potential of colour as a semiotic resource, Machin (2010) relates the following personal communication:

> A graphic designer recently told me that in a newspaper redesign they had changed the white they used to make it a 'purer, flatter, brighter white'. So the same colour but with different qualities. Why could this be? Clearly there are important symbolic meanings of both different hues of colour and their more subtle qualities.
>
> (Machin, 2010: 63)

Experts in the use of colour such as graphic designers are aware of the alterations in meaning that the selection of one particular hue, or variations in its quality, over another can have on the final product. The multimodal approach adopted in this chapter concurs in acknowledging that colour as a semiotic resource is capable of evoking several meaning potentials. Multimodal scholars, however, argue that studying colour as a valuable resource needs to be carried out systematically if such meaning potentials are to be justifiably brought about. To start with, this justification emanates from the confirmation that colour, as was the case with typography, can encode the ideational, interpersonal and textual metafunctions. Kress and van Leeuwen state that:

> Starting with the ideational function, colour clearly can be used to denote specific people, places and things as well as classes of people, places and things, and more general ideas.
>
> (Kress and van Leeuwen, 2002: 347)

As an example, they recall how in medieval times black would stand for penance; in many cultures nowadays, black is the prototypical colour used to signify death or mourning, so colour seems, indeed, capable of ideationally denoting meaning. Colour can also realize the interpersonal function, as when we try 'to impress or intimidate through "power dressing", to warn against obstructions and other hazards by painting them orange, or even to subdue people' (Kress and van Leeuwen, 2002: 348). Finally, colour is equally useful at the textual level as it can 'help create coherence in texts' (2002: 349). As was also the case with typography, the meaning potential of this semiotic resource is not to be viewed univocally, that is, a particular colour does not automatically project one sole signification. Contextualization, genre expectations, as well as the principle of relative value in relation to the surrounding signs (see the discussion of 'typographical weight' in the previous section), also need to be borne in mind. In order to account for a full semiotics of colour, Machin (2010), closely following Kress and van Leeuwen (2002), proposes a series of dimensions along which 'the meaning of colour schemes rather than individual colours' (2010: 69) can be assessed. Machin's emphasis on studying families rather than individual colours could help circumvent the danger of attempting to find a one-to-one, invariable relationship between a particular colour and a hypothetical meaning. Plus, it would also mean that the Systemic Functional Linguistics tenet of meaning based on the lexico-grammatical combination of semiotic signs would be borne in mind to discern the actual, *ad hoc* signification of this semiotic resource. The dimensions proposed by Machin are: 'brightness', 'saturation', 'purity', 'modulation', 'differentiation', 'luminosity' and 'hue'. Below, I first define these dimensions and continue by illustrating the way colour has been exploited in the Chick Lit book covers of my corpus. As a fully detailed, exhaustive description of every single colour nuance on the covers is an unattainable task here because of space restrictions, I limit my main analysis to pointing out the various dimensions of the general background colour and comment briefly on any other salient aspects. See Appendix 2 for a summary of colour use in my selection of novels.

Machin begins by defining 'brightness':

> The meaning potential of brightness rests on the fundamental experiences we have with light and dark. There is probably no culture that does not have a mass of symbolic meanings and values based on this distinction. Much of this meaning potential comes from the association of clarity and obscurity. [...] Bright can be associated with moods such as happy and dark with depression and sadness.
>
> (Machin, 2010: 70)

Kress and van Leeuwen (2002) discuss 'value', rather than brightness, mainly following the terminology used in colour theory. Machin's and Kress and van Leeuwen's concepts of 'brightness' and 'value', however, seem to concur on the fundamentals: 'The scale of value is the grey scale, the scale from maximally light (white) to maximally dark (black)' (Kress and van Leeuwen, 2002: 355). In lay terms, brightness is the quality we describe when we say that a colour is 'light' or 'dark', but essentially we are assessing how close or distant the particular colour is to white. A navy blue, for instance, is considered 'darker' than a sky blue, despite the hue – blue – being the same. A navy blue would also be darker than a canary yellow. Six of the novels opt for brighter colours, whereas the remaining four feature darker options. This does not entail, nevertheless, that the brighter colours on these covers do not differ in relation to other dimensions, as explained below. The brighter (that is, closer to white) colours used on the six novels are closest to what Chick Lit scholars have traditionally categorized as pastel, although pastel shades are best described in relation to saturation, not brightness. These brighter variants are shades of pink (very light red), blue, yellow and white. *Game Over, Lucy in the Sky, My Canapé Hell* and *The Devil Wears Prada* have turned, instead, to darker variants. The meaning potential emanating from brighter colours is, as Machin claims, associated with lightness and optimism. The vivacity of most of these covers certainly points in that direction, but this dimension, on its own, seems insufficient to justify such a claim. The second dimension, 'saturation', should help with this assessment:

> This is the scale that runs from most intensely saturated colour to the most diluted versions of the same colour (either towards pale and pastel or towards the dull and dark). Its meaning potential seems to lie in its ability to express emotional 'temperature'. Less saturated colours are more toned down, subtle, gentle, even peaceful or possibly moody. More saturated colours are emotionally intense, bold and engaging.
>
> (Machin, 2010: 70, 75)

Only the bright red of *Game Over* and the bright yellow of *The Undomestic Goddess* use saturation as their main asset; the remaining eight novels select a certain level of dilution, although only five of them can be acknowledged as being prototypically pastel, with lilac, soft pink, sky blue and off-white being the preferred choices. This assertion, however, needs some further refining as it refers primarily to the background of the covers. It is important to bear in mind that these book jackets are rather elaborate in their designs and tend to contain an array of different illustrations that, generally, use colour quite liberally. *Pants on Fire*, for instance, is one of the eight novels that resorts to a certain level of dilution and lies closest to the pastel end of the scale. As previously explained, this cover also features the embossed lettering of the title and name of the author, as well as a distinctive raising of the picture of a heart on the shorts that the woman on the cover is wearing. Embossing is not the only flourish on these letterforms, as each one is distinguished from the rest by being printed in shades of red all emphasizing a certain level of saturation. The heart on the hot pants is also embossed in a saturated shade of red, creating simultaneously a coherent cover at the textual level. The rather deliberate contrast between a diluted, pastel background and the saturated reds of the title is, as a consequence, quite striking and certainly appealing. Besides, it seems to confirm that the principle of relative value of the various colour dimensions (as was the case with the relative value of weight in typography) needs to be equally considered, for it is not simply the dilution of the background but the illusion of further dilution in relation to the saturated reds of the lettering and heart that seems at stake here. The final layout is, thus, quite noticeable and draws attention to it. To say that the primary way in which the interpersonal metafunction works for these covers is to attract the reader's attention might appear slightly reductionist. However, obviating such a crucial contribution might, equally, result in a central meaning potential associated with colour being overlooked. Besides helping with this aspect of the interpersonal metafunction, the main meaning potential of saturation, according to Machin, lies in 'its ability to express emotional temperature' (Machin, 2010: 70) which, in my corpus, is illustrated, on the one hand, by the boldness of the saturated red of *Game Over*, whose main character is ideationally depicted as opinionated and over-confident and, on the other, by the subtleness of the pale blue on *Conversations with the Fat Girl*, which projects the image of a gentle and docile individual.

Saturation is closely connected to the third dimension, 'purity', which is 'the scale that runs from "purity" to "hybridity". A pure colour might be a pure red or blue' (Machin, 2010: 76). This closeness between these two dimensions is illustrated in the corpus by the fact that the cover with the most saturated colour is also featuring the purest red (*Game Over*). The prototypical pastels and the rest of the diluted covers promote a kind of hybridity between reds and whites, or reds and blues, for instance. Kress and van Leeuwen (2002: 356) have suggested that the meaning potential arising out of the contrast 'pure versus hybrid' is linked to principles typical of modernist and postmodernist concerns. The former movement favoured ideologies characterized by certainty and security that were realized, they explain, in the paintings of Mondrian; postmodernism, on the other hand, celebrates mixture, the combined and the hybrid. Extremely pure colours, because they are seldom found in real life, might project a meaning potential evoking lack of realism. But the fact that the backgrounds of the covers generally shun this option does not entail that such 'unrealistic', pure hues are totally eschewed. *Alphabet Weekends, Pants on Fire, The Last Year of Being Single* and *The Undomestic Goddess* all employ pure reds (mainly), blues and greens not for the general background but for some objects also featuring on the cover. The first of these novels, for instance, exhibits drawings of the Eiffel Tower, what looks like a jug full of some refreshing drink, a bottle of Pimms and two glasses, as well as some gambling chips and a die. These illustrations are ideationally significant, for ideas such as adventure, travel, holidays and flying to some exotic locations are central to the plot of the novel. Textually, however, these illustrations are also linked by the purity of colour selected: for instance, the fruit slices inside the jug and glasses, the cap on the bottle of Pimms, and the die use a rather pure red, whereas the playing chips turn to a pure blue. The pure colours of these illustrations provide the cover with a slightly cartoon-like appearance, as is also the case in *The Undomestic Goddess* (pure red on the picture of a handbag and lipstick, pure blue on a bottle of some cleaning product). When used, purity is, therefore, expertly exploited and aids the ideational meanings as much as does the textual coherence of the covers.

'Modulation', the fourth colour dimension in Machin's inventory, encompasses what is generally described as the colours' shades:

> This is the scale that runs from colours that are fully modulated, that are more natural, which are textured with different shades, as colours are seen

> in the natural world, to flat colours with no such shades. [...] Flat, unmodulated colour may be experienced as simple, bold or basic. Highly modulated colour may be perceived as subtle and doing justice to the rich texture of real colour – or as overly fussy and detailed.
>
> (Machin, 2010: 77)

This dimension is one that my selection of novels has not favoured, as all the covers but one discards modulation. Modulated colours, like hybrid colours before, emphasize naturalness and realism – not something that Chick Lit book jackets are particularly concerned with. The modulation in *Lucy in the Sky*, the only novel to use it, depicts a sunset in which blue and purple gradually adjust until they metamorphose into fuchsia and pink, in a way reminiscent of a real sunset. There is a second novel, *The Devil Wears Prada*, which gives the illusion of modulation but not because the colours are gradually shaded but rather because the background is made up of five different strips in which different degrees of saturation seem to be creating modulation. The rest of the novels opt for colours that feel unrealistically flat, as if they are consciously denying any claim to realism. Characteristically, critics of the genre point out how impracticable, how virtually impossible to attain, the aims prototypically encoded in the genre are: perfect job, supreme appearance, heavenly and successful heterosexual relationship. It could be argued that, because the genre's authors are perfectly aware of the unlikelihood of what is being related in their stories, semiotic resources are purposefully utilized in a way that makes them look cartoon-like and without any pretension of truthfulness or authenticity. As will be discussed in Section 2.4.1, the way semiotic resources emphasize lack of realism can be said simultaneously to project very low modality. In sum, ideationally this combination of characteristics conveys a sense of playfulness over any other signification.

The fifth dimension is that of 'differentiation':

> This is the scale that runs from monochrome, which could be black and white or just shades of the same colour, to the use of many colours. This can be used to suggest timelessness as in black and white and might be used to make images seem symbolic rather than descriptive.
>
> (Machin, 2010: 78)

There is consensus in the corpus in relation to this dimension as all use polychromatic covers in which differentiation is emphasized, albeit to various extents. The meaning potentials arising out of differentiation can range widely from the sophistication sometimes attached to black and white combinations to the garishness found in compositions that over-use colour. The Chick Lit covers in my corpus cannot be said to abide by the former, but they should not necessarily be seen as the latter either. Interpersonally, differentiation helps to draw attention to these covers, whereas ideationally they highlight the slight frivolousness of the genre.

The sixth dimension, 'luminosity', does not seem characteristic or particularly useful for Chick Lit as it is not applied in any of the novels: 'This is the scale from luminous colour, which looks as though light is shining through it (e.g. coloured glass), to its opposite. Luminosity has a long history of being associated with the unworldly glow of magic and supernatural beings or objects' (Machin, 2010: 78). Finally, the last dimension to discuss is that of 'hue', which corresponds to what, in lay terms, we actually call the 'colour' of objects. Machin states:

> This is the scale from blue to red. On the blue side there are associations of cold, calm, distance and backgrounding. On the red side there are associations of warmth, energy, salience, foregrounding. [...] But for hue, meaning potential depends for a big part on all the above factors.
>
> (Machin, 2010: 79)

The general continuum of warmth to coldness is the meaning potential most characteristically emerging out of this final parameter, although, as Machin acknowledges, it might eventually depend on all the previous factors. Chick Lit might actually be quite useful to prove such dependence because half the novels in the corpus display colours that might be placed at the cold end of the scale, whereas the rest are best viewed as describing warmth. In the former group are *Alphabet Weekends, Conversations with the Fat Girl, Diamonds and Daisies, Lucy in the Sky* and *Pants on Fire,* but I would strongly hesitate to assign the meaning potential of 'coldness' to any of these novels. In fact, the genre, as a whole, could be potentially described as the fictional genre furthest away from any signification of 'emotionlessness' (see more on the role and language of emotion in Chapter 5). The hue of the various covers, consequently, cannot be reduced to expressing such dichotomous meanings on the warmth–coldness scale, and needs further contextualization.

In this respect, a discussion of the various colour dimensions is not complete without mentioning the hue most stereotypically mentioned in relation to Chick Lit, pink. Strictly speaking, only *Alphabet Weekends* has an overwhelmingly pink background, although seven of the other novels resort to some form of 'pinkness'. For instance, I am considering colour realizations that hybridize reds and whites as much as reds and blues so, although a novel such as *Diamonds and Daisies* might be best characterized as employing lilacs and light violets on its cover, in the context in which those two shades are utilized they become highly reminiscent of the pinkness associated with the genre. In *The Undomestic Goddess,* on the other hand, the drawings of a feather duster, a pastry cutter, a rose, and some stars and flowers dotted around the cover also use pink, albeit on a yellow background that clearly predominates. Koller's (2008) assessment regarding the values attached to 'pinkness' seems useful in bringing to the fore the way Chick Lit has appropriated this colour more than any other. Koller's research,[18] furthermore, combines a social semiotic and a cognitive semantics perspective, so her conclusions are backed up by the tools provided by two different disciplines:

> While associations with pink still overwhelmingly make a connection between femininity and its stereotypical values, as well as with sexuality, an emergent concept is that of fun and confidence. In artefacts and visual texts, pink is seen as gendering textual referents and as attracting female readers' attention, often in tandem with verbal components. A second function of pink is to index sexuality and sexual identity [...]. Finally, the emergent associations of pink with fun, independence and confidence find their visual reflection in the use of pink as a post-feminist colour indexing economically independent, hedonistic femininity.
>
> (Koller, 2008: 418)

Koller appears to have tapped into three crucial issues that might explain why this colour is so prototypically linked to Chick Lit and the values it encompasses, despite the fact that pink does not have to, nor does it, overwhelmingly always feature in every Chick Lit book jacket produced. First of all, the 'emergent concepts of fun and confidence' pointed out by Koller have also been repeatedly summoned up in my research as frequent ideological projections for some of the semiotic resources analysed here. Not simply the colour pink, but many other aspects (flourishes and a cartoon-like appearance arising out of contrastive pastels and excessive saturation, for instance) also coincide in projecting a sense of playfulness. Together with this ideational projection, gendering pink is interpersonally useful for attracting the reader's attention, a function which should not be overlooked[19] either. Pink is also acknowledged as being capable of indexing sexuality and sexual identity, and here, Koller argues, 'there is clearly a continuum from the emotional concepts of romance and love to their physical aspects' (2008: 413). In Chick Lit, both ends can be said to be present as, whereas successful romantic resolutions have become the backbone for the genre, the physical, sometimes openly lustful, aspects of romance are not avoided either. Finally, pink as a post-feminist manifestation signals values that should not be reduced solely to expressing fun:

> In this framework, pink is used to communicate fun and independence, financial and professional power without conforming to masculine norms, as well as femininity and self-confidence. Closely linked to consumerism, post-feminism sees the empowerment of women as a positive value but seeks to set itself apart from malicious stereotypes of feminists as humourless and mannish (Lazar, 2006).
>
> (Koller, 2008: 416)

The ideological characterization of Chick Lit protagonists as encoded in verbal markers is further elaborated in Chapters 3 and 4, in which the feminist claims made in some Chick Lit works will be addressed. As far as the non-verbal resource of colour is concerned, pink seems to have been re-worked and reclaimed to mark some distance with previous feminist stereotypes, especially those that might have likened feminism to humourlessness. Where, previously, we might have found a sterile association between pinkness and feminine clichés, a post-feminist take on the use of this colour sees an empowerment directly illustrated by embracing rather than rejecting pink. This embracement, closely linked to consumerism as pointed out by Koller, also resonates in Chick Lit concerns with fashion, appearance and issues regarding the urbanite existence of the prototypical Chick Lit novel protagonist. In sum, viewed from this perspective, it looks as if this new type of self-assured and hedonistic femininity projected by post-feminist ideologies is well served by the use of pink in Chick Lit. Furthermore, I have already argued that the notion of discursive import proposed by Nørgaard (2009: 147) in relation to typography could be extended to the semiotic resource of colour. Koller's (2008) conclusions here emanate from the analysis of multimodal realizations in leaflets, advertisements, websites and magazines, so the socio-cultural models that inform the associations of pinkness with gender and sexuality seem to have found a way to materialize themselves in a variety of discourses. Before the recognition of Chick Lit as a genre, it could be argued that these associations with pinkness had not, at least not so clearly, been discursively imported into the popular fiction arena. This transference of the meaning potential of the use of a semiotic resource onto a context in which it was not originally employed, therefore, seems to fit the notion of discursive import. Additionally, the same principle applies if we consider that the whole set of values specifically linked to Chick Lit has subsequently been imported into Chick Lit non-fiction discourse (Yardley, 2006: 25; see Section 2.2) where the colour pink is gendering a particular form of post-feminist femininity in relation to topics not culturally reminiscent of female matters, especially in relation to financial-help publications. Examples of the latter are Olszewski's *Live it, Love it, Earn it* (2010) and Hill's *Shoo, Jimmy Choo!: The Modern Girl's Guide to Spending less and Saving more* (2010).

In conclusion, the semiotic resource of colour can be described as functioning in tandem with that of typography to encode a few, but constant, significations in the corpus. Of all of them, suggestions of a carefree existence, slight frivolousness and ludic aspects are the most characterizing features of the books' covers. I am aware that this corpus is not, by any means, comprehensive, nor do I claim it to be. Instead, I consider this corpus to be representative of the above-mentioned significations because they all underscore some prototypical values associated with the genre.

The final part of this chapter looks at other multimodal realizations apart from those of typography and colour, especially as they are manifest in the key work of the genre: *Bridget Jones's Diary*. It is also an attempt at putting it all together in the context of one specific book cover.

2.4 Other Multimodal Realizations

2.4.1 Bridget Jones's Diary

This section focuses on the novel that is most recurrently singled out as marking the birth of Chick Lit as a genre, Helen Fielding's *Bridget Jones's Diary*[20] (see Figure 2.1).

Fig 2.1 The cover of *Bridget Jones's Diary*, by Helen Fielding (reproduced courtesy of Pan Macmillan).

There are two main reasons for delving into the multimodal components of this book jacket. On the one hand, as already pointed out, this work is the prototypical example of most of the values associated with Chick Lit fiction as, for many scholars (Ferriss and Young, 2006; Gill and Herdieckerhoff, 2006; Gormley, 2009; Modleski, 2008; Smith, 2008; Yardley, 2006; see Chapter 1 for more on the history of Chick Lit), it virtually prompted the creation of the genre. Second, and crucially, I consider the fact that the book jacket of the novel which is mostly associated with this genre has openly eschewed utilizing most of the semiotic resources that since its publication have become inextricably linked with Chick Lit. In fact, it was the repetitiveness of some of these semiotic resources that eventually put a particular stamp on the genre's book covers, as Modleski reminds us here:

> Noting this diversity, however, would go against the interests of publishers eager to capitalize on the tried and true. Hence, the novels' marketers attempt to make the books instantly recognizable to avid consumers by using similar cover designs (often pastel and usually picturing stiletto heels, purses, and other accoutrements of modern femininity). Marketing strategies thus work to obscure novels that may deviate in important ways from the original formula.
>
> (Modleski, 2008: xxii)

Although the analyses in previous sections confirm Modleski's assessment and corroborate the importance of the 'tried and true', the fact that *Bridget Jones's Diary* successfully avoids falling into the 'Chick Lit book cover' trap needs further investigation. This does not invalidate previous conclusions, for instance, in relation to how marketing strategies function as part of the distribution strata identified by Kress and van Leeuwen (2006: 7); nor does it cancel out the potential for meaning creation of such distribution technologies (see Section 2.2). However, it certainly raises some questions concerning the rationale behind the particular way in which semiotic resources have been put together on the cover of *Bridget Jones's Diary*, as they differ drastically from the rest of the novels in the corpus and, hence, encode different meanings to those associated with the genre. Pursuing all these aims, I revisit the notions of colour and typography but in relation to modality which, in Systemic Functional Linguistics, is traditionally considered one of the resources available for the projection of interpersonal meaning.

Van Leeuwen defines modality as:

> The social semiotic approach to the question of truth. It relates both to issues of representation – fact versus fiction, reality versus fantasy, real versus artificial, authentic versus fake – and to questions of social interaction, because the question of truth is also a social question – what is regarded as true in one social context is not necessarily regarded as true in others, with all the consequences that brings.
>
> (van Leeuwen, 2005a: 160)

In the verbal mode, modality is traditionally associated with (although not exclusively realized by) modal verbs which reflect a speaker's attitude to a particular utterance; modality is especially concerned with how speakers encode their commitment to the truth value of what is being stated. Multimodal analysts, however, argue that modality is not solely restricted to the domain of the verbal language:

> According to social semioticians modality is not restricted to language but is a multimodal concept. All means of expression have modality resources. The question of truth emerges in all of them, even if the kinds of truth they allow and the ways in which they express degrees of truth will be different.
>
> (van Leeuwen, 2005a: 165)

The seeming ubiquity of modality in all communicative interactions can also be explicated by its ability to encode interpersonal relations between interlocutors. Thus, non-verbal language also makes use of a series of resources to filter in the stance and attitude of the sign producer so the reality advertised in the text is necessarily always carrying the specific 'stamp' of that producer. Kress and van Leeuwen (1996) particularly focus on the modal encoding of visual images, although their initial proposal has been subsequently tested on further modes: for instance, see van Leeuwen's work on the modality of sound (1999) and typography (2005b, 2006, revisited below). Van Leeuwen (2005a) concretizes the markers of visual modality discussed by Kress and van Leeuwen (1996, 2006) on eight different dimensions: 'articulation of detail', 'articulation of the background', 'colour saturation', 'colour modulation', 'colour differentiation', 'depth articulation', 'articulation of light and shadow' and 'articulation of tone range' (2005a: 167). The realization of visual modality via these dimensions, however, depends on what Kress and van Leeuwen call 'coding orientation':

> Visual modality rests on culturally and historically determined standards of what is real and what is not, and not on the objective correspondence of the visual image to a reality defined in some ways independently of it.
>
> (Kress and van Leeuwen, 2006: 163)

This means that 'contextual factors such as genre and genre expectations are hence crucial to the assessment of modality, as is historical context' (Nørgaard, 2010b: 67). As far as visual modality is concerned, especially as realized in photography, Kress and van Leeuwen argue that naturalistic photography has traditionally been considered the norm against which other modal realizations were judged, so that the closer the photographic representation might be to the 'real', the higher the modality would be. However, in the scientific domain, for instance, diagrams might sometimes suffice whereas a photograph with high articulation of detail might detract from the communicative purpose of that particular interaction. The dimensions just mentioned, therefore, are not in themselves sufficient to explicate whether a visual composition is characterized by high or low modality. It is by considering those dimensions as they happen in a particular context that the real modality score can be discerned. Chick Lit books are no exception, so the way visual modality is realized needs to consider the contextual aspects surrounding their production. The rest of this section considers how these modality markers manifest in *Bridget Jones's Diary* and their significance in terms of the interpersonal metafunction.

As stated above, the main characteristic to highlight in relation to the book cover of what could be termed the 'quintessential' Chick Lit novel is its atypicality in relation to the semiotic resources employed. None of the books in my selection features a photograph on the cover, although, admittedly, that does not imply that photographic images are totally banned from these book jackets. For instance, recent editions of Adele Parks's works have swapped the drawings and illustrations originally featured for photographic material (see Note 17 for further information on this); film tie-in versions of some novels have also taken advantage of book covers to publicize further the movie version and have incorporated photographs of the main actress (*The Secret Dreamworld of a Shopaholic*, for instance). *Bridget Jones's Diary*, however, still stands out among the rest, not just because the cover features a photograph rather than drawings or illustrations, but more importantly because of the characteristics of the photograph and the meanings it seems to convey. The sepia-coloured photograph features a woman, smoking, who seems to be reading something which is difficult to make out. Since she is holding it out in front of herself, it would seem safe to assume she is reading a book but, because of the surrounding verbal markers, it might easily be her diary. There is quite a lot of wording on the page too: at the very top, there is an entry from what can be assumed to be her diary, followed by what seems like the reading on a digital clock. Some publicity information ensues, followed by the title and name of the author. The first means of visual expression identified by Kress and van Leeuwen, degrees of articulation of detail, 'form a scale which runs from the simplest line drawing to the sharpest and most finely grained photograph' (van Leeuwen, 2005a: 167), so the more articulation of detail, the higher the modality. It is not only hard to make out whether the woman on the cover is holding a book or a diary, but also the cigarette allegedly in her hand could, in fact, turn out to be a pencil or a pen. There is hardly any definition of the clothes she is wearing (it seems she has a dark jacket over a white shirt, but it is not easily discernible) or where she is actually standing. In sum, everything points at low modality being the main characteristic of the picture. The same applies for the second parameter, the degree of the articulation of the background, as it is not possible to ascertain where the woman is standing. Because the articulation of light and shadow disproportionately (in terms of naturalistic photography, that is) shows a preference for the former, it appears as if the woman is standing next to a window. But, she could equally have been positioned in front of an illuminated screen, for instance. The low degree of depth articulation does not help discern her actual position either. The poor articulation of detail, virtually zero articulation of background and depth, and the rather artificial effect of the illumination of the picture all confirm that this photograph is at the low modality end of the scale. The rest of the dimensions also underscore values that project very low modality; more importantly, these dimensions rely heavily on colour, a semiotic resource that has been thoroughly analysed in the corpus of novels, and that has proven particularly useful in projecting the ideational, interpersonal and textual metafunctions. Although there is some degree of saturation in relation to the darkest browns, it is not especially significant (mainly when viewed in the context of some of the covers in the corpus such as that of *Game Over*, for instance); colour differentiation is not underscored for the picture features the sepia version of what would have, otherwise, been a black and white photograph. This also implies that colours tend to be quite flat, so there is hardly any colour modulation either (for instance, the colour of her skin is nearly merged with the background) and the articulation of tone is virtually restricted to two (the light and dark versions of browns and beiges). In sum, all the dimensions realize very low modality. Ideationally, the whole composition is far removed from the values encoded in the jackets of the novels in my corpus and, I would add, from any other Chick Lit novel ever published. The whole composition appears to encode significations related to dullness, even dreariness for some readers, although, perhaps, it also projects meanings associated with the reflective and inward-looking nature of the diary-writing exercise. And yet, it seems to overlook completely the core component of playfulness that has since become a constant in the genre. Furthermore, because of the 'unattractiveness' of the cover, the interpersonal function of drawing readers' attention might be questionable, but this lack does not correlate with the success of the novel. Whereas other titles in the genre appear to rely heavily on rather elaborate book covers, one of the most successful novels in terms of sales and critical acclaim is not concerned with the same combination of semiotic resources. At this point it is necessary to remind ourselves that multimodal frameworks and paradigms tend to stay away from claims of univocal relationships between resources and meanings. However, in the context of the whole genre, this book jacket would appear to 'defy' most of the results and conclusions drawn from the analysis of some other examples of Chick Lit.

Interestingly, Nørgaard (2010b) proposes to view the semiotic resource of typography in light of modality too:

> The question remains whether and to what extent the concept of modality is applicable to the analysis of this semiotic mode [typography]. Does the visual side of written verbal language in any way signal 'as how true' or 'as how real' the typography itself should be taken? And, if yes, how can typographic modality be captured in our analysis?
>
> (Nørgaard, 2010b: 74)

Nørgaard concludes that typographic modality needs further investigation, as she has some concerns regarding whether the dimensions proposed by Kress and van Leeuwen are the most apt parameters to bring how it operates to the fore. In section 2.3.1 I have described in detail how typography encodes the three metafunctions in Chick Lit covers, but my assessments should perhaps be qualified further in terms of modality. It seems that, interpersonally, the typographic variants that emphasize script-like features do establish a particular connection with the reader as if they were inviting them to take part in their intimate thoughts, because of the high modality of the letterforms. That is, by being reminiscent of handwriting, these variants can be acknowledged to be closely representative of the 'reality' that is human writing. As a result, high typographical modality points at a close, intimate connection with the readers, who are invited to believe they are reading the direct thoughts being shaped by the hand of the writer. To strengthen even more the contrast with the rest of the genre, *Bridget Jones's Diary* is also successful at avoiding any typographical manifestation of penmanship; on the contrary, in relation to the rest of the novels in the corpus, the title can be described as non-sloping, not excessively curved, not connected, regular and void of any flourishes, which differs to a great extent from most of the novels in the corpus. In sum, there is very little on the jacket of *Bridget Jones's Diary* that reminds the reader of a prototypical Chick Lit book cover. Because the publication of this novel coincides with the outset of the genre, it can be argued that Chick Lit, as we know it nowadays, was still in its infancy and its characterizing traits were not yet fully developed. This does not detract from the fact that, for instance, Marian Keyes's *Watermelon* was published in 1996, virtually at the same time as Fielding's novel, but it already displays some of the defining aspects discussed in this chapter. All in all, it seems that in the context of the success of the genre that ensued, it is precisely the atypicality of *Bridget Jones's Diary* that helped it stand out among the sameness subsequently found among the rest of the novels.

2.5 Conclusion

This chapter has embarked on a description of Chick Lit as a genre from the perspective of the first point of contact that the readership has with the novels, the books' covers. Via the systematic approach that multimodality affords the analyst, it has been possible to conclude that some of the prototypical values associated with Chick Lit works already emanate from this first point of contact. Because multimodal stylistics intends to be complementary of, not substituting for, analyses of the language proper, this initial overview of the features of the genre is introductory, not exhaustive. One of the aims set out in the introduction to this chapter was to confirm, deny or question whether multimodal tools could form part of a stylistics apparatus of analysis. It is safe to conclude that multimodal frameworks are not only useful but perhaps should be referred to more regularly to bring to the fore core components of the meaning of literary works that are illustrated by semiotic modes other than the verbal. Finally, this chapter is the first step in bringing to the fore some of the characteristics of Chick Lit fiction. The findings here need to be contextualized by implementing a similarly methodical and systematic analysis of the language of the novels proper, which is the aim of the following chapters.

Chapter 3

Who is the 'Chick' in Chick Lit?

3.1 Who is the Chick Lit Protagonist?

In Chapter 1, I present an overview of what this genre has come to be perceived as, its main traits and its general characteristics. There I quote Gormley (2009), who provides a rather encompassing summary of what these main features are, including the fact that these novels depict 'the life, loves, trials and tribulations of their predominantly young, single, urban, female protagonists.' The aim of the present chapter is to look in detail at who these female protagonists are, at whether their age, marital status, and social and geographical locations are, indeed, so prototypically defining and such a constant in the novels, and at why these issues have become key aspects for the definition of the whole genre. In sum, the umbrella concern of this chapter is the characterization of Chick Lit women. Before I delve into this task, I reiterate what has been claimed in previous chapters regarding the prototypicality of the novels I focus on. Describing the vast array of heroines in the very many plots and storylines by now incorporated in Chick Lit (see Chapter 1 for more on this) would not be especially conducive to a fruitful and effective analysis of the genre's female characters. My aim, instead, is to look for the commonalities that have come to endow these women with their identity as part of a separate and instantly recognizable variety of popular fiction. Thus, I focus on some general traits despite the multifarious ways in which these have been subsequently reworked and refashioned in the novels. Pursuing this aim, this chapter adopts a double theoretical position (a similar approach is also undertaken in Chapter 5) so that the stylistic rigour of the monograph is maintained. The first part of the chapter is informed by theories from cognitive psychology, which allow me to explicate how readers flesh out aspects of the identity of the Chick Lit protagonist via the application of models used in social cognition. In the second part, I use a corpus stylistics methodology which, by being firmly anchored on computerized methods of language analysis, sheds light on how the features that jointly outline who the Chick Lit female is are linguistically realized. I intend to contrast whether and, if so, how the conclusions that the socio-cognitive perspective lets me draw correlate to results obtained via a corpus stylistics investigation. My main aim, therefore, is to contribute to the study of the genre with as comprehensive and thorough a characterization of the 'chick' in Chick Lit as possible.

The double take I adopt in this chapter is partly based on the work on characterization carried out by Culpeper (2001; see also Culpeper, 2000)[1] whose aims are to 'explore how the words of a text create a particular impression of a character in the reader's head' (2001: 1). The main focus of his research, however, differs from mine as he feeds from a variety of disciplines but eventually anchors his work in cognitive stylistics[2]. He explores the way readers are capable of interpreting characters by combining their prior knowledge with the cues emanating from the text. As he states, he is concerned with 'the process of characterisation rather than with character' (2001: 1). Although my own analysis is inspired by Culpeper's, I do not delve into the process of characterization in the same way he does. Instead, I turn my attention to the 'character' rather than the 'process'. Having said that, there are still plenty of commonalities between the way Culpeper tackles characterization and my own theoretical standpoints and subsequent practical analysis of the Chick Lit protagonist; these areas of agreement are, in the main, represented by the combination of top-down and bottom-up approaches for the analysis of characters. Employing a top down approach means that I take advantage of the models proposed in social cognition to explain how readers' prior knowledge of social structures shapes their interpretation of Chick Lit women; thanks to the corpus stylistics tool Wmatrix (Rayson, 2009) I also include a bottom-up perspective whereby the main semantic domains of a corpus[3] of Chick Lit works are considered in light of the social and otherwise categories that the socio-cognitive slant has highlighted.[4] In sum, I attempt to account fully for characterization in Chick Lit by balancing out a multidisciplinary perspective that combines theoretical tenets from cognition and corpus studies.

One distinctive trait of the Chick Lit's chick that has been accorded special relevance in a variety of scholarly work (Hanson, 2004; Marsh, 2004; Whelehan, 2000, 2005) is the claims to feminism made by the women in these novels. Despite the fact that this issue is dealt with briefly here in relation to some of the social categories to which these women belong and which the socio-cognitive slant highlights, the relationship between female characters, feminist and post-feminist concerns deserves a fuller account than could be provided here, so this discussion is resumed and fully developed in Chapter 4. Thus Section 3.2 sets off by introducing some theoretical aspects on socio-cognitive models which can account successfully for the way readers rely upon prior knowledge for character impression formation, followed by a practical application of these models to a series of prototypical novels. Next, in Section 3.3, these results are viewed in light of corpus stylistics tenets and, more specifically, in connection with the semantic components of the language of the novels. As explained below, the software used allows the researcher to tag the language of the novels in a variety of ways, from prototypically grammatical aspects such as parts of speech, to keyword analysis and semantic tagging. Because I am interested in looking at certain themes and topics that encode the social categories that a socio-cognitive approach brings to the fore, grammatical and keyword taggings do not render themselves so advantageous a tool for my interests.

This does not mean that looking at the way some parts of speech, for instance, behave cannot help investigate other aspects of the novels. Here, though, I focus on whether a computerized methodology can bring out, in a more comprehensive and accurate way, the semantic aspects of the texts that jointly project and characterize the themes, topics and subject-matter of the novels and that bring to light who these women are, where they work, what they like, or what they talk about. For that aim, I have compiled a corpus of six novels amounting to a total of around 650,000 words which has been run through Wmatrix (Rayson, 2009); the computerized tagging resulting from the software analysis brings about a series of enlightening comparisons. For instance, first, I focus on certain semantic categories that appear to feature more prominently in my novels than in the texts that these are contrasted with; then, and most interestingly, I consider some other semantic realizations which the software picks out as being under-represented in relation to those contrasting texts. These two sets of comparisons provide some rather elucidating results and interesting food for thought because the series of social categories that a socio-cognitive perspective appears to highlight do not always find a fully matched correlate in the computerized analysis of the same data.

3.2 Social Cognition and Characterization

This section investigates how theoretical proposals emerging from social cognition can help explain readers' ability for character interpretation. This first half of the chapter closely follows the characterization model proposed by Culpeper (2001) although, for my own interests here, I restrict the variety of perspectives that he borrows from to aspects of research on social cognition.[5] As previously mentioned, Culpeper ultimately frames his characterization model within cognitive stylistics as his aim is 'to show how a representation of character (an impression of character) might be constructed in the mind during the process of reading' (Culpeper, 2001: 34). Strictly speaking, though, this chapter is not to be understood as a faithful illustration of work on cognitive stylistics, although it is still informed by some of its general principles.

Culpeper's model of characterization emerges from the intricate connection of a series of cognitive, discoursal, linguistic and other aspects that pertain to and help explain text comprehension. Based on Meutsch's (1986: 324) framework for literary analysis, Culpeper proposes a general description of text comprehension in which aspects of characterization are also fundamentally embedded. In his proposal, the following set of components jointly aid text processing: 'control system', 'prior knowledge', 'situation model', 'textbase' and 'surface structure' (Culpeper, 2001: 35). Each element, Culpeper argues, is dynamically related to the rest and also contains some specific aspects directly related to characterization. Briefly, the control system 'oversees the entire comprehension process. [...] Part of the literary control system will be "reading for character"' (2001: 36); prior knowledge 'concerns the knowledge held in long-term memory which can be used in the comprehension process. A subset of this knowledge will contain information that is relevant to the understanding of character' (2001: 36); in the situation model, 'prior knowledge and textual elements combine to create a meaning representation – our sense of what the text is about. Part of the situation model may (depending on the text type) constitute our impression of a character' (2001: 36); the textbase is 'a meaning representation, but unlike the situation model it only includes the propositional content of the text. Some of these propositions will, of course, relate to character' (2001: 37); finally, the surface structure 'of the text [...] will include the particular linguistic choices attributed to characters' (2001: 37). Such a rich array of constituents evidences that characterization occurs as a result of a multifaceted process which is, as pointed out before, embedded in text comprehension but, due to space constraints, I cannot afford to look into all the various parts of the text comprehension model here. Instead, I focus specifically on the roles of 'prior knowledge' and 'surface structure', for which I exploit theoretical proposals from social cognition and some linguistic aspects brought to the fore by corpus stylistics, respectively. As previously mentioned, I am not concerned with the whole process of characterization but with those aspects of the process which can help render clear what elements specifically embody the essence of the Chick Lit female.

Focusing on prior knowledge means that what readers 'know' is important, first, for text comprehension and, second, for fleshing out who the chick in Chick Lit is. How that knowledge is stored and how it operates is described in the application of psychology and other cognate disciplines' tenets to literary texts, so defining a few basic key concepts here should be advantageous for my own endeavours. For instance, the brain is said to store information as both long-term memory and short-term working memory; whereas the former is meant to function in a more permanent way, the latter is more active and feeds information onto the long-term domain (Culpeper, 2001: 58). In relation to the latter, a distinction that scholars generally work with is that of 'episodic' versus 'semantic' memory (Tulving, 1972). As Culpeper summarizes:

> The general idea is that information which has been analysed and interpreted in short-term working memory is provisionally held as an 'episode' in episodic memory. [...] Semantic memory [...] contains more general abstract knowledge.
>
> (Culpeper, 2001: 59)

This distinction is not without its problems either, as it is not very clear where the boundaries of episodic and semantic memory lie, although for the most part scholars prefer to see them as part of a continuum rather than as discrete categories. It is not immediately obvious either how events that are initially held in episodic memory come to form part of semantic memory. For my own purposes, I focus on the notion of semantic memory because it is there where the kind of prior knowledge which readers activate for text processing and characterization seems to reside. The choice of plural for the noun 'readers' in the previous sentence is intentional because most components of this prior knowledge are presumed to have been collectively experienced rather than pertaining to the individual; as Culpeper states, 'it is also this knowledge which authors can assume – at least to some extent – to be shared amongst their readership. Indeed, it is the shared nature of semantic memory that led van Dijk (1987, 1990 for example) to suggest that it be called "social memory"' (2001: 60). It ensues, therefore, that considerations of how prior knowledge influences text comprehension should encompass a social component; if, by default, any model of characterization should be able to cope with social aspects too, then social cognition seems capable of offering the right tools to tackle such an enterprise. Social cognition is generally defined as:

> A branch of social psychology that involves the study of the processes and structures that determine and are determined by knowledge of self and others.
>
> (McCann and Higgins, 1990: 15)

Pennington (2000) elaborates on what is the realm of this discipline and argues that there are

> [...] three cognitive processes [...] that we apply to our social world. First, information we receive about other people (and ourselves, for that matter) is *interpreted*; this means that information is given meaning often by both the social context and our previous experience, cultural values, etc. [...] Second, social information is *analysed*, this means that an initial interpretation may be adjusted, changed or even rejected. [...] Third, social information is *stored in memory* from which it may be recalled or retrieved. [...] Theory and research in social cognition may equally be about other people, ourselves, and, which is most likely, about ourselves in interaction with other people.
>
> (Pennington, 2000: 2)

Social cognition, therefore, is a discipline that incorporates the social domain into the study of human cognition. Following Pennington, the way people perceive and interact with the social world can be seen as a threefold process: 'interpretation' of the information surrounding us, 'analysis' of this input, and 'storage' for possible future recall. Crucially, thus, research in social cognition argues that the social world needs to be seen as encompassing other individuals as well as ourselves, so, social cognition, as a discipline, investigates people's perceptions of other people. Besides this clearly defined object of study, social cognition also contemplates the differences between the cognitive processing of 'social' and 'non-social' categories, 'social' here understood as pertaining to people. Hence, social cognition research concerns itself with whether our perception of other people and the way we process information about them differs from the way we perceive objects (see Brewer, 1988; Cantor and Mischel, 1977, 1979; Rumelhart, 1984). In general, scholars tend to agree that the ways social and non-social categories are processed display more similarities than discrepancies, although this is an aspect on which I do not dwell any further in this chapter. In the rest of this section, I focus exclusively on how people perceive other individuals.

Social cognition researchers benefit from applying the notion of 'schema' that they borrow from schema theory.[6] Fiske and Taylor (1991) define it as:

> A cognitive structure that represents knowledge about a concept or type of stimulus, including its attributes and the relations among those attributes. [...] Schemas facilitate what is called top-down, conceptually driven, or theory-driven processes, which simply means processes heavily influenced by one's organized prior knowledge, as opposed to processes that are more bottom-up or data-driven.
>
> (Fiske and Taylor, 1991: 98)

Schemas (or schemata) provide a further way of explaining how prior knowledge is organized in the human brain and also how it operates. Viewing these schemas in light of their connection to the social world, Culpeper narrows down his research interests by specifically focusing on 'social schemas' (Culpeper, 2001: 76). He highlights the relevant role that these 'high-level cognitive structures that contain links between social categories' play (2001: 77), and he goes on to add that 'when a category is activated, so too is the network of which it is a part. It is this network that I shall describe as a social schema' (2001: 77). Prior knowledge, therefore, is not to be understood as a mass of unconnected and jumbled-up pieces of information but rather as being organized in a series of compartments, structures and connecting networks which effectively determine the top-down half of information processing. When those domains draw together and systematize clusters of information about the social world, they are specifically referred to as social schemas. Because these social schemas function as higher-level cognitive structures, Culpeper suggests that we utilize other ways of conceptualizing individuals in our social world. He argues that the social categories that people use in their perception of others can be seen as three broad groupings structured according to the information these groupings hold:

> *Personal categories*: These include knowledge about people's preferences and interests [...], habits [...], traits [...], and goals. [...]
> *Social role categories*: These include knowledge about people's social functions. They include kinship roles [...], occupational roles [...], and relational roles. [...]
> *Group membership categories*: These include knowledge about social groups: sex, race, class, age, nationality, religion and so on.
>
> (Culpeper, 2001: 75–6)

Individuals are seen as part of a particular personal category because they may display certain interests (playing golf, for instance), habits (biting their nails), traits (being shy), or goals (to achieve celebrity status). Second, social role categories allow us to define a person as a parent (kinship role), or in relation to their professional dedication (occupational role), or as being friends, lovers or partners (relational role). Finally, we also pigeonhole people in specific groups which are determined, for instance, by biology (sex category), by whether people are Caucasian or Oriental, for example (race), by their social status (class), their age, etc. As with any classification, Culpeper's is not to be seen as exhaustive; on the contrary, the boundaries should be understood as fluid and further categories can also be added. Van Dijk (1987), for example, suggests that we also evaluate people according to the category 'appearance'; more importantly, he argues that the categories that structure our knowledge of people also determine certain attitudes and evaluative links (described below) towards them and these categories include

> [...] 'appearance', 'gender', 'age', 'occupation', 'role', or 'class', as well as the (inter)actions associated with these categories, which also underlie our prototypical beliefs about other people.
>
> (van Dijk, 1987: 192–3)

The inclusion of 'appearance' issues in the list above confirms something that also rings true in relation to Chick Lit: the way people *look* is an aspect influencing our assessment of other individuals so it does have a place in the social evaluation of others. The appearance category includes those features of a person's physical aspect that are reasonably controllable, that is, can be relatively easily changed, enhanced or adorned. In relation to Chick Lit novels, scholarly work has repeatedly highlighted that physical appearance is not just another factor in the general description of women but a crucial one:

> Although the Bridget Joneses and Jemima Js of the new millennium are free agents relative to their sister characters of past centuries, their freedom is mitigated by [...] the self-imposed and culturally sanctioned tyranny of hating their own bodies. [...] These novels point to something greater than a narcissistic obsession with one's physique or sexual desirability; in virtually every novel, being thin has not only romantic but also financial rewards and repercussions. Looks are a form of currency that aid not only one's search for a mate but also one's ability to secure that promotion, get that next job, and become a fully realized human being.
>
> (Umminger, 2006: 240)

For Umminger, thus, such an excessive preoccupation with weight issues as the only possible way in which these women can felicitously succeed in the rest of their lives can only be negatively assessed. The fact that some aspects of the social world, such as appearance issues, are capable of bringing out further cognitive connections that result in evaluative reactions is illustrated by van Dijk's notion of 'attitude schemata' (1987, 1988). As Culpeper summarizes:

> It is particularly important to note that social schemata include links across the three category groupings. [...] [S]ome of these links form evaluative beliefs (that is, may be considered positive or negative features). Such evaluations constitute what van Dijk (1987, 1988) refers to as 'attitude schemata' [...] and provide a link to the notion of ideology. Different groups would have had different attitudes, or different attitude schemata, associated with the schema for a particular group.
>
> (Culpeper, 2001: 77)

Umminger's assessment confirms that the recurrent preoccupation that Chick Lit women have with their appearance can indeed be met by rather negative reactions; so it appears that behind Umminger's rather antagonistic view of these women's obsession with being thin lie certain attitude schemas that reject the enslaving signification that Chick Lit women attach to weight issues. Besides, whereas Umminger echoes one of the appearance issues that most characteristically typify what the Chick Lit protagonist worries about, her weight, looks and appearance matters extend to many other aspects such as being in possession of fashionable clothes, shoes and accessories, or subjecting themselves to the latest beauty routines. Because appearance has a special role to play in relation to the depiction of Chick Lit women, I incorporate it into Culpeper's 'group membership category'; thus, in our capacity as readers, our ultimate perception (positive or negative) of these female characters is as much determined by their preoccupation with their looks as it is by their sex, race, class or nationality.

By now, it should have become clear that Culpeper's characterization model which I take advantage of in this chapter advocates the applicability of social cognition tenets to the analysis of fictional characters. Essentially, the principles and processes that are put in motion when we assess other individuals also get to work when we encounter characters in fictional contexts. But the fact that the latter are, fundamentally, non-actual means that the way we conceptualize them cannot be totally likened to the way we perceive individuals in the real world. Characterization in fictional contexts must necessarily involve some further processes that do not apply in real life. As Culpeper explains:

> I would argue that first impressions of characters are guided by the implicit models offered by social schemata. Such schemata, once activated, offer a scaffolding for incoming character information. Moreover, they allow us to make further knowledge-based inferences and thereby flesh out our impressions of character [...]. However [...] we also need to take on board knowledge about fictional character types. Thus, we need to consider yet another group of categories which we might label 'dramatic role'.
>
> (Culpeper, 2001: 86-7)

Essentially, the non-actuality of fictional characters means that a different set of schemas is activated in character comprehension; character conceptualization is enriched by the addition of the dramatic role category to the already existing information about the social world. Whereas in the actual world social categories will suffice for a felicitous assessment of individuals as part of a specific personal, social or group membership category, in fictional contexts these need to be appropriately complemented by knowledge that caters specifically for their fictionality. Culpeper goes on to add that

> The notion of dramatic role [...] does not concern the individuality of a character, but the universal roles that underlie narratives and plays. [...] Dramatic role knowledge, however, is not isolated from the kind of information that is used in the perception of real people.
>
> (Culpeper, 2001: 87)

These dramatic roles do not operate outside of, but in conjunction with, the social categories that pertain in the real world. More interestingly for my own purposes in this chapter, Culpeper also argues that dramatic role knowledge is not concerned with individual manifestations of particular characters but with the universality of certain types, which brings this knowledge in line with the notion of genre. As Culpeper explains:

> Dramatic roles are closely tied to genre. Our knowledge about different genres – comedies, tragedies, romances, Westerns, detective stories, and so on – includes a set of associated dramatic roles. Thus, recognising the genre one encounters can lead to the activation of a set of dramatic roles, which in turn may guide one's perception of the characters.
>
> (Culpeper, 2001: 87)

The social categories that allow people to understand other individuals are, therefore, not sufficient to account for fictional characterization, so readers (or film watchers or theatre audiences, for that matter) activate additional schemas to complement their prior social world knowledge. These additional schemas are so directly aligned with the notion of genre that, only when a particular genre is identified, is one set of dramatic roles triggered over any other. When Chick Lit readers interpret characters in the novels, they do so by also recognizing that these belong in a specific genre, so, by implication, the dramatic roles that allow readers to flesh out Chick Lit women should also concurrently confirm the independent identity of the genre. I am arguing, thus, that accepting the existence of the dramatic role category can assist a stylistic analysis of Chick Lit in further ways because it indirectly emphasizes the novels' coherence as being part of a specific genre and might even help tighten existing definitions of this form of popular fiction. For instance, because Chick Lit is framed within the general umbrella category of popular fiction, the particulars of the three social groupings previously mentioned and developed below might be better understood in light of the ultimate aims and objectives of the genre which, by and large, underscore the entertainment aspect over social or ideological concerns (this is amply developed in Chapter 5), for instance. As Smith (2008) also does, it could be argued that, like many other genres, Chick Lit is simply a product of its time and hence duplicates aspects and messages of the society that begets it:

> I argue that this literature is adept at revealing and/or reflecting the society that produced it, interfacing with the dominant ideologies of the time period, and challenging, rather than deploying, the ideologies transmitted by women's magazines, self-help books, romantic comedies, and domestic-advice manuals.
>
> (Smith, 2008: 16)

Smith is specifically interested in investigating the way Chick Lit projects what she terms the 'Cosmopolitan culture and consumerism' which frames this genre but which equally permeates other popular manifestations such as fashion magazines, romantic comedies and self-help books. Because of the ubiquitous presence of the values embodied in the Cosmopolitan and consumer cultures (see also Knowles, 2004b), readers do not find it difficult to activate those already-existing elements of their social knowledge when fleshing out Chick Lit women, as the social schemas generating that prior social knowledge are based on contemporary social realities experienced by them. The million-dollar question concerning the projection of those realities in Chick Lit, and which can tip the scales regarding a definition of Chick Lit, is whether the reproduction of such current issues highlights a self-reflective, ironic, and challenging attitude, as Smith (2008: 26) suggests, or whether readers are actually failing to read between the lines and simply embracing the consumerism (among other values) which Chick Lit seems to be firmly embedded in. The answer to such a query, I argue, has repercussions for the notion of the genre itself. Smith goes on to ponder along similar lines because, despite arguing that Chick Lit novels challenge rather than deploy certain ideologies which are, otherwise, present in magazines and romantic comedies, for instance, she still has some misgivings regarding the ultimate effects that tracing this reality on to the novels has on readers:

> While I voraciously consume these magazines each month, I am simultaneously disturbed by and wary of the messages that they impart to their readers, and I see the negative effects that these images and articles can have upon their consumers when I teach *Bridget Jones's Diary* in my college classes. Many young women in my classes speak fervently about their *identification* with Bridget, and I worry that they, like Bridget, are unable to dissect or critique the messages conveyed to them everyday by consumer culture.
>
> (Smith, 2008: 19; italics mine)

As I suggest above, attempting to explain this slightly contradictory, certainly controversial, duality whereby Chick Lit is the consumerism-progeny of its time but still purports to replicate certain values in an ironic, challenging way, has repercussions for the notion of Chick Lit as a genre. Should we abide by Smith's preoccupation in the above quotation, then some readers are unable to discern and be critical about those negative aspects of consumer culture that they are constantly bombarded with, and that Chick Lit also incorporates. Instead, we might want to advocate that the incorporation of consumerism and 'Cosmopolitan culture', which in Chick Lit has a clearly defined strand in relation to appearance and looks, is simply Chick Lit's ironic, playful, even flippant, way of dealing with contemporaneous social messages that Chick Lit authors and/or readers might not necessarily condone or abide by. This is certainly an issue which scholarly research on the genre does not seem to agree on. What seems to be more clearly confirmed, however, is the fact that readers partially flesh out Chick Lit characters thanks to the dramatic roles which are, by now, specifically associated with the genre and differentiated from some closely related ones such as romantic fiction (further connections and discrepancies between Chick Lit and romances are discussed in Chapter 4). But, as explained, dramatic roles on their own do not suffice for fictional characterization, as 'first impressions of characters are guided by the implicit models offered by social schemata' which 'once activated, offer a scaffolding for incoming character information' (Culpeper, 2001: 86), so the way these social categories function deserves a few more thoughts.

Chick Lit female characters 'remind' readers of real-life people. Despite the fact that dramatic roles can account for the genre's women being portrayed as ditzy but genuine, quirky but cute, for instance, there are many other traits which bring these women much closer to the current reality of the twentieth and twenty-first centuries. Some argue (see below) that behind Chick Lit chicks lies an attempt at a quasi-faithful representation of certain female values and beliefs drawn from our social world which would subsequently invite the readership to recognize, sympathize and maybe even empathize with those real-life values. This issue has received ample attention in a variety of scholarly work on Chick Lit:

> More telling than any of these economic indicators, however, was the veritable explosion of discourses about Bridget Jones. She became an icon, a recognisable emblem of a particular kind of femininity, a constructed point of identification for women. Newspapers set out to find the 'real' Bridget Jones or sent 'genuine Bridget Joneses' to review the films. Bridget generated instant recognition among many young heterosexual women; as Imelda Whelehan (2002) has argued, part of the success of the book lay in the 'that's me' phenomenon whereby Bridget became regarded not as a fictional character but as a representative of the zeitgeist.
>
> (Gill and Herdieckerhoff, 2006: 489)

Gill and Heidieckerhoff, on the one hand, and Whelehan, on the other, are not alone in highlighting that Chick Lit has been especially successful at accommodating female attitudes, values and behaviours highly reminiscent of issues pertaining in the real world of contemporary women. Smith, in turn, states that 'characters, readers, and authors are so similar that often, in defining the genre, critics collapse the genre's characters, readers, and writers' (Smith, 2008: 7); Bernard (1999), on the other hand, in a review of *Bridget Jones's Diary* for American audiences, considers that

> [d]espite a few cultural discrepancies, many American women embraced the character with giddy *self-recognition*. She was a kind of resilient anti-heroine who veered between the pathetic and the courageous in her quest for love, sex, and an acceptable pair of opaque black stockings. In America, as in England, Bridget was embraced as an iconic thirtysomething Everywoman.
>
> (Bernard, 1999; italics mine)

Critical perspectives[7] on the genre not concerned with discussing socio-cognitive aspects in the same way I have presented here still confirm the direct influence that categories that belong in the social world exert in the novels, as if the latter had transposed real women onto the page. Readers, thus, can easily activate their prior knowledge on social categories for the interpretation of certain messages which authors seem rather keen to replicate in fictional form. In fact, for some, the success of the genre relies precisely on the way these novels count so heavily on readers not just recognizing these messages, but identifying with them in the 'that's me' manner pointed out by Whelehan above (2002: 55). In the next section, therefore, I look in detail at how this transposition from the real world to the fictional world takes place and what consequences this has for our understanding of the chick in Chick Lit.

3.2.1 Social cognition and Chick Lit

The theoretical discussion presented in the previous section bears witness to this discipline's capability to equip stylisticians and literary critics with models that can successfully account for how we come to interpret characters the way we do. I now move on to assess a group of Chick Lit novels in light of the social categories and groupings proposed by Culpeper above. Five novels have been looked at to analyse which social categories are employed to literally flesh out the Chick Lit female and whether there are commonalities between the various chicks in the five novels. Then, I investigate the connection of the above to dramatic role schemas and consider whether by being at work in the various novels they underscore the coherence and identity of the genre. The novels are Helen Fielding's *Bridget Jones's Diary* (1996) [BJD], Sophie Kinsella's *Can you Keep a Secret?* (2003) [CKS], Adele Parks's *Game Over* (2001) [GO], Fiona Walker's *Lucy Talk* (2000) [LT] and Imogen Edwards-Jones's *My Canapé Hell* (2000) [MCH]. My assessment of women in these novels focuses exclusively on the main characters, mainly because of space constraints, but also because most Chick Lit novels are essentially structured around this one individual, with the rest of the characters and plot-lines subordinated to her. As Mlynowski and Jacobs explain:

> The single most important element of your chick lit novel is your main character. No matter what kind of story you're aiming to write [...]. What readers love about chick lit is that the heroine is them – but with more attitude, more courage, or maybe just more shoes. She is Everywoman, with quirks and problems that are believable yet larger than life. She's confident yet insecure. Smart but naïve. Lovable yet flawed.
>
> (Mlynowski and Jacobs, 2006: 64)

There is no shortage of websites[8] that, just like Mlynowski and Jacobs's publication above, also advise on how to write your female protagonist. Mlynowski and Jacobs, moreover, seem to suggest that, by its very nature, putting together the various characteristics of this protagonist involves crossing ontological boundaries and transposing onto the page the traits of the reader herself. Assuming character-reader identification, as Mlynowski and Jacobs do, must undoubtedly also facilitate readers' character impression formation because apparently they would only need to trigger already-stored prior knowledge about realities of their own. Mlynowski and Jacobs also provide a list of recommendations for character depiction as follows:

> You have to create a character sketch that will work for you [...]. To get you started, here are some preliminary details. [...] Name; age; physical description; education; five words that describe her personality; where does she work? Is she good at her job? Why? Or why not?; Her dream job, or dream life; Things that annoy her; Her bad habits; What people like about her; Her roadblocks to happiness; The person she trusts most (and why); The person she should trust most (and why); Her dream guy; What she does to relax; Before the book began, the best day of her life, the worst day of her life.
>
> (Mlynowski and Jacobs, 2006: 70–1)

This craftsmanship sketch for Chick Lit characterization consists, in essence, of the same 'bullet-points' that would be triggered as social schemas in real-life person impression formation. Therefore, to put flesh on the bones of a Chick Lit female felicitously, a writer needs to spell out convincingly the same three basic groupings of social categories used for people: for instance, this can be achieved by highlighting personal categories in the form of 'her bad habits', or social role categories by identifying 'her dream job' and 'her dream guy', and group membership categories by including information about this chick's 'education'.

These three broad groupings help us characterize people according to a series of parameters. The personal category concerns our knowledge about individuals in their capacity as people, and allows us to learn about their preferences and interests, habits, individual traits, and goals. The first commonality found among the five novels is in relation to their preferences and interests, as three of the five protagonists engage in self-help book reading: Lucy from LT, Bridget from BJD, and Abigail from MCH. Obviously there are other interests not shared by the five women, such as the fact that Lucy (LT) enjoys organizing parties for her friends and Cas's interests (GO) are mainly determined by her sexual prowess. There is less agreement in relation to their habits, but they coincide again with regard to the traits by which they are mostly known: 'scatterbrained', 'disorganized', 'inefficient' and 'needy'. As concerns their goals, these are mainly determined by the plot-line of each novel: Lucy (LT) is intent on recovering from a break-up with her boyfriend, Cas (GO) is bent on maintaining her successful career, and Emma (CKS) wants to finally get rid of her habit of keeping secrets. In sum, they are resolved to better themselves and dispel any trace of failure in their lives; whether they are successful or not, is a different matter. As an illustration, consider the following:

> Dear Mo,
> Very productive weekend so far. Have sent out invitations for Halloween party, sorted my tights drawer, thrown everything past its sell-by date out of the fridge and cleaned the bathroom even though it's Jane's turn on the roster. [...] She says I'm suffering from displacement activity syndrome because Greg hasn't called me. I told her that was rubbish and set about polishing the telephone for the fifth time. [...] She tried to persuade me to go with her to a line-dancing night at her riding school, but I was far too busy removing built-in grime from cooker hob, and cleaning lime-scale from the kitchen taps with the toothbrush Greg keeps here for overnight stays. [...] Might just tidy my bedroom again.
>
> (LT: 5–6)

Lucy (LT) illustrates some of the features in the personal category above. Lucy is obsessively needy, insecure (this cleaning spree is prompted by the fact that a woman has answered her boyfriend's phone) and over-dependent. After this incident, her goal is simply to find out who that woman is and whether her boyfriend is actually cheating on her. Towards the end of the novel, she shifts her goal towards recovering from the break-up until she eventually gets together with a different man.

The social role category (kinship, occupational and relational roles) also exhibits similarities among the five novels. These women always feature as 'daughters', so their kinship role and family connections seem underscored, although the focus is still on them rather than on the members of their families. Their occupational role varies but only within the professional domain, that is, these women are never manual workers or housewives, for instance. They are part of a new generation of urban professionals whose careers determine their lives to a considerable extent: Emma (CKS) is a marketing assistant, Abigail

(MCH) is a journalist, and Cas (GO) is a successful television producer. Their relational role is, nevertheless, the trait that these characters are especially known for, especially since and, probably because of, *Bridget Jones's Diary*: these women are either single at the beginning of the novel or have a boyfriend who ends up being replaced by the figure of the new and better man. The relational role also describes friendship links among characters, an aspect that has been highlighted by some scholarly work. Lucy (LT), Cas (GO), Bridget (BJD) and Emma (CKS) are all described in their capacity as friends of other characters; however, the underlying nature of some of these friendship links is not always defined in positive terms:

> Many heroines are depicted as naïve and passive, constantly surprised by events [...], surpassed by men in terms of career opportunities [...] or tricked by 'evil,' 'scheming' female characters who compete for their chosen heroes [...]. This latter theme draws on the old notion of women as manipulative, particularly in relation to men. Thus, despite a popular belief that chick lit portrays strong female friendships, in fact other women are frequently represented as competitors and therefore not to be trusted.
>
> (Gill and Herdieckerhoff, 2006: 494–5)

Abigail (MCH), for instance, deserts her close mates in exchange for her new life as an entertainment journalist who reports on the lives of celebrities; order is, nevertheless, eventually restored and she returns to her old friends who she so cherished before work commitments changed her. It is important to remember the notion of attitude schemata (van Dijk, 1987, 1988) discussed above, as it highlights the evaluative associations (positive or negative) that social categories can trigger. As Gill and Herdieckerhoff (2006) point out, the characterization of these women is based on widely spread stereotypes concerning the manipulative and competitive nature of some women, especially with regard to other women and most clearly when they are fighting for the attention of the prototypical male. In Chick Lit, female friendships seem to be particularly conducive to exploiting those stereotypes and this can result in some readers evaluating this restrictive presentation of women rather negatively. As discussed in Section 3.2 in relation to appearance issues and consumer culture, whether this is done in a challenging way so that stereotypical versions of women as manipulative and scheming are viewed in a new light, or whether it is perpetuating such a view, is something that the readership must determine by themselves.

The final grouping is group membership category. The type of knowledge in this category is based on sex, race, class, age, nationality, religion and, as discussed earlier, appearance. The variations between the characters seem less marked than among the previous categories. Only Cas, the protagonist of *Game Over*, seems to be slightly more affluent than the others. Apart from that, they are all middle-class (or upper-middle-class) women, in their late twenties or early thirties, white, British, and profess an obsessive preoccupation with their appearance, as in the next extracts:

> I've championed the 'what normal people look like in designer clothes' corner. I've been dressed up in hipsters, bumsters, I've donned blonde and dark wigs to see if blondes really do have more fun. I've [...] test driven the micro skirt, the tube skirt, the split up the side skirt and all in the name of fashion.
>
> (MCH: 4)

> Am now convinced that I have the figure of a TellyTubby. Feel so paranoid that I rejected the sexy little mini-dress I'd packed for tonight [...]. We ate in a country pub [...] I had a small tuna salad. Feel famished.
>
> (LT: 109)

There are no explicit references to religion or spiritual beliefs in these five novels, but this does not mean that these traits are not present in other Chick Lit works, especially in some of the most recent offshoots of the genre such as Christian Lit or Church Lit.

To sum up the way social categories illustrate readers' impression formation, it is important to highlight that, in the real world, the various categories are not always activated equally when we interact with other real-life beings. In relation to person perception, Culpeper (2001) states that there are two possible ways of forming our impressions:

> Sometimes a category may indeed suffice, and sometimes we may form an impression more on the basis of information about a particular individual than any category [...]. The first alternative involves a greater emphasis on top-down processing and results in a 'category-based' impression [...]. The second alternative involves a greater emphasis on bottom-up processing and results in a 'person-based' or 'attribute-based' impression: the impression is made up of the individual attributes of the target person.
>
> (Culpeper, 2001: 83)

It is possible that impression formation comes as a result of 'person-based' processing which emphasizes the individual attributes of the person in question rather than their being part of the categories discussed above. Impression formation of fictional characters can also be triggered by any of these two means, but the processes that allow category-based and person-based impression formation differ in nature:

> Category-based processing means greater emphasis on the prior knowledge categories relevant to character in forming an impression of character; person-based processing means greater emphasis on the textbase in forming an impression of character.
>
> (Culpeper, 2001: 83)

In Chick Lit, impression formation is less marked by bottom-up processes so it does not tend to originate in 'person-based' or 'attribute-based' impressions. Instead, perceptions seem to be mainly 'category-based' or top-down, as shown by the similarities in the social groupings analysis applied above. This, in turn, limits the scope for individuality in the portrayal of these women, although, alternatively, it strengthens the coherence of the genre. The repetitive nature that this lack of distinctiveness generates results in the reinforcement of the part played by the dramatic role category. So, if social schemas form the skeleton of the character, a slightly more particularized presentation of the various 'chicks' is still determined, to a great extent, by the dramatic role knowledge that shapes the eventual rendition of individual women and our processing them, as firmly lodged in Chick Lit. These female characters resemble one another because Chick Lit writers closely follow certain generic conventions in the depiction of these women, so that what could initially be understood as a stereotypical presentation, reminiscent of a quasi-reactionary, sterile depiction of women, can be equally justified by the authors' interest in adhering to the specific 'ideal woman' somehow expected from these works.

3.2.2 Social cognition and feminism

Recognizing the role that social schemas play in forming character impression is not the only way in which a socio-cognitive analysis can shed light on Chick Lit women. Attitude schemas (van Dijk, 1987, 1988) and the evaluative beliefs associated with them are also employed in our perception of individuals. These evaluations of beliefs and knowledge, Culpeper states, are closely linked to the concept of ideology, which together with the social schemas and dramatic role categories discussed in the previous section can account more comprehensively for Chick Lit characterization. Although aspects of feminism are revisited in a more detailed way in Chapter 4, especially in relation to the linguistic realizations of transitivity and speech and thought presentation, I briefly approach here how social cognition principles can equally shed some light on these claims to feminism. The role played by these ideological feminist concerns befits my discussion here because of the open relationship that these novels set up between their female characters and feminist beliefs and values. For example, Jemima, a friend of Emma's in *Can you Keep a Secret* defines what the notion of feminism means for her as follows:

> 'I'm being a feminist, actually,' retorts Jemima. 'We women have to stand up for our rights. You know, before she married my father, Mummy went out with this scientist chap who practically jilted her. He changed his mind three weeks before the wedding, can you believe it? So one night she crept into his lab and pulled out all the plugs of his stupid machines. His whole research was ruined!' [...] 'Do you think you should just let men walk all over you and get away with it? Great blow for feminism.'
>
> (CKS: 280)

The possible traits that a 'feminism' schema could comprise would, most certainly, vary from one individual to another, but some of the most likely aspects would include knowledge of women's rights, knowledge about women's inequalities, the denouncement of such inequalities, at times activism, and so on. Before Jemima in the above quotation had related her own version of feminism, she had clarified that 'revenge is a speciality of mine' (CKS: 279). Jemima's words encode a rather peculiar definition of feminism which essentially likens the ideological message contained in this political, social, literary and otherwise movement to revenge specifically targeted at cheating male partners. Other novels also display a slightly unorthodox perception of feminist concerns, such as Jenny Colgan's *Amanda's Wedding* (1999) in which the flippant Amanda Phillips justifies her decision to keep her maiden name as a feminist stance:

> 'Darlings!' said Amanda, with an edge in her voice. 'This is my BIG NEWS!'
>
> [...] 'Anyway, by sheer coincidence I spoke to the castle's people and they gave me his mother's number, and she had his home number and it was just across London, so we got together and we had so much in common; [...] and now I am going to be Lairdess Amanda Phillips-McConnald!' finished Amanda, all in one breath.
>
> There was a silence.
>
> 'Hey, his name's Phillips too?' said Fran.
>
> 'No, no! You see, I'm keeping my name and taking his name. It's a feminist statement, really.'
>
> (Colgan, 1999: 11–12)

The take of these women on feminism sounds, at the very least, rather unorthodox. Their apparent support and adherence to a feminist ideology is not used as a platform to fight for women's rights or to denounce inequalities but as a source of comedy. Resorting to a comedic treatment of otherwise serious matters is actually a recurrently employed tactic of the genre (see Marsh, 2004). For instance, their obsessive worry with looks and appearance tends to be accompanied by a humour component, as in the following:

> Come on, I'm not the first, nor will I be the last, woman to try a homespun, crash-course, Pygmalion-like transmogrification with the aim of netting something delectable in the staminate department. [...] I did all that walking-up-the-stairs-instead-of-taking-the-lift thing. I cut the fat off my ham when I made ham sandwiches, but I didn't melt away into a pre-pubescent nymph, so I cut out ham altogether, and other meats, too, pretty soon after. In fact nothing ever passed my lips unless it was nutritionally valuable and had been interrogated in terms of fat and calorie content.
>
> (Parks, 2002: 24, 25)

The female in question here is Cas from Adele Parks's *Larger than Life* (2002) who, in order to get Hugh, the love of her life, needs to completely reinvent herself, especially in the looks department. Because discussing the latest beauty trend or the ultimate piece of advice on diet matters is, more often than not, done in such exaggerated terms, this constant concern for looks could be seen not just as an ironic presentation of current social trends but also as an opportunity to bring in comedy to the plots. The customary humoristic depiction of some of these contemporary social issues might, thus, need to be re-evaluated as embodying and projecting elements of the dramatic role knowledge rather than the prior social knowledge. The fact that these novels accommodate a playful twist to the presentation of certain contemporary social values strengthens the part played by the dramatic role and hence reinforces these women as a particular fictional type. Additionally, the combination of certain social categories and dramatic role information, inclusive of comedic aspects, also bolsters the identity of the genre, for this felicitous mix becomes prototypically representative of Chick Lit and no other fictional form. As I develop in Chapter 5, the reader has come to expect this combination and even feels cheated when it is not delivered to her.

If the humour component is taken out of the equation, nonetheless, the mocking nature with which some feminist issues seem to be presented could perhaps generate an anti-feminist reading of these novels. The producers of the genre, being women themselves, are leaving the door open for a kind of rebuke of their novels as quasi-reactionary[9] which has, in turn, provided critics with much scope for discussion. Whelehan (2000), for instance, originally expressed a certain uneasiness with the rather unconventional treatment of feminist concerns in Chick Lit as illustrated in *Bridget Jones's Diary*:

> Bridget neatly expresses the tensions of a woman who recognises the rhetoric of feminism and empowerment, but isn't always able to relate this to her fulsome desire for a hero from a Jane Austen novel. […] The second crucial lesson is that 'after all there is nothing so unattractive to a man as strident feminism.' […] *Bridget Jones* might be seen as a 'post-feminist' text in the sense that feminist values are situated as somewhere in the past.
>
> (Whelehan, 2000: 136, 137)

She furthers her assessment by discussing the confessional style of this novel which is used to 'encourage the reader to identify with Bridget's vulnerabilities. But in doing so, the reader also becomes complicit in the view of feminism as too prudish, judgemental and unattractive' (2000: 137). Despite the fact that Whelehan's reading of the novel here is perfectly legitimate, it could also be argued that evaluating Bridget Jones's connection with feminism as 'prudish and unattractive' might deprive the novel of its humour component. In fact, Whelehan herself softens her appraisal of the same issue in some of her later work:

> In previous publications I have found myself being more dismissive about these works, since it is easy to classify them as retroactive and merely souped-up, sexed-up versions of the classic Mills & Boon romance.
>
> (Whelehan, 2005: 16)

Whelehan, therefore, concludes that these novels exhibit certain developments in relation to some 1960s and 1970s women's writing. She adds that Chick Lit has still been able to accommodate feminist concerns by voicing those issues that older forms of feminism apparently failed to address as First- and Second-Wave Feminism were based on some social circumstances which, simply, do not suffice any longer to account for the specific situations of the twentieth- and twenty-first-century realities. For instance, in her comparison of the way feminism is nowadays dealt with to the feminist bestsellers of the 1970s, Whelehan observes that:

> Both groups of books tell us something about their contemporary cultural context and both suggest that, much as feminism of the Second Wave was truly life-changing in the impact it has had on social policy, the law and politics over the years, there were mistakes and deficiencies which left certain women out in the cold.
>
> (Whelehan, 2005: 5)

Although accusing these authors of a 'sitting-on-the-fence' mentality could be an alluring proposition for some, contextual factors affecting late twentieth- and early twenty-first-century readers need to be borne in mind too. In so far as these female figures fail to display the type of political commitment of their 1970s counterparts, for instance, Chick Lit's relationship with feminism is, simply, flawed. But inasmuch as this genre attempts a faithful representation of current social concerns, inclusive of the career, relationship and even appearance pressures women are under, the connection of these novels with feminism is atypical but, still, similarly valid. For instance, their characters' obsession with looks might be viewed not as a failure to cater for feminist concerns but as empowering. Chick Lit authors seem to have endowed their female characters with voices that relish the discussion of beauty routines, fashion interests or weight worries. If this is the case, a characterization of twenty-first-century femininity does not conflict with, but is instead fully endorsed by, an extensive treatment of appearance schemas that simply reflect the type of external contextual pressures that a Cosmopolitan-reading generation of women seems to be under. In Chick Lit, that vision of femininity does not seem at odds with feminist messages either.

To end the discussion of Chick Lit in light of social cognition principles, it is worth revisiting the social schemas discussed above and, more importantly, the evaluative beliefs that they can generate. Culpeper (2001: 77) emphasizes that these evaluative beliefs, manifested in attitude schemas, are ultimately tied up to the notion of ideology, as my discussion of feminism has also underscored.

However, there seems to be another significant side to these cognitive structures and the kind of evaluation they activate:

> Van Dijk also suggests that these evaluative beliefs may be associated with emotive aspects, such as like and dislike (1987: 188–9). How emotive and affective aspects are dealt with in a cognitive model and whether they belong there at all is controversial [...]. With regard to characterisation, my model needs to cope with emotive aspects, since sometimes authors construct characters in order to create particular emotional effects.
>
> (Culpeper, 2001: 78)

Emotion research and its connection to the genre and its readers are amply discussed in Chapter 5. Here, I restrict my discussion of emotional aspects to the links they have with characterization as, in Chick Lit, character impression formation appears to rely on the activation of a series of cognitive[10] structures inclusive of prior social knowledge, dramatic role knowledge, evaluative considerations of feminism, and, finally, an important affective side. Chick Lit authors, for the most part, work under the premise that the happy-ending formula is an essential prerequisite of the genre and that formula does not appear to be too far from readers' expectations either. These expectations, as I go on to explain in Chapter 5, have led me to suggest elsewhere (Montoro, 2003, 2007) an alternative label for the genre, namely 'Cappuccino Fiction', because the happy unfolding of these novels underscores the 'feel-good' factor and 'sweet' taste that readers are left with when finishing them, just like after drinking a nice cup of your favourite cappuccino. The upbeat emotions that these novels evoke in the reader, therefore, would play yet another fundamental role in the commercial success of the books; together with the various aspects developed in this section, the role of these emotive aspects could be ultimately genre-defining.

The conclusions that an analysis of the various socio-cognitive aspects described thus far have allowed me to draw, nonetheless, can still be strengthened by looking more closely at the language of the novels themselves. After all, the top-down processes that get to work in character impression formation represent only half of the equation. Section 3.3 shifts its focus radically; I aim my attention at the language of the novels by implementing a corpus stylistics analysis which, by its very nature, illustrates how a bottom-up perspective can complement, confirm and perhaps also challenge some of the conclusions so far drawn.

3.3 Corpus Stylistics Approach

The analysis above seems to have proved reasonably solidly the advantages of using frameworks from social cognition to clarify, if not totally resolve, characterization issues in Chick Lit. Thanks to the application of these frameworks, the chick in Chick Lit has been literally 'fleshed out' so that we have learned about her stock characteristics, including information regarding her job, her kinship, interests and preoccupation with looks, among some other concerns. Once more I come back to the issue of prototypicality and representativeness in my depiction of Chick Lit women but, on this occasion, my claims are more directly related to the methodology I implement in this part of the chapter. The prototypicality I have underscored elsewhere in this monograph takes on a special meaning here because of the statistic significance I look for in my application of corpus stylistics principles. The analysis in the following section describes prototypicality with regard to regular, consistent, stereotypical and cumulative uses of language and, in particular, of certain semantic domains that are over-represented in the novels. Having said that, I also look at other semantic groupings that seem to be under-used in relation to the reference corpus I measure them against, because they can equally shed light on characterization in Chick Lit. Because of the outcomes of the first half of this chapter, I pay special attention to those semantic domains which have a correlate in the social groupings or dramatic roles discussed above, but I do not neglect looking at others which can informatively complement characterization aspects of these Chick Lit women. In doing so, I want to illustrate the notion of prototypicality with the solid support of results from a computerized, as opposed to a manual, investigation of the novels. In sum, I am interested in augmenting but, at the same time, critically contrasting the socio-cognitive evaluation just presented. The rigour of the stylistic approach that I am after in this monograph is, obviously, behind this comparison. First, though, I explain what corpus stylistics is generally understood to be, and which software I have made use of for my analysis. Then, I discuss the results of this application in my corpus of novels. I conclude by advocating the usefulness of multidisciplinary and multimethodological research in the way I do here, not simply as a way to avoid complacency in our investigative endeavours but also because ultimately I aim to provide a thorough depiction of Chick Lit as a genre, rather than as it manifests in the individual novels, a task which can be clearly aided by the complementarity of a variety of disciplines.

3.3.1 Corpus stylistics

Corpus stylistics is a recent development within stylistics which, despite its status as a relatively newcomer to the discipline, is nonetheless proving particularly advantageous and befitting to the objectivity and rigour of stylistics. As Mahlberg and Smith state:

> The term 'corpus stylistics' has come to be used to refer to an emerging field that aims to combine questions from literary stylistics with approaches from corpus linguistics [...]. In contrast to some of the more computational approaches to stylistics such as stylometry, one may want to see methods

> in corpus stylistics mainly as complementing interpretation and detailed manual analysis.
>
> (Mahlberg and Smith, 2010: 450)

The basic premise underlying a corpus stylistic approach, therefore, is the computerized analysis of data so that it can augment, rather than substitute for, the manual analysis of texts; it is precisely this complementary role that appeals for my own investigation here. As is commonplace in corpus linguistics, the basic methodological principle of using a computer to assess linguistic patterns in literary texts can be approached from a variety of perspectives. This variety, nonetheless, tends to be narrowed down to three major approaches and methodologies, the so-called 'corpus-assisted analysis', 'corpus-based analysis' and 'corpus-driven analysis'. The first of these categories 'uses large reference corpora to assist the analysis of a single text. Corpus-assisted analysis may be carried out in order to validate (or invalidate) the stylistician's intuition about the stylistic effects of particular linguistic structures' (McIntyre, 2013). Researchers selecting this kind of analysis (see O'Halloran, 2007) work with already-existing corpora against which they can check the specific words, expressions or themes that their manual work, intuition, or already-existing scholarly research may have highlighted as especially significant in the text under scrutiny. McIntyre goes on to add that corpus-assisted analysis does not require particular expertise or specialized skills, something that might appeal to those not versed in computing. Corpus-based and corpus-driven analyses, on the other hand, consider the target text as a corpus in its own right that is then run through some piece of software to try and draw conclusions based on the outcomes of that analysis. The difference between corpus-based and corpus-driven analysis '(as described by Tognini-Bonelli, 2001; see also Francis, 1993) is that the former uses corpus analysis to validate existing theories and hypotheses, while the latter uses the results of corpus analysis to formulate new theories and hypotheses' (McIntyre, 2013). This distinction, however, does not always hold; in fact, it tends to collapse when these two approaches are put into practice in stylistic analysis. Another distinction of relevance for my own purposes is that of 'intratextual' versus 'intertextual' analysis:

> When such analysis is focused entirely on the target text in order to extrapolate information relating to that text alone, this is *intratextual* analysis (Adolphs, 2006). When such analysis is supplemented by comparing the target text against a reference corpus, this is *intertextual* analysis (Adolphs, 2006).
>
> (McIntyre, 2013)

Accordingly, the analysis of the Chick Lit novels I present in Section 3.3.2 uses a mixture of corpus-based and corpus-driven analysis on the one hand, and is characterized by its intertextual nature on the other. My investigation sets out to consider pre-existing proposals on the language that possibly characterizes

Chick Lit women based on the conclusions drawn from looking at the novels via the models and frameworks of a completely separate discipline (that is, social cognition). Thus, I check whether the preoccupation of these women for their image, for instance, results in an over-representation of certain semantic domains which can prove that these women do indeed 'talk' so much about their appearance, bodies and looks. Having said that, this computerized methodology also allows me to look at my data independently of those original pre-existing proposals so I consider certain semantic domains that, by being under-represented, might actually question concerns previously highlighted as illustrative of Chick Lit women. Finally, I define my approach as intertextual because I look into the spread of a series of semantic domains in relation to the group of fictional texts that the software of my choice uses for comparison.

The software tagging my corpus and also providing the reference corpus for comparison is Wmatrix (Rayson, 2009). Wmatrix uses USAS (UCREL Semantic Analysis System; see Rayson *et al.*, 2004) developed at Lancaster University's Centre for Computer Corpus Research on Language (formerly the University Centre for Corpus Research on the English Language, UCREL). Wmatrix can tag the target corpus for keywords, parts of speech, and semantic categories as well as generate frequency lists, keyword lists, n-grams and collocates. The semantic tag-set used by Wmatrix was initially based on McArthur's (1981) *Longman Lexicon of Contemporary English,* although that original classification has been subsequently revised to account for some inconsistencies and to

A general and abstract terms	B the body and the individual	C arts and crafts	E emotion
F food and farming	G government and public	H architecture, housing and the home	I money and commerce in industry
K entertainment, sports and games	L life and living things	M movement, location, travel and transport	N numbers and measurement
O substances, materials, objects and equipment	P education	Q language and communication	S social actions, states and processes
T time	W world and environment	X psychological actions, states and processes	Y science and technology
Z names and grammar			

Table 3.1 Hierarchy of major discourse fields (Archer *et al.*, 2002: 2)

generally improve the accuracy of the tagging. The revised tag-set is arranged according to a hierarchy of 21 major discourse fields (as shown in Table 3.1) expanding into 232 category labels.[11]

In this chapter, I focus exclusively on the results of the semantic tagging (SEMTAG) illustrated in Table 3.1 because, despite the fact that keyword analysis and part of speech keyness can undoubtedly also shed some light on the general linguistic structure of the corpus, the former offers clearer opportunities for contrasting the outcome of my socio-cognitive analysis and, hence, complementing it in light of characterization issues. A further advantage of focusing on the semantic tagging is summarized by Walker:

> My study also demonstrates that Wmatrix's semantic functionality can help with the stylistic analysis of a larger text (in this case a novel) by identifying themes within the text, and locating potentially important sections of text for further investigation that might have been missed by (the more established) keyword analysis, thus making Wmatrix a useful addition to the stylistician's tool-kit.
>
> (Walker, 2010: 364)

Although keyword analysis is by now a well-established approach used in corpus linguistics and corpus stylistics, I concur with Walker above that investigating the semantic characteristics of the target corpus by paying attention to the frequency (or, indeed, under-recurrence) of semantically-related groups of words rather than frequently-used words might bear fruitful benefits; in my case, focusing on semantic domains befits my interests especially well in so far as I can contrast whether the various schemas discussed in the previous section are linguistically embodied in certain lexical items related to each other by virtue of their semantic closeness.[12]

The target corpus is made up of six Chick Lit novels amounting to a total of about 650,000 words; for ease of reference I refer to it as my *Chick Lit Corpus*. The six novels are *Bridget Jones's Diary* (H. Fielding, 1996), *Getting Rid of Matthew* (J. Fallon, 2007), *Pants on Fire* (M. Alderson, 2000), *The Last Year of Being Single* (S. Tucker, 2003), *The Other Woman* (J. Green, 2004) and *The Secret Dreamworld of a Shopaholic* (S. Kinsella, 2000). The corpus contains data that spans a period of 11 years as I wanted to include a sufficiently significant chronological spread. My choice of novels in this section purposefully differs from those investigated in Section 3.2.1 (except for *Bridget Jones's Diary* which throughout the monograph has been kept as a constant because of its prototypicality as the original embodiment of Chick Lit); I want to avoid the possible circularity that using the same novels might bring about as my aim, after all, is more in tune with discussing Chick Lit characterization in the whole of the genre than in the individual novels. This also raises some issues regarding the notion of 'aboutness' (Philips, 1989) that basically refers to the content of the text, to what the text is 'about'. By building up the *Chick Lit Corpus* using novels other than those studied in the previous section, I try to circumvent the danger of the computerized analysis showing results that might simply replicate the 'aboutness' of the novels under investigation. If, as is my contention here, these novels coherently coalesce in belonging to a well-defined genre, then further examples of prototypical Chick Lit works should also be able to provide solid results about the genre, irrespective of the works used. As explained below, this tactic paid off as, for the most part, Chick Lit's cohesiveness has been sufficiently substantiated. Finally, a further reason why I have abstained from looking at keywords in this analysis is summarized here by McIntyre:

> Interpreting long key word lists thus demands a reliable procedure in order to distinguish those words that are simply statistically significant, and those which are both statistically and interpretatively significant. Many of the words in a key word list will be indicative of the content of the text – what is often termed its 'aboutness' (Philips, 1989). Such words can in many cases be disregarded.
>
> (McIntyre, 2013)

The distinction between 'statistically' and 'interpretatively' significant is crucial to determine a sound assessment of the target corpus. As McIntyre suggests, keyword lists very often highlight words that are statistically significant because they would be used rather frequently and would also underscore the content of the text, what the text is 'about'. But the researcher needs to be discerning so as not to overemphasize the relevance of those words at the top of these lists and she should search, instead, for those results that might be interpretatively relevant. For instance, McIntyre states that 'we would expect proper nouns to turn up as key, since character names are often specific to one novel.' (2013) A frequency keyword list of the *Chick Lit Corpus* does indeed contain proper nouns such as 'Helen', 'Dan', 'Matthew' and 'Sophie', among many others, but looking at these in isolation does not aid my aims in this chapter. Instead, I focus exclusively on keyness with regard to semantic domains. Whereas I analyse the statistical significance of the themes and topics projected by the *Chick Lit Corpus*'s various semantic domains and whether they correlate to the social groupings and dramatic role categories discussed in the previous section, I do not neglect considering keyness by other means, as I also look into how interpretatively significant the under-representation of some other categories is for the characterization of Chick Lit women.[13]

The intertextual stance of this section also means that the *Chick Lit Corpus* is not viewed in isolation but in light of one of the reference corpora provided by the software. The reference corpora in Wmatrix (Rayson, 2009) are extracted from the British National Corpus (BNC) Sampler, a sub-corpus of the entire BNC containing a fiftieth of the total amount of words – about two million words. The BNC Sampler is divided into Spoken and Written sub-corpora in, roughly, a 50–50 ratio, with further sub-divisions making up each half, as summarized in Table 3.2.

Spoken (990,704 words)		*Written (1,010,690 words)*	
Context-governed (496,852)	Demographic (493,852) [by socio-economic class]	Imaginative (231,663)	Informative (779,027)
Leisure (136,606)	I (AB) (164,933)	Drama (23,786)	Pure science (32,974)
Educational (80,463)	II (C1) (98,700)	Poetry (30,144)	Applied science (117,685)
Business (134,275)	III (C2) (137,686)	Prose fiction (177,733)	Social science (29,868)
Public/Institutional (145,508)	IV (DE) (92,533)		World affairs (277,128)
			Commerce & finance (92,057)
			Arts (51,645)
			Belief & thought (43,626)
			Leisure (134,044)

Table 3.2 BNC Sampler Corpus (2,001,394 words) (Rayson, 2009; available online at http://ucrel.lancs.ac.uk/bnc2sampler/sampler.htm)

The first decision facing the corpus stylistics researcher is the selection of the appropriate sub-corpus to measure her data against. As discussed by Culpeper (2009) and also developed in Chapter 5, the issue of comparability of the two corpora needs to be carefully considered, as gauging the linguistic components of the target material against the characteristics of non-comparable texts could bear results that might be skewed or simply insufficiently representative in statistical or interpretative terms. Because of the fictional nature of my corpus, the BNC Sampler Written Imaginative sub-corpus seems the most appropriate choice so the results obtained should reveal important aspects about my target text. On a less positive note, though, the BNC Sampler Written Imaginative sub-corpus does not discriminate between drama, poetry or prose fiction; the genre conventions that these three major sub-sections represent and which inevitably also result in differing linguistic characteristics for each genre could be used as a convincing argument to discredit the comparability of the *Chick Lit Corpus* and the BNC sub-corpus. The software does not currently allow for the various sub-sections of the Written Imaginative sub-corpus to be used in isolation. Because prose fiction represents, by far, the largest component of the Written Imaginative sub-corpus (177,733 of 231,663 words; that is, over two thirds of the whole amount), I still consider its comparability with my own corpus feasible. Future research should perhaps contrast other reference corpora closer in kind, but this is one aspect that, unfortunately, I cannot develop further in this chapter.

Finally, there remains some clarification regarding the way Wmatrix obtains comparative results and identifies keyness. Walker (2010) explains that:

> The test Wmatrix uses to ascertain keyness is log-likelihood (LL), and keyword/POS/concept lists are ranked by LL value, with the highest values (and therefore most significant items) at the top of the lists. Often when using keyness lists, the analyst will decide a cut-off level of significance or keyness to shorten the list.
>
> (Walker, 2010: 369–70)

Wmatrix uses the log-likelihood (LL) statistical method to compare the target and reference corpus; this method is based on the possibility that the outcomes of the comparison are brought about by error or chance. Wmatrix establishes the following LL cut-off points:

> 95th percentile; 5% level; $p < 0.05$; critical value = 3.84
> 99th percentile; 1% level; $p < 0.01$; critical value = 6.63
> 99.9th percentile; 0.1% level; $p < 0.001$; critical value = 10.83
> 99.99th percentile; 0.01% level; $p < 0.0001$; critical value = 15.13
> (Rayson, 2009; available online at http://ucrel.lancs.ac.uk/wmatrix/)

This means that the higher the LL cut-off point (15.13), the lower the possibility that the statistical significance of the results is fortuitous. The nature and size of the corpus, the type of text being analysed, as well as other circumstances will determine which LL is most conducive to gaining meaningful results. On occasions, setting a low cut-off value might result in an unmanageably large number of key items to analyse that would hinder rather than aid the analyst's job. In my case, I have selected the highest LL cut-off value offered by the software that provides a 99.99th percentile degree of confidence in relation to the statistical significance of the results. The interpretative significance, nonetheless, still necessitates the subsequent close scrutiny on the part of the researcher, as I explain below; for instance, for some of the categories studied, the LL cut-off point I used needed lowering so that certain figures could be contextually interpreted.

3.3.2 The results

In what follows I analyse the results emerging from the comparison of the *Chick Lit Corpus* and the BNC Sampler Written Imaginative sub-corpus. A certain amount of subjectivity in the selection of results to discuss is unavoidable as, primarily because of space constraints, I do not delve into all the semantic categories that the comparison brings about. Instead, I look at those groupings which I deem most illustrative of characterization issues in Chick Lit. As a reminder, I have used a 15.13 LL cut-off value, so any score above that figure is statistically significant in relation to the reference corpus. For ease of presentation, I divide my discussion into two parts: I first deal with those semantic categories whose presence is positively marked in relation to the reference corpus, that is, those categories that are more commonly used in the Chick

Chick Lit Corpus compared to BNC Sampler Written Imaginative: selected positive scores			
	Tag	*LL*	*Semantic Category*
1.	S3.2	+252.83	Relationship: Intimacy and sex
2.	I2.2	+109.48	Business: Selling
3.	X2.6–	+86.79	Unexpected
4.	O4.2+	+76.16	Judgement of appearance: Beautiful
5.	T1.3	+74.07	Time: Period
6.	F2	+69.34	Drinks and alcohol
7.	S3.1	+67.48	Personal relationship: General
8.	F1	+58.32	Food
9.	F3	+57.73	Smoking and non-medical drugs
10.	A5.3–	+37.38	Evaluation: Inaccurate
11.	X8+	+35.80	Trying hard
12.	X9.2–	+34.59	Failure
13.	E4.1+++	+22.38	Happy
14.	S1.2.6–	+17.24	Foolish
15.	E4.1+	+16.72	Happy
16.	S5–	+16.10	Not part of a group

Fig 3.1

Lit novels, followed by those other categories which, on the contrary, score below the threshold of the reference corpus. Figure 3.1 contains the 16 most significant semantic categories out of the total 62 groupings which scored above the 15.13 cut-off value.

Archer *et al.* (2002: 1) explain that the semantic tags used by the software 'show semantic fields which group together word senses that are related by virtue of their being connected at some level of generality with the same mental concept.' By considering semantically-related lexical items as part of groups thus, Wmatrix is able to underscore keyness at levels beyond the keyword; it should ensue, therefore, that solid claims with regard to the linguistic characteristics of a particular corpus can be made on the back of semantic keyness. Furthermore, the higher the score of the category in question, the more reasonably safe the conclusions drawn will be. The first of the categories in Figure 3.1 with a positive LL score of +252.83 is 'S3.2 = Relationship: Intimacy and sex'. This semantic tag includes 'terms relating to relationships that are intimate and/or sexual, or to a person's sexual orientation' (Archer *et al.*, 2002: 27). The concordances in Figure 3.2 illustrate some of the entries in this category.

Out of the 158 components of the 'S3.2 = Relationship: Intimacy and sex' category, the top ten tokens are 'love', 'fuck', 'boyfriend', 'kiss', 'girlfriend', 'sexy', 'hug', 'kissed', 'kissing', and 'sleep_with'; further instances are realized by items such as 'lover', 'couples', 'hugging' and 'flirtatious'. The considerably high score of this category highlights the first commonality between the corpus stylistic analysis and the socio-cognitive appraisal of characterization in Section

S3.2 = Relationship: Intimacy and sex	LL = +252.83
ince pointless as have no	**boyfriend**. Behave sluttishly
combusted through joy and	**sexual** promise), alcohol units
work), calories 1258 (	**love** has eradicated need to pig
cards. Toy with idea of	**flirting** energetically with any
hem play. Perfect. Fell	**in love** with him. Five years goin
with food. Lose shoes.	**Cuddle** and kiss in public. Feel
ldn't marry Paul . I was	**sleeping with** someone else. How can
ed and then cover me with	**kisses**. But she wasn't often so

Fig 3.2

3.2.1, which makes this figure not just statistically significant but also interpretatively relevant. The relational role (part of the social role grouping) by which Chick Lit women are, by and large, best known is undoubtedly the constant search for a heterosexual romantic liaison which permeates most Chick Lit works. As also discussed above, Chick Lit heroines appear somehow to fail to be content if the resolution to their ever-present fixation on romantic affairs is not a felicitous one. The over-representation of the 'S3.2 = Relationship: Intimacy and sex' category in light of the data in the Written Imaginative sub-corpus seems to confirm that this obsession is indeed a trait by which these women can be defined. In a nutshell, Chick Lit women can be safely said to talk, discuss, chat, or think about loving relationships a lot as the linguistic realization in the novels clearly demonstrates.

The relational role, however, has also been discussed with regard to the depiction of these women as friends. The semantic tag-set of Wmatrix (see Table 3.1) does not contain a category including items whose semantic affinity encodes exclusively the concept of 'friendship'; the category whose semantically-related components stand closest to this notion is 'S3.1 = Personal relationship: General'. This grouping includes 'terms relating to relationships in general; prototypical examples: accompanying, buddy, camaraderie, compadres, companionship, cronies, escort, friendship' (Archer *et al.*, 2002: 27). Once more, the positive LL score +67.48 suggests that the relational role of friendship is indeed an inherent trait of these female characters. For instance, consider the examples in Figure 3.3.

S3.1 = Personal relationship: General	LL = +67.48
work out. Love the	**friends**, better than extended
old and enduring	**friendship** but at the same time
friends than lovers or	**partners** or spouses. She said
desire was joined by	**companionship** and profound respect.
she was difficult to	**get on with**, or incompetent
inging. That's what	**friends** were for. What Rachel
though, is that her	**friendship** made Helen feel better
without close female	**friendships**. Of course I have Fran

Fig 3.3

'Friendship' as part of the relational role, however, has also been discussed above in connection with attitude schemas. As Gill and Herdieckerhoff (2006) point out, relationships among Chick Lit women often exploit the stereotype of the scheming and manipulative girlfriend who is only interested in pursuing her own agenda, especially as far as attracting the attention of the token male is concerned. Despite the positive score of the 'S3.1 = Personal relationship: General' category which suggests that friendships are indeed an over-represented topic in the *Chick Lit Corpus*, the issue of what kind of friendships these women are involved in does not seem to be so clearly illustrated, so to substantiate linguistically Gill and Herdieckerhoff's claims further proof would be needed. This might be viewed as a slight shortcoming in the possible conclusions that a computerized analysis feasibly allows us to draw; that is, although the examples in Figure 3.3 and the positive score of this category do assist the identification of a general linguistic correlate to the relational role of friendship, they fail to discern crucial aspects concerning this schema which critics such as Gill and Herdieckerhoff (2006) pick up on. For instance, the convincing LL score for the 'S3.1 = Personal relationship: General' grouping (+67.48) does not illustrate whether the lexical items in this category specifically describe friendships among women (more on this below); more importantly, this value does not clarify whether, and if so how, the attitude schemas that might lead some readers to evaluate negatively friend relations are linguistically realized.[14] Despite the fact that the interpretative potential of the results come, on this occasion, slightly short in relation to the clear support that these statistics convey in the case of other semantic categories, the over-representation of the 'S3.1 = Personal relationship: General' in the *Chick Lit Corpus* cannot be overlooked either, because it still substantiates, for the most part, the fact that friendship is important for the Chick Lit female. Moreover, this crucial role is further supported by the 'S5– = Not part of a group' category with a LL value of +16.10. Although, the items in this category are less frequently used than those in the 'S3.1 = Personal relationship: General' above, their presence, albeit indirectly, still indicates how much Chick Lit chicks rely on being part of a social network; for instance, see the concordances in Figure 3.4.

S5– = Not part of a group	LL = +16.10
keeper, but it keeps the	**loneliness** at bay, and, as horrific
I'm not so good at being	**on my own**, and anyway, he has his p
lways felt so isolated and	**lonely**, and I think the only way
Lisa shrugs. 'Maybe she's	**lonely**. Maybe she lived for her
frustration, cry with the	**loneliness** and responsibility of it
home to the predictable if	**lonely** safety of her little family
Undeniably, Helen was the	**outsider** who had breezed in and ruin

Fig 3.4

To sum up, Chick Lit chicks dislike feeling alienated or friendless as the positive score of this group and the concordances above highlights; it is mainly by considering their distaste for loneliness in tandem with the over-representation of the 'S3.1 = Personal relationship: General' group that the role of friendship is not simply brought to the fore but also greatly strengthened. It can be argued (as is the case with other categories as well) that it is the combination of the various categories rather than the categories on their own that is effective; that is, characterization comes as the result of the cumulative effect of a series of semantic groupings that facilitate character impression formation. The interpretative significance of the apparent shortcomings of some of the results, therefore, needs contextualizing; suffice it so say that, in relation to the social role, and more specifically, relational aspects, a corpus stylistics approach is still capable of enlightening characterization aspects.

The corpus stylistics slant of this section, however, seems to have found an especially well-stocked set of linguistic correlates for the personal grouping, as eight out of the selected 16 entries in Figure 3.1 exemplify how the personal traits of the Chick Lit female are 'linguistically' fleshed out. It is important to remember that most corpus stylisticians (see Archer *et al.*, 2009; Mahlberg 2007a, 2007b; Mahlberg and Smith, 2010; McIntyre and Archer, 2010) underscore the interpretative role of the researcher with regard to the validity of a computerized analysis of texts, as my analysis on the notion of friendship also points out. In corpus stylistics, a computational approach is understood as a valuable instrument to add to the stylistician's toolkit, but a tool nonetheless. Thoroughly checking results is still the responsibility of the analyst. My analysis on Chick Lit is no exception to this rule, as proven by the fact that certain semantic groupings which, initially, did not seem to indicate straightforwardly a direct linguistic link with the social groupings highlighted by the socio-cognitive approach, on closer inspection, turned out to be especially useful to account for female characterization. As described above, identifying people according to the personal category allows impression formation with respect to their interests, habits, traits and goals (Culpeper, 2001: 75). Thus, the novels analysed in Section 3.2.1 confirm these women's penchant for reading self-help books, or personality traits such as being 'scatterbrained', 'inefficient' or 'needy'. Several semantic groupings of those in Figure 3.1 vouch for a similar characterization. For instance, the positive half of the 'X2.6– = Unexpected' category ('X2.6 = Expect') groups together lexical items which depict a certain level of expectation; the minus sign of the category in my results indicates a negative position in the expectation semantic scale, hence, it encompasses items that project significations related to unexpectedness, unpredictability or surprise. The comparison of the *Chick Lit Corpus* and the reference corpus gives the 'X2.6– = Unexpected' grouping a positive LL score of +86.79 which shows a rather convincing level of over-recurrence in the novels. But it is by examining some of the concordances in detail that female characterization becomes apparent as the examples portray women who seem to 'wonder' about things, women who are 'surprised' at

X2.6– = Unexpected	LL = +86.79
her cheek . I stop,	**amazed** at seeing Lisa this
and I look at her in	**surprise**. She's looking really
and nearly keel over in	**astonishment**. Admission 5.00. I fe
'No I wasn't, I was	**hopeless**! I was paddling around
a year ! It makes me	**wonder** what I 'm doing, being
'I say, as though	**astonished**. You wouldn't believe
I spend in a year.	**On impulse**, I pull the chequebook
her irritation at the	**whimsical** expression. 'But I love

Fig 3.5

events, or 'astonished' at what may have happened. Consider, for instance, the concordances in Figure 3.5.

It could be argued that these examples and, perhaps by extension many others, do not unequivocally clarify in convincing terms that only female characters have authored this semantic illustration of 'unexpectedness', so, once more, the statistical analysis seems to fall short with regard to the possibility of an insightful analysis. However, two circumstances back me up in advocating that this semantic category does, indeed, evince one of the most prototypical traits of Chick Lit women, namely their lack of assertiveness, self-confidence or conviction, and, hence, it also avers the validity of a corpus stylistics approach. On the one hand, the novels included in the corpus were chosen because of their prototypicality; the danger of circularity was, hopefully, circumvented by adhering to the criteria on the prototypical Chick Lit novel discussed in multiple examples of scholarly work, as defined in Chapter 1. That prototypicality means that the main character (or the I-narrator and character in the case of first-person narration) is, by default, female, so most of the linguistic realizations (of this or any other category for that matter) necessarily concern the females in the novels rather than the males. This leads directly to the second supporting reason I mention. As will be addressed when the negative scores are discussed, the 'S2.2 = People: Male' category is convincingly under-represented, with an LL score of –249.48, which proves that these novels overwhelmingly favour a female presence over their male counterparts. Although caution needs to be exerted so as not to overemphasize the significance of results or advocate a full extrapolation to texts other than those included in the target corpus, it seems that the statistics are solid enough to confirm my proposals here so that, as far as personal characterization goes, Chick Lit chicks can be described as unconfident, hesitant and uncertain among some other traits. For instance, the same sense of insecurity is supported by the 'A5.3– = Evaluation: Inaccurate' and the 'X8+ = Trying hard' categories which show LL values of +37.38 and +35.80 respectively, as illustrated in Figures 3.6 and 3.7.

The first of these semantic groupings, 'A5.3– = Evaluation: Inaccurate', assembles evaluative items which, because of the negative specification of the

A5.3– = Evaluation: Inaccurate	LL = +37.38
thinner. 5 a.m. What's	**wrong** with me? I 'm completely
I knew it. This is all my	**fault**. If I were a better person,
their marriage was a huge	**mistake**. He was nowhere near ready f
to, and sometimes we make	**mistakes**, and sometimes we do things
Could I have been that	**wrong**? 'Flattered by her attention
in the newspaper about a	**mix-up** at a bank. I loved this story

Fig 3.6

X8+ = Trying hard	LL = +35.80
on being sophisticated or	**hardworking** but on staying warm and
of whole day's bloody	**effort** and hydro-electric body-gene
es 3826. Spent the weekend	**struggling** to remain disdainfully
'Hello? 'I 'm trying my	**damnedest** to be polite, to try to hid
mobile, I am winning a	**battle**, on the way to winning the
A tart, you mean? 'Linda	**attempts** to make a joke. 'Linda
Helen made a half-hearted	**attempt** to tidy up, knowing that

Fig 3.7

tag, depict lack of accuracy; the second, 'X8+ = Trying hard', brings together those words whose signification concerns effort or resolution. Meanings regarding lack of accuracy are primarily realized by items such as 'wrong', 'fault' and 'mistake', which point out that these women recurrently worry about their having behaved erroneously or whether events in their lives are due to their incompetence and fault. Despite this sense of wrongdoing encoded linguistically in examples such as those in Figure 3.6, they do not stop trying hard to address and accommodate their apparent blunders, as illustrated in Figure 3.7. Their continuous efforts do not always felicitously translate into a sense of achievement, as the semantic category 'X9.2– = Failure' seems to point out. The statistical significance of the 'failure' category in relation to 'X8+ = Trying hard' is minimal, decreasing from an LL value of +35.80 for the latter to an LL score of +34.59 with respect to the former, although its interpretative value is clearly one of support and reinforcement for those other semantic categories which paint the Chick Lit female in a very particular, not always especially flattering, light. For instance, consider the concordances in Figure 3.8.

To recap, so far the femaleness of the Chick Lit chick is portrayed in relation to her lack of self-confidence and her sense of uncertainty regarding events in her life; there is also a deeply ingrained sense of inadequacy on her part so that whatever event in her life may have developed unsuccessfully is as a direct result of her own wrongdoing; despite these flaws, she never stops trying to improve things, a course which is, more often than not, inevitably met by a subsequent sense of failure. This somewhat negative depiction is complemented by the

X9.2– = Failure	LL = +34.59
te Marmalade. Am disastrous	**failure**. Michelin-star cookery? K
an overwhelming sense of	**defeat** that I have to put it in
for me after the two-day	**fiasco** before . They said I was
just left it, admitted	**defeat** in the face of such self-ab
kidding? My marriage is a	**failure** and I'm on my own. 'Do you
when in the hell it all	**went wrong**. It's been eight week
way she was going to admit	**defeat**. She had all her eggs in o
t's just me, I 'm such a	**fuck-up**. I know I'll regret this

Fig 3.8

S1.2.6– = Foolish	LL = +17.24
us all. Feel incompetent	**fool** and as if everyone else in
I was making a complete	**prat** of myself behaving like a
diculous. It probably was	**ridiculous**, but I couldn't help feel
fully. 'You are so bloody	**gullible**. Anyway, I agree with Fra
Maybe I 'm just being	**naive**, but I can't see him
my dad. 'It's the most	**ridiculous** idea I've ever heard.
Janice. So, ' I say	**inanely**. 'I hear Tom 's got limed

Fig 3.9

'S1.2.6– = Foolish' category (LL=+17.24) which also strengthens the adverse presentation of these women (Figure 3.9).

It seems, thus, that some of the characteristics of Chick Lit women highlighted in Section 3.2.1, namely being 'needy' or 'inefficient', do not simply find a clear linguistic correlation in the results emerging from a corpus stylistic approach but are also reinforced by quite a few others. Furthermore, I discuss above that the issue of prototypicality of Chick Lit takes on a special meaning in this chapter as it is the statistical significance which a corpus stylistics approach grants access to that can more rigorously confirm the traits already highlighted by other means. These figures underscore the regular, consistent and, most importantly, cumulative effect of the various semantic categories in a way that other approaches cannot do. It is, therefore, not simply the presence of the various semantic groupings in isolation, but their collective and aggregate effect that can, literally, help flesh out the chick in Chick Lit.

The somewhat unfavourable stance on the women of the genre encoded in the categories above, nonetheless, is partially exonerated by the presence of two 'Happy' groupings: 'E4.1+++ = Happy' with an LL value of +22.38 and 'E4.1+ = Happy' which scores +16.72 on the same likelihood scale; these are exemplified in Figure 3.10.

The 'plus signs' indicate a positive position on the semantic scale of 'happiness', so the 'E4.1+++' category differs from its cognate 'E4.1+' as a matter of degree. Despite the negative traits in Chick Lit female representation

E4.1+++ = Happy	LL = +22.38
say, trying not to sound too	**thrilled**. 'In fact … I'd probably p
nanger and I feel a thrill of	**exhilaration**. 'I fail to see' Well,
No, Rachel. I mean it, I 'm	**thrilled**. I just, I don't know what
E4.1+ = Happy	LL = +16.72
rapist. She was loud and	**funny** and called a spade a fucking
silence, then screams of	**delight** coming from the kitchen.
anyway. I want to have	**fun**. This is not a fun house and I
osest she had ever got to	**euphoria** and that it was like when

Fig 3.10

discussed above, the two 'Happy' groupings are a reminder of the intrinsic feel-good factor that identifies the genre, as, after all, one of the main reasons why readers approach these novels (see Chapter 5) is the happy resolution which they have vehemently come to expect. Additionally, this feel-good factor as well as the 'negative' depiction of femaleness as insecure or needy can be jointly assessed in light of the 'that's me' (Whelehan, 2002: 55) phenomenon described above and which I revisit in relation to group membership categories below. It could be argued that painting such a negative image of femaleness is no accident but, instead, a deliberate strategy of the genre, because this less than flattering presentation of femaleness is always combined with the upbeat sentiments that characterize the resolution of the story. Thus, Chick Lit authors seem to have ably strengthened the effect of the eventual feel-good factor by also emphasizing these women's imperfections because the very many blunders they are responsible for somehow humanize them. Underscoring those flaws makes these chicks more human, which might eventually foster readers' identification with those character traits that seem so reminiscent of aspects in their own lives. In turn, 'celebrating' those shortcomings also make Chick Lit women come out all the more triumphant when those errors and blunders are eventually overcome. In fact, for some, this attempt at some apparent authenticity with regard to a real representation of twentieth- and twenty-first-century women is the real secret of the genre's success and this faithful tracing on to paper of real women's concerns allegedly also necessitates the portrayal of certain negative aspects.

I2.2 = Business: Selling	LL = +109.48
er or sound-bites or unique	**selling** points. That each has equal
as doing so in Surrey. Had	**bought** a plot of land that overlook
own space and that John has	**bought** her a TV and that he is very
Some boring course about	**customer** focus and how you can get mo
pers about editorial. Meet	**advertising** company in Kings Cross
I go out at lunchtime and	**buy** a short red skirt. I never
ider this to be a practical	**buy** I believe I will get lots of

Fig 3.11

There are some other results in Figure 3.1 that directly evoke some of the components of the group membership category, the final grouping identified by Culpeper (2001: 75). Of these, it is undoubtedly the various references to appearance issues that deserve special attention. Before addressing those, the 'I2.2 = Business: Selling' category with a rather convincing LL value of +109.48 needs mentioning too, as it points out certain consumerism aspects typical of Chick Lit urban society (Figure 3.11).

The preoccupation with Cosmopolitan culture and consumerism (Smith, 2008) is, nevertheless, primarily embodied in women's obsession with appearance issues which two entries in Figure 3.1 illustrate directly; a further three not included there also merit attention: in the first group we find 'O4.2+ = Judgement of appearance: Beautiful' with a convincing LL value of +76.16, and 'F1 = Food' with an LL score of +58.32; in the second, we have the 'B1 = Anatomy and physiology', 'B4 = Cleaning and personal care', and 'B5 = Clothes and personal belongings' categories. To start with, the 'O4.2+ = Judgement of appearance: Beautiful' (+76.16) is illustrated by the concordances in Figure 3.12.

O4.2+ = Judgement of appearance: Beautiful	LL = +76.16
t on. What about that	**lovely** cerise two-piece you used
der and women get less	**attractive**, so all those twenty-t
d. 'She's incredibly	**attractive**, isn't she?' 'Mmm,
ast going, 'That's a	**pretty** dress, darling . Cut!
re can I find a really	**nice** black skirt under £60 I
now, with my sleek,	**chic** conservative clothes,
, but not too high,	**elegant** shoes, they can't bel
pretend race with 'our	**glamorous** hostess Phoebe Trill'

Fig 3.12

The positive score for this category suggests that appearance is more recurrently discussed in the *Chick Lit Corpus* than in the reference corpus. Scholarly work on Chick Lit (Marsh, 2004; Umminger, 2006) has particularly focused on the way appearance issues gain special significance when they pertain to the domain of the female body. Body concerns, as the prototypical example of Bridget illustrates, often translate into an unhealthy preoccupation with food consumption so that reaching the ideal in life is inexorably linked to achieving the ideal weight. Once more, the results from a corpus stylistics approach are quite enriching as the 'F1 = Food' grouping which a positive LL score of +58.32 demonstrates (Figure 3.13).

As the concordances in Figure 3.13 indicate, the obsessive worry about weight issues in the novels does not exactly translate into a total avoidance of lexical items relating to food. In fact, their recurrence confirms that these women employ those terms more often than they are used in the reference corpus. The recurrence of these items can equally suggest that these women discuss food even though they might still deny themselves

F1 = Food	LL = +58.32
6.45. Return with forgotten	**groceries**. 6.45–7. Assemble shepherd
roceries. 6.45–7. Assemble	**shepherd's pie** and place in oven
Diet Coke (me) and cheese	**pizza** with extra mushrooms and appl
sex ? 'Catherine fruit and	**chocolate**, and he does things Freddie
ee bottles of Sauvignon. Nö	**food**). Sarah `Have you over bee
id he ? 'Sarah `Yes . With	**cherries** on top. And lots of whipped
on top . And lots of whipped	**cream**. Eleven p.m. Catherine gone
s to where to go and what to	**eat** and where to stay. Hopefully

Fig 3.13

any culinary satisfaction. Admitting that food is not something to fear but something to enjoy could be seen as a sign of weakness in relation to their obsessive concerns with appearance, for their ideal weight can hardly be combined with gastronomic indulgence. This can be described as a further manifestation of the 'that's me' phenomenon (Whelehan, 2002: 55) whereby readers are invited to sympathize and even empathize with such predicaments and sacrifices. The 'F1 = Food' semantic grouping is, actually, not the only category which might bring into question some of the conclusions on the genre drawn by scholars that do not focus exclusively on the linguistic make-up of the novels. In connection with appearance issues, for instance, there is yet a further category (Figure 3.14) which stands out among the rest because of its negative score in relation to the reference corpus, that of 'B1 = Anatomy and physiology' (LL = –81.07).

The convincing negative score of this semantic group, which includes lexical items semantically related by their reference to parts of the body, shows that the novels in my corpus pay less attention to anatomical matters than the texts in the reference corpus. The fact that the score is not borderline but solidly grounded on the negative side certainly provides food for thought regarding previous scholarly assessments of these women's preoccupation with body matters. In order to understand this unexpected result further, I searched for other semantic categories that might also project significations reminiscent of female concerns for their looks. Wmatrix's hierarchy of semantic domains (see

B1 = Anatomy and physiology	LL = –81.07
eath my clothes, my entire	**body** is covered in scales . But I
ked stunning: skin clear,	**hair** shining. I caught sight of
telling you nobody wants	**legs** like a stick insect . They
ight about my concept of my	**body** in relation to men, and, i
watching Erica Parnell's	**face** as it changes . As realizati
ngled voice, aware that my	**cheeks** are flaming. 'Derek, have
don't like what I see. My	**skin** 's green, my mouth is dry a
d my hair's sticking to my	**skin** in clumps . But worst of all

Fig 3.14

Table 3.1) includes the 'B4 = Cleaning and personal care' category which brings together lexical items relating to domestic and personal hygiene, and the 'B5 = Clothes and personal belongings' category that clearly assembles terms that denote clothing or other personal items. Because Chick Lit chicks' worry with looks is also often discussed in relation to beauty routines and shopping sprees for clothes or shoes, these two semantic domains seem like the obvious choice to measure my corpus against. Surprisingly but most interestingly, these two categories clearly embodying topics prototypically associated with the women in Chick Lit score below the pre-established 15.13 cut-off value, so their recurrence is not on a par with some other categories in the corpus. The 15.13 cut-off figure, as explained previously, offers a 99.99th percentile degree of certainty that the results have not come about simply as the result of error or chance. In order to find whether these two categories feature at all in my corpus, I lowered the LL cut-off value to 6.63 which, nonetheless, still offers a 99th percentile level of accuracy. Only when the cut-off value is lowered do the B4 and B5 categories feature with a positive score of +10.55 and +7.12 respectively (Figures 3.15 and 3.16).

B4 = Cleaning and personal care	LL = +10.55
have facials from a local	**beauty therapist** and it was here I no
Nine a.m. have to be at the	**hairdresser's** to get my hair coloured
a.m. facial with Lisa,	**beautician**. Mobile phone rings.
s. Sophie was checking her	**make-up** in a small hand-bag mirror w
d go to work . I washed and	**moisturised** my face with his impressi
preferred being a fashion	**stylist**. There were more opportunities
rom the Ladies. With fresh	**lipstick** on. `Are you going down to

Fig 3.15

B5 = Clothes and personal belongings	LL = +7.12
ohn buys me a pair of leather	**trousers**. I try on lots. He
that were soft and cuddly,	**clothes** that always felt wonderful to
where Linda's Biba-inspired	**clothes** and Twiggy-inspired figure mad
lf in a pair of classic black	**trousers** and white shirt, a silver cha
Loan. Unfortunately 'buying	**clothes** and makeup' was not deemed a s
cool is that ? Choosing any	**outfit** I like from the wardrobe! I
l shoe back with the bias-cut	**georgette**, it was so ug, we were all

Fig 3.16

Therefore, the results emanating from the categories discussed here seem to cast some doubt on whether certain tenets that have been considered a given in relation to Chick Lit as a genre do indeed find a linguistic correlate in the novels. On the one hand, the body issue and over-obsessive preoccupation with appearance so often described by scholars do not seem to manifest linguistically, as references to anatomy are under-used with regard to other fictional genres. Second, although beauty products and clothes do feature more recurrently than in the reference corpus, they are nonetheless still not so overwhelmingly present in linguistic terms as is, for instance the 'S3.2 = Relationship: Intimacy and sex' category previously analysed with an LL value of +252.83. It might be, therefore that, after all, Chick Lit chicks do not talk so much about clothes, beauty products or shoes as they are deemed to do. I mention above that it is important not to overemphasize the significance of results or to extrapolate conclusions from the novels in my corpus to the whole of the genre. Perhaps an even larger corpus might be needed to allow for more compelling results, although I still maintain the solidity of the conclusions that the combination of several disciplines allows me to draw in this chapter.

The final categories with a positive score to discuss, for the most part, project what has been defined above as the 'aboutness' of the novels: 'T1.3 = Time period', LL score of +74.07; 'F2 = Drinks and alcohol', LL score of +69.34; and 'F3 = Smoking and non-medical drugs', LL score of +57.73. As a matter of fact, the three categories are greatly influenced by the aboutness of *Bridget Jones's Diary*, the first because of the diary style, the second and third explained by the over-recurrence of lexical terms related to drinking and smoking.

More interesting, however, are the final three categories I analyse because they are under-represented in the *Chick Lit Corpus* when compared to the BNC Sampler Written Imaginative sub-corpus: 'S7.1+ = In power', LL = –816.03; 'S2.2 = People: Male, LL = –249.48'; and 'S4 = Kin', LL = –56.35'. To these three, obviously, the previously discussed 'B1 = Anatomy and physiology' needs to be added. The first of these groupings collects items 'depicting power/authority/ influence and organisation/administration' (Archer *et al.*, 2002: 28). It is realized in the following concordances (Figure 3.17).

S7.1+ = In power	LL = –816.03
st be some sort of policing	**committee** to stop this from happening
a.m.phone sex. This time a	**board meeting**. On the table. In front
lse's job and that several	**board members** didn't know I had b
, This is not the way to	**handle** it. But I was in too deep.
again, and when I finally	**manage** to regain my composure I do
never see Linda as the	**omnipotent** matriarch of the family
ay, so I didn't bother to	**organize** anything . Still, at least
never 152 mind, she 's the	**boss**. And her office is pretty a

Fig 3.17

The negative score of this semantic grouping is high enough to suggest that some element of characterization is involved in this overwhelming statistic. It can be argued that the depiction of the needy individual outlined so far is, once more, linguistically supported by this category concerning a lack of real power. Furthermore, the fact that the 'S2.2 = People: Male' is also substantially under-represented, as the LL value (–249.48) demonstrates, safely confirms that the under-recurrence of lexical items indicating authority, influence and organization do indeed pertain to the women of the novels. Finally, the semantic category 'S4 = Kin', which convincingly throws a negative LL value of –56.35, clearly refers to the kinship role included in the social category grouping described by Culpeper (2001: 75). Some examples of how this grouping materializes can be found in Figure 3.18.

S4 = Kin	LL = –56.35
years to come, boring their	**daughters** rigid by going 'You know
ly silver lining in cloud of	**mother's** criminality was that it mi
nd is the one out of all the	**family**(including Paul) I most like
to win . Even with his new	**sister-in-law**. I like being part of
is is what I want . A proper	**family**. Nice people. People who
wedding and being Paul's	**wife**. 'Sarah' But couldn't it be
where is my errant younger	**brother** anyway? 'continued Dan. 'U
family? Uncles? Aunts?	**Grandparents**?' 'Nope, and it's fine.

Fig 3.18

The top 10 words in this category are 'mother', 'mum', 'family', 'dad', 'father', 'wedding', 'parents', 'married', 'wife' and 'husband', which also suggests that, despite the under-recurrence of this grouping, female kinship is still more statistically significant than male relations as the top two words prove. The categories illustrating negative scores, therefore, enrich our understanding of characterization issues in Chick Lit because they bring to the fore aspects which might have been previously mentioned or discussed in the critical assessment of the novels but which, up to now, had not been sufficiently evidenced with the linguistic support provided by a corpus stylistics analysis.

3.4 Conclusion

Although it is difficult to extrapolate results from the analysis of some works to the whole genre, the diverse approaches I take in this chapter both reinforce and bring into question some conclusions regarding Chick Lit characterization which other scholarly work has drawn on the back of, perhaps, less rigorous analyses. It is not my intention here to do away with the scholarly validity of those multifarious analyses that Chick Lit has already given rise to, as all my citations in this and other chapters prove. However it seems that it is the actual linguistic make-up of the novels that might confirm or challenge previous appraisals. As a corpus stylistics approach demonstrates, there are certain concerns prototypically associated with Chick Lit and its women that simply do not find a linguistic match in the novels. This, obviously, also has repercussions for the definition of the genre itself. A more diverse set of novels might be needed in order to firmly aver the characteristics of Chick Lit, so my challenging certain givens here simply highlights that more work is needed on this matter. This is tackled further in Chapter 4, which deals specifically with one amply discussed aspect of these novels, their relationship to feminism. I conclude the present chapter by advocating the usefulness of multidisciplinary research methods as well as the combination of top-down and bottom-up approaches as this comprehensiveness is what will ultimately allow a realistic definition of Chick Lit as a genre.

Chapter 4

Chick Lit in Context

4.1 Chick Lit Contextualized

This chapter embarks upon the discussion of certain issues already raised throughout this monograph but which still require further fine-grained clarification. I aim to provide more explicit insights into two specific matters, namely Chick Lit's relationship with feminism and its genre status in connection with cognate forms of popular fiction such as romances and romantic fiction.[1] Feminism has been approached in Chapter 3 (Section 3.2.2) mainly as it relates to aspects of social cognition and attitude schemas. The relationship between Chick Lit and romances is discussed primarily in Chapter 1 (Section 1.3) where I attempt to formulate a plausible definition of the former and look closely at its connections with the latter; the possible status of Chick Lit as a fully-fledged genre is also addressed in Chapter 3 (Sections 3.2 and 3.2.1), this time in connection with dramatic role schemas and the part they play as genre-defining aids. By providing a joint account of these two aspects, I intend to contextualize Chick Lit further so that its status as a genre, self-standing or otherwise, can be more neatly fine-tuned. My objectives here are backed up by plenty of scholarly work which has previously highlighted issues similar to mine here: for instance, see Hanson (2004), Henry (2004) and McRobbie (2004), for analyses of the relationship between Chick Lit and feminism; and Harzewski (2006), Kiernan (2006) and Whelehan (2005) for studies on the status of Chick Lit as an independent genre and discussions on how it relates to more traditional romances.

The kind of double assessment of Chick Lit I propose to implement in this section additionally brings to the fore that romances have also been assessed through a feminist lens (Coddington, 1997; Jackson, 1993; Jones, 1986; Snitow, 1986). Thus, the connection between modern romances and Chick Lit, on the one hand, and the representation of femaleness in either, on the other, is worth investigating further for it can bear fruitful results for a definition of both Chick Lit and its sister genres. This last statement, nonetheless, already highlights that I am not suggesting that the dissimilarities between these various manifestations of popular fiction – Chick Lit and romances, that is – are strikingly divisive. On the contrary, there are plenty of commonalities between them; however, this does not mean that possible discrepancies are not worth looking into either. Following the stylistics outline of this monograph, the main difference between this chapter and the previously mentioned academic work on these matters is the fact that I analyse Chick Lit by focusing mainly on the language of the novels, more specifically I look at whether transitivity patterns (Halliday 1994; Halliday and Matthiesen, 2004) and Leech and Short's model of speech and thought presentation (1981, 2007; Semino and Short, 2004) can shed light on Chick Lit in a way that other approaches cannot do. Therefore, my aim here is to complement some of the assessments previously made on romantic fiction, Chick Lit, and their connection with feminism based on the evidence emerging from a linguistic analysis of a series of Chick Lit and romance novels.

The methodology I follow in this chapter differs from the methods I employ elsewhere in the book. For instance, I do not use the corpus stylistics approaches used in Chapters 3 and 5, nor do I adopt the multimodal take of Chapter 2. This does not imply that I leave aside my intention to firmly abide by the rigour demanded by stylistics and repeatedly claimed in this monograph. I still observe the accuracy and exactness of a stylistic analysis but, essentially, this chapter derives from manual as opposed to computational work for the reasons I go on to explain below. In a way I follow more traditional approaches to stylistics research, what Ronald Carter calls 'steam stylistics':

> It is a term with which Carter's immediate colleagues are becoming increasingly familiar, and one which is always used by its creator to refer, in the most positive sense, to that body of stylistic work which continues to achieve thorough, convincing, and mind-expanding results year on year without the aid of new advances in computer technology, or reference to cutting-edge research in cognitive science. Though sometimes eclipsed by the sheer novelty of cognitivist and corpus methodologies, 'steam stylistics' (normally premodified with 'good, old-fashioned ...' by Carter) comfortably equalled those approaches for innovation and experimentation.
>
> (Gavins, 2005: 405)

Eschewing the 'help' of computers, or disregarding the newness of the latest interdisciplinary development within the field, still leaves the analyst with the honest and worthy option of a more traditional, manual stylistic study of those issues which she might consider of relevance. In fact, the two general frameworks I go on to explain in the following sections and which I subsequently apply to the novels did not, at first glance, appear to be related in the sense of being capable of bearing out an interpretatively significant outcome for my interests here. However, once the language of the novels was doubly analysed from the perspectives of these two models, they did indeed confirm that looking at transitivity patterns, on the one hand, and complementing this analysis with Leech and Short's speech and thought presentation model, on the other, can help contextualize the genre by clarifying where Chick Lit stands in relation to other cognate forms. As far as the issue of feminism is concerned, I revisit its relationship with Chick Lit using tenets from Systemic Functional Linguistics (SFL) which I also borrow in Chapter 2, but this time I look mainly at how the ideational metafunction materializes in verbal and mental processes. Transitivity is the grammatical system that illustrates the way we encode experiential meaning in language via certain 'processes' with which 'participants' engage and which are framed by various 'circumstances'. Halliday's transitivity model traditionally identifies six different types of processes: *material, mental, relational, behavioural, verbal* and *existential* (Halliday and Matthiessen 2004: 170); only mental and verbal processes are dealt with in this chapter, not because the rest are not capable of bringing out essential aspects about the language of the novels, but because I am interested in looking at the way chicks in Chick Lit both talk and think; that is, I want to consider how their voices and thoughts are linguistically projected. Furthermore, looking at transitivity patterns has already been used to shed light upon the way femaleness is portrayed in romantic fiction (Ryder, 1999; Wareing, 1994). By looking at, mainly though not exclusively, material processes and the role of participants in relation to those processes, both Ryder and Wareing conclude that the prototypical female of romances is portrayed as a largely passive participant, whereas male actors behave as their active counterparts. No other study seems to focus exclusively on verbal and mental processes in the way I do here. This tactic, however, paid off, as looking at mental and verbal clauses, despite providing some interesting insights into the novels, also brought to the fore that a transitivity analysis fails to account fully for some other crucial linguistic characteristics of these works. So, after searching for instances of mental and verbal processes to evaluate how they signal linguistically female characters' voices and thoughts, I then supplement that analysis with an examination of the type of speech and thought presentation categories that respectively project what they say and what they think (especially in relation to whether women's messages are verbalized in their own words or whether, instead, they are mediated via a narrator).

The conclusions I subsequently draw from the combination of approaches can be said to have been inductively reached rather than deductively proposed, something that is also directly determined by my attempt to avoid the problems associated with circularity in research. For instance, as I go on to explain below, I select six novels from which different extracts are carefully analysed. Inevitably, selecting material implies a certain imposition on the part of the researcher who can, even inadvertently, fall into the circularity trap by attempting to 'define' a particular object of study but pre-empting and, perhaps, undermining and even invalidating that attempt on the back of the choice of data. In order to explain how I chose the material for analysis in as innocuous a way as possible and to avoid the circularity snare, it might be worth revisiting briefly the general outline on romance and romantic fiction introduced in Chapter 1. There I discuss that the origin of the term romance goes as far back as the Greeks (Regis, 2003) but that modern romance is far more commonly associated with novels in which the happy resolution of a heterosexual romantic relationship forms the backbone of the narrative. Second, critical appraisals of romances and romantic fiction also underscore the ample variety of narrative forms into which, according to The Romantic Novelists Association, these novels can materialize: 'general fiction, women's fiction, historical, romantic comedy, chick lit, sagas – even spooky – as well as romance. [...] It embraces Jilly Cooper's 900 pages as well as the 187 Harlequin Mills & Boon category romances[2] which are published every month; multi-generational sagas and Regency romps; deeply serious meditations on life and flippant twenty-somethings' metropolitan shenanigans' (Romantic Novelists' Association, http://www.rna-uk.org/index.php?page=romanticfiction).

Third, some other studies of romances add the 'publication style' component, whereby these novels might be best differentiated by whether they appear as part of a series or as individual titles, what the Romance Writers of America website calls 'series or category romances' and 'single-title romances' (http://www.rwanational.org/cs/the_romance_genre). Finally, Regis (2003) further clarifies that the prototypical romance novel is structured around eight narrative components: '*a definition of society* [...]; the *meeting* between the heroine and hero; an account of their *attraction* for each other; the *barrier* between them; the *point of ritual death*; the *recognition* that fells the barrier; the *declaration* of heroine and hero that they love each other; and their *betrothal*' (2003: 14). The intrinsic complexity involved in setting the boundaries between what can be defined as romance, whether it differs from romantic fiction, and where Chick Lit stands in relation to these two forms leads me to conclude in Chapter 1 that, for the purposes of this monograph, it is better to conceive of the notions of romance and romantic fiction as synonymous.

This decision, nonetheless, still does not dispel all doubts concerning the possible circularity trap in my choice of novels for analysis. Because I want to assess how a transitivity and a speech and thought presentation analysis can shed light on the way women's voices and thoughts are linguistically realized, I compare two Chick Lit novels with two other sets (inclusive of two novels each) of prototypical romances, but I base my choice of novels on publication style rather than on any other characteristic of those mentioned above, as this seems to be the only aspect which can be more clearly and easily verified; hence I compare two Chick Lit works with what I, for ease of reference, name 'standalone' and 'series-embedded' romances.[3] This criterion is by no means problem-free, nor does it bear the definitive signs of distinction between romances and romantic fiction and, indeed, Chick Lit as, for instance, the standalone category can also include novels published as part of a trilogy. However, one distinct difference between these two categories is the fact that authors publishing their novels as independent books are, for the most part, not circumscribed by the general structural frame in which series-embedded novels are produced. For instance, the Mills & Boon website (http://www.millsandboon.co.uk/) lists, among others, the following series in which their books are published: 'Blaze', 'Cherish', 'Desire', 'Historical', 'Intrigue',

'Medical' and 'Modern'. As an example, consider Mills & Boon's pre-defined outline that all romances published in the 'Medical' romances should adhere to:

> Do you love handsome, big-hearted doctors? Are you a fan of *ER*, *Grey's Anatomy*, *Nip/Tuck*, *House*? In Medical Romance you'll find our trademark devilishly alluring doctors – as well as the highs and the lows, warmth and passions, of medical life! Medical Romance is first and foremost about heart-racing romance, with the added bonus of pulse-raising medical drama that throws our heroes and heroines together...even when they might not want to be!
>
> (Mills & Boon, http://www.millsandboon.co.uk/AAMedR.asp)

Standalone romances, therefore, are freer from the constrictions of the series so authors are allowed to develop their plot any way they wish to. Although not totally free from controversy, I still maintain this criterion as the way to avoid circularity in my choice of novels for comparison with Chick Lit.

All of the above issues highlight that my claims on Chick Lit, its relationship to feminism and the possibility of further contextualization, especially as far as its place in the genre cline is concerned, come as a result of an *a posteriori*, empirical approach. The chapter is thus divided into two main parts: an examination of the mental and verbal processes that realize some of the transitivity patterns of a series of novels, on the one hand, and the application of a speech and thought presentation framework to the same material. These two approaches also explore the way a linguistic analysis can bring to the fore the way feminist concerns are dealt with in these forms of popular fiction. Before I delve into this double investigation I initially provide a summary of the main theoretical tenets that characterize the two models that frame this chapter, which I now move on to explain.

4.2 Theoretical Principles

In this section I introduce the main tenets of the two theoretical frameworks I apply to the novels in Section 4.3, starting with a general description of transitivity and following on with an outline of Leech and Short's speech and thought presentation model.

4.2.1 Transitivity

Transitivity can be initially described as the grammatical system that projects experiential meaning as defined in Systemic Functional Linguistics (SFL). As discussed in Chapter 2, SFL is based on the premise that language is organized around three metafunctions, the ideational, the interpersonal and the textual metafunctions:

> It is clear that language does – as we put it – construe human experience [...] there is no facet of human experience which cannot be transformed into meaning. In other words, language provides a theory of human experience, and certain of the resources of the lexicogrammar of every language are dedicated to that function. We call it the ideational metafunction. [...] At the same time, whenever we use language there is always something else going on. While construing, language is always also enacting: enacting our personal and social relationships with other people around us. [...] We call it the interpersonal metafunction, to suggest that it is both interactive and personal. [...] But the grammar also shows up a third component, another mode of meaning which relates to the construction of text. [...] We call it the textual metafunction.
>
> (Halliday and Matthiessen, 2004: 29–30)

These three metafunctions have been studied here in Chapter 2, where the application of these SFL principles is discussed in relation to instances on non-verbal communication. Of the three metafunctions above, however, I focus exclusively on the ideational metafunction (which some authors such as Nørgaard, 2003, following Eggins (1994; 2004), refer to as 'experiential'). This ideational metafunction gets to work because certain lexicogrammatical components of language project the way human experience is linguistically construed:

> Our most powerful impression of experience is that it consists of a flow of events, or 'goings-on'. This flow of events is chunked into quanta of change by the grammar of the clause: each quantum of change is modelled as a figure – a figure of happening, doing, sensing, saying, being or having. [...] All figures consist of a process unfolding through time and of participants being directly involved in this process in some way; and in addition there may be circumstances of time, space, cause, manner or one of a few other types. [...] The grammatical system by which this is achieved is that of TRANSITIVITY (cf. Halliday, 1967/68).
>
> (Halliday and Matthiessen, 2004: 170)

Halliday and Matthiesen (2004) further explain that the figures of happening, doing or sensing they identify contain three elements, some of them compulsory and some optional or secondary, that allow the encoding of experiential meaning via the ideational metafunction: the *processes*, the *participants* and the *circumstances*:

> 1. a process unfolding through time
> 2. the participants involved in the process
> 3. circumstances associated with the process.
>
> (Halliday and Matthiesen, 2004: 175)

Because experiential meaning is varied in nature, processes are varied too. In fact, in SFL there are six different process types: *material, mental, relational, behavioural, verbal* and *existential*[4] (Halliday and Matthiesen, 2004: 170–1). *Material processes* 'are processes of doing in the material world and can be identified by asking "What did x do?"' (Nørgaard, 2003: 29). *Mental processes* 'are concerned with our experience of the world of our own consciousness' (Halliday and Matthiesen, 2004: 197). *Relational processes* are 'those of identifying and classifying' (Halliday and Matthiesen, 2004: 170). *Behavioural processes* are meant to be on the 'borderline between "material" and "mental" [...] processes: those that represent the outer manifestations of inner workings, the acting out of processes of consciousness (e.g. *people are laughing*) and physiological states (e.g. *they were sleeping*)' (Halliday and Matthiesen, 2004: 171). *Verbal processes,* in turn, are 'on the borderline of "mental" and "relational" [...]: symbolic relationships constructed in human consciousness and enacted in the form of language, like saying and meaning (e.g. the "verbal" clause *we say,* introducing a report of what was said: *that every fourth African is a Nigerian*)' (Halliday and Matthiesen, 2004: 171). Finally, 'on the borderline between the "relational" and the "material" are the processes concerned with existence, the *existential,* by which phenomena of all kinds are simply recognized to 'be' – to exist, or to happen' (Halliday and Matthiesen, 2004: 171). The richness of SFL's transitivity framework is obvious; besides, it renders itself rather well to a practical application for the analysis of actual stretches of language as the myriad of scholarly articles and monographs employing a transitivity analysis can vouch for. More interestingly, a considerable number of these publications deal specifically with literary language. For instance, the now classic article by Halliday (1971), 'Linguistic function and literary style: An inquiry into the language of William Golding's *The Inheritors*', set up the standards with regard to the study of the ideological metafunction through the application of a transitivity analysis. His endeavours have been widely replicated in other instances of scholarly work; for instance, for my own interests here, another classic in which an application of the transitivity framework specifically considers issues regarding femaleness and social power (or more accurately, lack of it) is Burton's 'Through glass darkly: Through dark glasses' (1982), which analyses an excerpt from Sylvia Plath's *The Bell Jar* ([1963] 2005)[5] and highlights the dehumanizing effect that the electric-shock treatment that Plath endures has on the female protagonist.

By focusing only on the way verbal and mental processes are exploited in my set of novels I want to bring to the fore the way Chick Lit women (as well as those in standalone and series-embedded romances) talk and think. This interest, however, is also spurred and justified by the outcome of my investigations in Chapter 3. As mentioned, some of the classic examples of academic research that have taken advantage of a transitivity analysis have drawn attention to the traditionally passive role that females are endowed with either in prototypical examples of romances or some other forms of literary fiction. The female character in *The Bell Jar,* for instance, is stripped of any volition, power of decision and, ultimately, her own humanity because the material processes in which she is a participant eschew portraying her as actor, a role which is, instead, transferred to the electric-shock machine that makes her body contort with pain in the psychiatric hospital where she is admitted for treatment. A second example is that of Wareing (1994), who looks at some modern romances and concludes:

> My aim has been to provide a stylistic framework for exploring how female characters are recuperated into a traditional passive role in sexual and romantic encounters, even when the characters appear to subvert or reject patriarchal values in other areas of their lives. From the analyses above, it is evident that the tradition of the passive heroine is deeply rooted in the norms of novel writing. The stylistic patterns which are most frequently used in the representation of a female protagonist create her as the object, and not the originator of desire, and view her through the eyes of a male observer, fragmenting her body for his speculation.
>
> (Wareing, 1994: 136)

Similar conclusions are echoed by other scholars; more importantly, most of these studies rely mainly, although admittedly not exclusively, on the role of material processes to justify their claims of female submissiveness, very often, especially towards the males in the story. This means that the male counterpart in the novels that Wareing investigates, for instance, is provided with a kind of prominent role as an action-generating individual contrary to the recipient role of the female; she simply becomes the passive participant in whichever action the male initiates. In SFL terms, these males are the 'actors' whereas the females become the 'goal'. However, one aspect that justifies my attempts to further contextualize Chick Lit with regard to its sister genres, standalone and series-embedded romances, is the fact that maleness has been proven to be under-represented in Chick Lit. As discussed in the previous chapter, a corpus stylistics analysis of the *Chick Lit Corpus* (see Sections 3.3.1 and 3.3.2) highlights that the group of prototypical Chick Lit novels that make up my corpus is characterized by the under-use of lexical items that refer to maleness, grouped by the software used for analysis under the category 'S2.2 = People: Male'. The comparison of my corpus with the BNC Sampler Written Imaginative sub-corpus pre-loaded in Wmatrix (Rayson, 2009) gives a statistically significant LL (log-likelihood)[6] score of –249.48; as a reminder, I explain in Section 3.3.1 that I use the highest cut-off point (15.13) for my comparisons so that the results obtained can be said to be statistically pertinent. Thus, any result above the 15.13 cut-off point suggests that the category to which that result refers is over-represented in relation to the reference corpus and, likewise, anything below it confirms that the semantic category under comparison is less used than the same group of lexical items in the reference corpus. Because the 'S2.2 = People: Male' category is widely under-represented with regard to the corpus it is measured against, I conclude that the female voice in Chick Lit is given some relevant prominence in relation to the male perspective. Consequently, my interests here are not so much an examination of women's role in the genre measured against their male counterparts, but an analysis of the kind of voice that these women are endowed with, both in terms of the 'symbolic relationships constructed in human consciousness and enacted in the form of language, like saying and meaning', that is verbal processes (Halliday and Matthiesen, 2004: 171), and their 'inner experience, the processes of consciousness' (Halliday and Matthiesen, 2004: 170), or mental processes. Mental clauses are divided into four types: cognition, emotion, desideration and perception, that is, processes of 'thinking', 'feeling', 'wishing' and 'perceiving' (in a physical sense). The participants involved in these clauses are the 'senser', who is typically human or human-like, and the 'phenomenon' or that which is felt, sensed or thought:

> The Senser is, logically enough, the participant who senses, that is, who thinks, prefers, sees, etc. [...] The phenomenon is consequently that which is sensed, ie thought, preferred, seen, etc., by the Senser.
>
> (Nørgaard, 2003: 31)

Verbal processes, on the other hand, are 'clauses of saying, as in *What did you say? – I said it's noisy in here,* with *you, I* functioning as Sayer. [...] "Verbal" clauses [...] accommodate three further participant functions in addition to the Sayer: (1) Receiver, (2) Verbiage, (3) Target' (Halliday and Matthiessen, 2004: 252, 255). Nørgaard (2003) further defines these participant functions as follows:

> The Sayer, who is the central participant of Verbal process clauses, is the participant who does the saying, commanding, suggesting, responding and other literal or symbolic verbal acts. [...] The Verbiage is that which is said or signalled by the Sayer in a Verbal process clause when not constituted by a projected clause: 'He requested a break', 'She asked me too many favours'. The Receiver of the Verbal process clause is sometimes represented in the clause and may be preceded by the preposition 'to'. [...] The Target is a slightly different participant that occurs in what Martin, Matthiessen and Painter (1997: 126) call 'judgemental verbal processes' such as 'praise', 'criticize', 'insult', 'abuse'. [...] A Target may occur together with a Receiver as in 'Our boss constantly praises Clive to the rest of us', of which 'Clive' is the Target and 'the rest of us' the Receiver.
>
> (Nørgaard, 2003: 33)

Therefore, I want to investigate whether, by looking at verbal processes and their various participants, we can learn about what these female characters have to say and how they verbalize it; similarly, investigating mental processes should provide an accurate picture of the way 'thinking' is effectively worded in these works, but it might also highlight whether 'feeling', 'wishing' and 'perceiving' are actions that Chick Lit women engage in.

Finally, some word of clarification concerning my choice of methodology is needed here. Above I explain that the method of analysis I employ in this chapter is more in line with a traditional, manual examination of data than has been the norm in other chapters: what I refer to as 'steam stylistics'. This shift is not whimsically decided but directly motivated by the widely-acknowledged current inefficacy of computational tools to deal with transitivity patterns:

> For the purposes of the chapter, I have consciously set aside the inescapable fact that the initial transitivity analysis still has to be done, and that it can be extremely time-consuming. There is software which is available to help speed up the process of functional analysis. [...] As yet, however, these programmes cannot easily handle different layers of analysis [...] and in any case some basic steps in applying the analytical methods outlined here are difficult to do except by hand.
>
> (Thompson, 2008: 30)

Computers, therefore, seem unable to cope with the intricacy and multilayered components of a transitivity analysis in an accurate and, hence, trustworthy way. As Thompson discusses here (see also Bartsch *et al.*, 2005), there is some software which can help the process along, but the general consensus, at least at the moment of writing this chapter, is that the problems and extra effort needed to actually take advantage of those programmes far outweigh the benefits. Thus, the mental and verbal processes I look at in my set of novels have been analysed by tallying the various instances of either category, as I explain in Section 4.3.

4.2.2 Speech and thought presentation

Speech and thought presentation is a framework widely discussed in stylistics (Leech and Short, 1981, 2007; Semino and Short, 2004; Simpson 1993; Short 1996[7]) although not necessarily always in conjunction with a transitivity analysis. In this chapter I demonstrate that the former can not only complement the latter, but can also cope with certain deficiencies that a transitivity analysis appears to display, especially with regard to the endeavours that occupy me here. Although the combination of these two frameworks bears very interesting and explanatory results with regard to the contextualization of Chick Lit I pursue here, I refrain from extending their applicability to texts, literary or non-literary, other than those under scrutiny in this chapter, despite my own intuitive suspicions that this combination of frameworks might actually render itself rather profitable for other analyses too. As far as a transitivity analysis is concerned, Nørgaard (2003) points out that, in spite of its applicability and its worth as an analytical tool, the model seems incapable of coping with certain idiosyncrasies typically, although not exclusively, occurring in literary registers:

> A character may, of course, occur repeatedly as the participant of this type of process with implications for the interpretation of the text, though very often in literature, instances of saying do not involve Verbal processes such

> as 'say', 'shout', 'whisper', 'answer', etc. but occur as direct speech without the inquit [...] A similar problem will emerge with the analysis of texts that contain considerable amounts of stream-of-consciousness or free indirect speech.
>
> (Nørgaard, 2003: 79)

A transitivity approach, thus, can help analyse verbal processes and the consequent effects they have in texts only in those cases in which the processes are explicitly marked by verbal forms indicating the occurrence of a speaking activity. What Nørgaard, however, rightly points out here is that speech is not always indicated by the presence of an introductory verb projecting the verbal process and, also, that the absence of the reporting verb introducing a verbal clause does not invalidate the existence of the verbal activity itself, nor, more importantly, the reader's perception of such an activity taking place. In these cases the verbiage, that is, that which is being said, is foregrounded and the process itself downplayed because it is dispensed with. For instance, consider the following excerpt extracted from Nora Roberts's *Megan's Mate* (1996) which, as explained below, is one of the novels chosen as prototypical examples of standalone romances:

> 'Dutch, what the hell's wrong with you? Are you drunk?'
>
> 'A nip or two of rum never rattled my brain.' He glared over Nathaniel's shoulder at Coco. 'It's her that's acting snockered. Out of my way, boy, I've got a thing or two left to say.'
>
> 'You've finished,' Nathaniel corrected.
>
> 'Out of his way.' All eyes turned to Coco. She was flushed, bright-eyed, and regal as a duchess. 'I prefer to handle this matter myself.'
>
> Megan tugged gently on her arm. 'Coco, don't you think you should go inside?'
>
> 'I do not.' She caught herself and added a friendly pat. 'Now, dear, you and Nate run along. Mr. Van Horne and I prefer to handle this privately.'
>
> (Nora Roberts, *Megan's Mate,*1996: 372)

All four characters (Megan, Coco, Mr. Van Horne and Nathaniel/Nate) hold the floor at some point during their conversation and are, thus, allowed some turns, but there is only one form explicitly describing a verbalization process, 'corrected'. A transitivity analysis, therefore, could be said to come slightly short of providing a full picture of the way speaking actually occurs. A speech presentation model can help account for cases such as the one above and, so, can complement rather than completely substitute for a transitivity approach.

The speech and thought presentation model most widely adopted in stylistic research is that of Leech and Short (1981, 2007) which, since its inception 30 years ago, has been much revisited and adjusted. The various reworkings of the model have been more recently analysed using computational tools in what was eventually published as *Corpus Stylistics. Speech, Writing and Thought*

Presentation in a Corpus of English Writing (Semino and Short, 2004). Semino and Short's publication is, to date, the most thorough version of the speech and thought presentation model in terms of the number of categories, criteria for identifying these categories and variety of texts they draw upon to come up with the new speech and thought taxonomy. The label 'speech and thought presentation' is, in fact, obsolete in Semino and Short (2004). Their extensive work on the linguistic reporting of speech and thought – also addressed in the second edition of *Style in Fiction* (Leech and Short, 2007) – has drawn attention to the fact that the original classification failed to account for the way 'writing' is linguistically reported. In relation to this third category, it is worth quoting Semino and Short at length here:

> In our previous publications, what we here call 'speech, writing and thought presentation' (SW&TP) was referred to as 'speech, thought and writing presentation' (ST&WP). The earlier ordering was mainly a consequence of history. The speech and thought presentation scales have been known, and discussed, by scholars for some considerable time, and the writing presentation scale has only recently been separately isolated and systematically described. We adopt the 'SW&TP' ordering in this book to reflect the fact (with which we have gradually come to detailed terms during our work) that the speech and writing presentation scales exhibit considerable similarities in form and function, whereas the thought presentation scale, because it has a different ontological status, has a weaker, analogical, relation to the other two discourse presentation scales.
>
> (Semino and Short, 2004: 18)

The SW&TP scale, thus, contains a rich array of different categories that fully describe how discourse, understood as an umbrella term to include speech, writing and thought, is linguistically presented. Another difference with the original model is the fact that the early formulation by Leech and Short (1981) was primarily brought to light to account for the presentation of speech and thought in fictional texts. The 2004 model incorporates newspaper news reports and (auto)biographies, so its new scope is far broader; besides, the initial objective regarding the description of fictional speech and thought presentation has been much expanded and used for other purposes too (see Jeffries, 2007; McIntyre *et al.*, 2004; McKenzie, 1987; Roeh and Nir, 1990). Finally, the 2004 model also spells out clearly the criteria followed by the authors to decide on the number and types of categories, the boundaries between these categories, and whether there are instances of overlapping:

> On the one hand there are the more formal, structural criteria for differentiating among the categories. These relate primarily to graphology (e.g. quotation marks, italics, paragraph boundaries), syntax (e.g. structural relations between clauses, grammatical mood) and deixis (including

> tense and pronouns). On the other hand, there are the more pragmatic, contextual and inference-based criteria, which are to do with judgements concerning the likelihood that someone might have said, thought or written something at a particular point. They therefore involve assessments as to whether the context and/or lexical choices in a particular stretch of text could reflect the views and/or verbal repertoire of particular individuals. These decisions result from inferences made on the basis of the co-text, the context and general background knowledge, and are therefore less clear-cut and more probabilistic than the decisions made on the basis of structural criteria.
>
> (Semino and Short, 2004: 223)

Admitting that there are both formal and functional criteria to consider when assigning one particular textual instance to one category or another also highlights that these parameters help with the decision but, by no means, always result in satisfactory, clear-cut distinctions. For the purposes that occupy me here, nevertheless, I do not delve into the rich array of categories in Semino and Short's version of the model, simply because most of the SW&TP groups do not feature in my sample of texts or, when they do, their presence is negligible so they do not merit discussion. The categories that need addressing are direct speech (DS), indirect speech (IS), free direct speech (FDS) and free indirect speech (FIS) as far as speech presentation is concerned, and direct thought (DT), indirect thought (IT), free direct thought (FDT) and free indirect thought (FIT), with regard to the presentation of the characters' thinking processes; in sum, the more 'canonical' forms of speech and thought presentation. In what follows I only provide a theoretical description of these two sets of categories; for a full account of the speech, writing and thought presentation model readers are referred to the full version developed in Semino and Short (2004).[8]

Traditionally, direct speech (DS) is associated with the verbatim (or nearest) reproduction of what someone has said, whereas in indirect speech (IS) someone else reports in their own words the content of that other person's utterance. This basic premise, however, is far more complex, as 'direct speech (DS) and indirect speech (IS) [...] [are] distinguished not just in terms of their formal linguistic features, but also in terms of whether the words and grammatical structures of the original utterance [...] [are] presented, as well as its propositional form' (Semino and Short, 2004: 9). The difference between direct and indirect speech is not just structural and formal but also involves the faithfulness claims to the original made in the reported clause so that the closer to the propositional and structural content of the former, the more in line with direct speech. Leech and Short (2007: 255–6) illustrate the two categories with the following examples:

a) He said, 'I'll come back here to see you again tomorrow' = DS
b) He said that he would return there to see her the following day = IS

Beside the functional distinction between the two forms, indirectness is formally signalled by a series of graphological and syntactic markers:

> (i) The inverted commas around the reported speech, which indicate that quotation is occurring [...] are removed, thus making the reported speech dependent on the reporting verb.
> (ii) That dependence is marked explicitly by the introduction of the subordinating conjunction *that.*
> (iii) The first- and second-person pronouns change to third-person.
> (iv) The tense of the verb undergoes 'backshift', as does the time adverb, *tomorrow,* which becomes *the following day.*
> (v) The 'close' deictic adverb *here* changes to the more remote *there.*
> (vi) The verb of movement changes.
>
> (Leech and Short, 2007: 256)

So, whereas assigning particular instances to either category should be based on criteria that are as easily verifiable as possible, the co-text, the context and the general background knowledge, as described above, also need to be taken into consideration. It is important to highlight the varying narrative effects achieved by employing one form or another, especially because IS can purposefully foreground the presence of the reporter; in fictional accounts that reporter tends to be the narrator through whose voice the uttered words are reported (although obviously other characters and/or narratees can also fulfil that role). This means that the claims to abide by the original can have varying degrees of adherence, so the stronger those faithfulness claims, the closer the reported speech will be to the alleged voice of the characters producing the original speech; on the other hand, the more the mediation of the narrator is made present, the further away from the original the reported clause would be felt to be. The speech presentation scale is made of categories other than DS and IS; for my purposes here, I am describing free direct speech (FDS) and free indirect speech (FIS). The main distinguishing feature highlighted in the original formulation of these two categories is that they, somehow, appear freer than the non-free varieties:

> Direct speech has two features which show evidence of the narrator's presence, namely the quotation marks and the introductory reporting clause. Accordingly, it is possible to remove either or both of these features, and produce a freer form, which has been called FREE DIRECT SPEECH: one where the characters apparently speak to us more immediately without the narrator as an intermediary.
>
> (Leech and Short, 2007: 258)

The combination of frameworks I use in this chapter is particularly useful to highlight instances of the freer forms of speech presentation (as well as thought, to be discussed later). It was mentioned above that a transitivity analysis seems to fail an investigation of those verbal processes in which the reporting clause is absent from the sentence. Looking at those same clauses from the vantage point of a speech and thought presentation model means that the speech-presentation capability of free direct forms is still acknowledged despite the absence of the reporting verb. A similar scenario is found in those instances in which indirect speech is freed from the mediatory effect of a reporting clause:

> FIS is normally thought of as a freer version of an ostensibly indirect form. Its most typical manifestation is one where, unlike IS, the reporting clause is omitted, but where the tense and pronoun selection are those associated with IS.
>
> (Leech and Short, 2007: 260–1)

As will be explained in Section 4.3, of the four speech categories that do feature in my set of novels, IS and FIS turn out to play a rather minor role when compared to DS and FDS; the fact that Chick Lit novels, standalone and series-embedded romances all eschew the more distancing effect of indirect and free indirect forms in favour of the immediacy of direct or free direct speech is, therefore, worth investigating.

In relation to free direct forms and their status as separate categories to the direct forms, Leech and Short's original proposal has been called into question, first by Short (1988), and more recently in the new version of the model proposed by Semino and Short (2004):

> We have already mentioned that, while Leech and Short (1981) presented FDS and FDT as presentational categories in their own right, we have come to view the free direct forms merely as sub-variants of the direct categories.
>
> (Semino and Short, 2004: 194)

The main matter of contention in relation to whether free direct forms should be defined as independent from their direct counterparts is based on functional rather than formal grounds, so that it seems, at times, hard to justify the direct/free-direct distinction with regard to faithfulness claims. Semino and Short's computational approach (2004) set out to test whether the functionality of these two categories warrants their presentational separation by attempting to stick to the formal differences in as thorough a way as possible; their analysis still ran into a series of ambiguous cases so they eventually settled for the DS, FDS or DS-FDS tagging which follows the following parameters:

- The direct tag DS was used where (i) there were quotation marks, (ii) there was a reporting clause [...], and (iii) the reported segment immediately followed or preceded the relevant NRS[9] within the same paragraph [...]
- The portmanteau tags DS-FDS were used where (i) there were quotation

marks, (ii) there was an NRS or some other speech presentation category performing the introductory function of an NRS from the reported segment. [...]

- The free direct tags FDS were also used where there were no quotation marks, or where, even in the presence of quotation marks, there was no reporting clause.

(Semino and Short, 2004: 196)

The problem of distinction between the forms, therefore, seems less than resolved, although Semino and Short conclude that 'the experience of coding the corpus suggests that this interface does not correspond to a category distinction, but merely to a clinal distinction between variants of the same category' (2004: 197). Delving into the analytical detail that this issue deserves falls well outside the scope of this chapter. For my own interests, though, I maintain the separation between the categories mainly on formal grounds. Because I take advantage of both a transitivity and a speech and thought presentation approach, I am especially concerned with those cases which the former model may have missed out on highlighting precisely because of the absence of the reporting clause. As the formal definition of free direct forms contemplates that verbal processes (as well as mental processes) materialize as free direct speech (and thought) because of the absence of the inquit, I give preference to the formal parameters and maintain the free direct categories as separate from the direct ones.

Finally, the thought categories can be formally aligned with speech categories, although their functional and ontological status is characteristically different. The four thought categories that feature in my novels are direct thought (DT) and indirect thought (IT), on the one hand, and free direct thought (FDT) and free indirect thought (FIT), on the other. The graphological and grammatical markers that help discriminate between the direct, indirect and free direct/indirect speech forms are also in operation with regard to thought presentation, although it is important to remember that the 'representation of the thoughts of characters, even in an extremely indirect form [...] is ultimately an artifice' (Leech and Short, 2007: 270). As developed below, an analysis of the thought categories proves especially fruitful because it helps contextualize Chick Lit's genre status and it also aids to spell out how it differs from standalone and series-embedded romances in a way that other analyses seem less capable of doing. One last clarification concerns the methodology I follow here; despite the fact that, as described in relation to the new SW&TP model devised by Semino and Short (2004), corpus and computational tools prove successful for the analysis of speech and thought realizations, I abide by the manual analysis preferred in this section. The 'steam stylistics' approach of this chapter allows me to view the speech and thought patterns of the novels in conjunction with the verbal and mental processes discerned in the transitivity half of my examination. Although, strictly speaking, my selection of excerpts could have been investigated using a corpus stylistics approach, the small-scale sample I use would not have warranted statistically significant results. Despite the dangers of extrapolating results outside the realm of the investigated excerpts, the interpretative value of the manual analysis I do undertake should not be underestimated either, as it is backed up by the tallying of linguistic markers in a way not attempted previously in other studies of Chick Lit.

4.3 The Analysis

In this section I attempt to contextualize Chick Lit further by implementing a linguistic analysis of the transitivity patterns and the speech and thought realizations of a selection of excerpts. I consider the linguistic make-up of Chick Lit but I also measure it against some other extracts taken from standalone and series-embedded romances. Finally, I assess whether the linguistic aspects of the three sets of novels I look into attest to the connection repeatedly mentioned by scholars between feminist issues and Chick Lit, and discuss whether the outcome of a linguistic analysis can complement, support or, even, contest such a connection with feminism. In sum, I aim to provide further evidence concerning where Chick Lit stands as a genre in relation to other forms of popular fiction. In pursuing these aims I have looked at six samples of 10,000 words each, respectively extracted from six different novels (a total of 60,000 words). The novels have been selected according to the criteria discussed in previous sections so that the dangers of circularity are kept at bay as much as possible. The novels are Helen Dunne's *Trixie Trader* (TT) (2001) and Liza Palmer's *Conversations with the Fat Girl* (CFG) (2005) in the Chick Lit group; Nora Roberts's *Suzanna's Surrender* (S'sS) (1991) and *Megan's Mate* (M'sM) (1996) illustrating standalone romances; and Ally Blake's *Billionaire on her Doorstep* (BDS) (2007) and Julie Cohen's *All Work and no Play* (AWnP) (2007) as series-embedded romances. The page ratio of the extracts selected varies from work to work but the samples all amount to about 10,000 words and are representatively spread through the whole novels. The figures I present here are the result of counting and adding up the markers for the different linguistic aspects I discuss, that is, I tally the number of instances of mental and verbal processes first; I follow that with an account of the occurrences of the four mental processes types (cognition, desideration, emotion and perception); then I look at the various cases of speech presentation and, finally, at the realizations of thought presentation. As explained before, I refrain from making claims regarding the statistical significance of my data and eschew extrapolating the relevance of my results beyond the scope of my own investigation here. However, I do highlight the interpretative potential of the figures I present because they are assessed on the back of reasonably large samples (for a manual analysis, that is) which are also representatively spread throughout the novels, so they amply illustrate the three different manifestations of popular fiction I investigate.

The triad of categories into which I split popular fictional romances (understood in its broadest sense) has been investigated by other scholars who also consider that popular romances can branch out, more or less neatly, into a series of sub-divisions and sub-categories. More importantly, some of these researchers draw upon linguistic analyses to suggest that popular romances do fall into a series of sub-categories. Opas and Tweedie (1999) (see also Opas-Hänninen and Seppänen, 2010) investigate romances (exclusive of prototypical examples of Chick Lit) and conclude:

> Looking at our results as a whole and comparing them with those of Biber and Finegan (1989), some interesting findings emerge. It seems that our data fall primarily into three categories, the Steel texts, the Regency texts, and the Harlequin texts, with some texts from each category overlapping with other categories. [...] This suggests that there are different types of romantic fiction and that they can be separated, at least to some extent, from each other.
>
> (Opas and Tweedie, 1999: 97)

Opas and Tweedie (1999) specifically focus on the use of stance markers in romantic fiction (see Chapter 5 for more on the notion of stance and the language of evaluation) and, by means of computational methods, are able to confirm that, within the general category of romances, linguistic usage varies to the extent that some different categories can be indeed established. More interestingly for this chapter, they separate out what they call the 'Steel texts' from the 'Regency' and 'Harlequin' texts. These three groups do not exactly correlate with those used here (Chick Lit, standalone and series-embedded romances), especially because the sub-categorization of romances I initially work with is based on publication style rather than on structural or linguistic parameters to avoid a circular discussion of the object of study. Opas and Tweedie's (1999) classification, nonetheless, still interests me because of the firm linguistic criteria on which their categories are based, which proves that some kind of distinction is possible when the language of the novels is studied. In what follows, I consider whether transitivity patterns and speech and thought presentation can similarly back up the tripartite classification based on publication style that I have tentatively proposed, and whether this helps strengthen the status of Chick Lit as a well-defined genre on its own linguistic merits.

The same interest to find linguistic support for issues that have been repeatedly raised in relation to Chick Lit also motivates the examination of the connection between Chick Lit and feminism (see Hanson, 2004; Marsh, 2004; Whelehan, 2000, 2005). Chapter 3 (Section 3.2.2) discusses whether tenets from social cognition can help understand the way some Chick Lit characters formulate strong feminist claims. In the present chapter, I focus on whether a linguistic analysis of the two aspects described can give some countenance to those claims too. For instance, one of the issues concerning the Chick

Lit-feminism correlation raised in Chapter 3 is the somewhat unorthodox understanding expressed by the women in the genre with regard to what this social, philosophical, political and literary (among other aspects) movement entails:

> 'Wait ... wait. It's this book called *What Men Want*. Right ... "If you have a beautiful sister, or friend, rest assured that your boyfriend is HAVING THOUGHTS ABOUT SEX WITH HER."' [...]
>
> 'I mean isn't that revolting? Aren't they just ...?'
>
> 'Shaz, can I call you back later?'
>
> Next thing Shaz was accusing me of being obsessed with men when I was supposed to be a feminist. So I said, if she was supposed to be so uninterested in them, why was she reading a book called *What Men Want?* It was all turning into a hideously unfeminist man-based row when we realized it was ridiculous and said we'd see each other tomorrow.
>
> (Helen Fielding, *Bridget Jones: The Edge of Reason*, 1999: 20)

This extract from *Bridget Jones: The Edge of Reason* is symptomatic of the rather oblique understanding of feminism that these heroines tend to profess. The unconventional (for some, plain flaky) treatment of feminist issues in Chick Lit has been amply approached from a variety of perspectives, some of which are worth reflecting upon before implementing the linguistic analysis of the novels. For instance, Hanson (2004) discusses *Bridget Jones's Diary* (1996) and comments that:

> From the start of the book ('9st 3') to its finish ('do as your mother tells you!'), *Bridget Jones's Diary* seems to endorse a preoccupation with the construction of the female body in relation to the male gaze, and femininity, not feminism, is seen as the route to empowerment. The book thus seems to offer a kind of lipstick feminism that assumes that a woman's best weapon in life is a floaty white dress in a romantic setting.
>
> (Hanson, 2004: 17)

The label 'lipstick feminism' suggests that in *Bridget Jones's Diary* (and, by extension, in the prototypical Chick Lit novel) the kind of femininity that embodies women's preoccupation with body image, clothes, shoes and general appearance far outweighs concerns with feminism multifariously understood as any kind of political, social or philosophical involvement with women's rights. Hanson develops her argument and adds:

> Feminism has always defined itself against femininity, at least since Mary Wollstonecraft [[1790] 1994] attacked genteel femininity and 'that weak elegancy of mind, exquisite sensibility, and sweet docility of manners, supposed to be the sexual characteristics of the weaker vessel' (73). Feminism/femininity has been a foundational binary opposition, and it has

> been assumed that the two categories are mutually exclusive. Might it be that this binary opposition is now being unravelled, as it is recognised that the two terms are mutually dependent rather than mutually exclusive? To suggest this is not to suggest that we live in a post-feminist or post-ideological world, but to entertain the possibility that feminist beliefs may have entered the mainstream more fully than we realise.
>
> (Hanson, 2004: 25–6)

According to Hanson, feminist beliefs do not necessarily have to be considered missing from the prototypical Chick Lit woman's discourse simply because there is a rather marked emphasis on femininity, perhaps a more marked sense than is embraced in other forms of women's fiction. If this is the case, then, a less belligerent but still equally valid version of feminism would be encoded in Chick Lit claims to feminism. In relation to the dichotomy femininity–feminism in Chick Lit and whether this duality is conceived of differently in its sister genres, Gill and Herdieckerhoff (2006) argue:

> In this brief analysis we have explored some of the themes and characterisations of contemporary chick lit. We have shown how romances have indeed changed in significant ways, but that the modes of femininity and of heterosexual coupledom on offer in contemporary chick lit are neither straightforwardly more progressive nor more retrogressive than in earlier popular romances such as those from the Harlequin or Mills and Boon stable.
>
> (Gill and Herdieckerhoff, 2006: 498)

Gill and Herdieckerhoff envision heterosexual romantic liaisons as one of the possible manifestations of femininity and conclude that, in this respect, Chick Lit seems to echo the same type of ideal 'heterosexual coupledom' generally perpetuated in romances. Having said that, they also add that:

> Chick lit articulates a distinctively post-feminist sensibility characterised by an emphasis on neo-liberal feminine subjectivities and self-surveillance and monitoring; the notion of the (sexual) body as the key source of identity for women; discourses of boldness, entitlement, and choice (usually articulated to normative femininity and/or consumerism); and a belief in the emotional separateness of men's and women's worlds. It is also characterised by an entanglement of feminist and anti-feminist discourses.
>
> (Gill and Herdieckerhoff, 2006: 487)

This rather encompassing rendition of the topics and themes that characterize Chick Lit as a genre in its own right concludes that 'an entanglement of feminist and anti-feminist discourses' is, nonetheless, still possible. Furthermore, Gill and Herdieckerhoff also underscore that some of the genre's defining traits are actually more in line with a 'post-feminist sensibility' than with feminist matters. This leads to a third major stance with regard to the connections between Chick Lit and feminism, or more accurately, its relationship with certain topics reminiscent of feminism in combination with some other issues more in tune with post-feminist concerns. Ferriss and Young (2008: 1–2) analyse what they call Chick culture which they define 'as a group of mostly American and British popular culture media forms focused primarily on twenty- to thirtysomething middle-class women. Along with chick flicks, the most prominent chick cultural forms are chick lit and chick TV programming.' Chick culture, thus, is a more comprehensive way of understanding which discourses and media paradigms actually encompass some of the themes dealt with in Chick Lit. For Ferriss and Young, at the core of Chick culture lies an enmeshed post-feminist, not feminist, ideology, although they later concede that the transitional evolvement from feminism to post-feminism should perhaps be seen on a cline rather than as antithetical positions separated by irreducible differences. Ferriss and Young (2008) illustratively summarize what they deem to be the most prototypical tenets of feminism and post-feminism that are worth quoting at length here:

> Feminism:
> - Reliance on political action, political movements, and political solutions;
> - The primacy of equality; resistance to and critique of the patriarchy;
> - Choice is collective – it refers to women's right not to have children and to enter careers and professions formerly closed to them;
> - A rejection – or at least questioning – of femininity;
> - Suspicion of and resistance to media-driven popular culture and the consumerism it supports;
> - Humor is based on the disjunction between traditional women's roles and women as powerful, independent people.
>
> Postfeminism:
> - The personal as political; agenda is replaced by attitude;
> - A rejection of second-wave anger and blame against the patriarchy;
> - Choice is individual – whether of family, career, cosmetic surgery, or nail color;
> - A return to femininity and sexuality;
> - Pleasure in media-driven popular culture and an embracing of the joys of consumerism;
> - Humor is based on the discrepancy between the ideals put forward by both feminism and the media, and the reality of life in the modern world; as such, the humor of postfeminism is often ironically self-deprecating.
>
> (Ferriss and Young, 2008: 3–4)

The bullet points in the post-feminism half of the quotation seem to ring truer with regard to the prototypical Chick Lit novel than those in the feminism group. However, the dichotomy feminism/post-feminism does not seem to be entirely resolved, and ticking most of the boxes in Ferriss and Young's otherwise thorough summary of features still does not fully satisfy all scholars with regard to an unequivocal categorization of Chick Lit as post-feminist despite the feminist claims that Chick Lit women make. In sum, Chick Lit can project the notion of femaleness multifariously as the above scholarly appraisals prove, sometimes in a way that might stand closer to post-feminist positions, other times in a way that emphasizes a clinal relationship between feminism and post-feminism. For instance, on the one hand, as suggested by Hanson (2004), femininity should not be necessarily understood as being at odds with some of the Chick Lit women's feminist claims; second, Chick Lit can also illustrate femaleness as the embodiment of what Gill and Herdieckerhoff (2006) call 'heterosexual coupledom'; third, femaleness can be conceived of as an expression of ideas which are situated half-way between feminist and post-feminist ideals. These otherwise sound descriptions of the Chick Lit–feminism relationship demonstrate that this is not, by any means, a settled or resolved matter. What seems to be missing from most of the scholarly work on the Chick Lit–feminism dichotomy is a linguistic analysis that might help disentangle some of the complexities rightly highlighted by research on the matter. Looking at the linguistic make-up of the novels could actually shed light on those otherwise perfectly sound non-linguistic parameters used by some scholars to gauge the connection between Chick Lit and feminism, which I now move on to address.

As explained previously, I focus exclusively on the way mental and verbal processes are exploited in my selection of novels, not because the rest of processes (material, relational, behavioural and existential) are incapable of enlightening aspects of Chick Lit and the romances but because I am interested in analysing how the linguistic voice and thoughts of the chicks in Chick Lit are realized. I thus consider all the predicators in the various samples and look for occurrences of mental and verbal processes in the six novels under scrutiny. The results are graphically arranged in Figure 4.1.

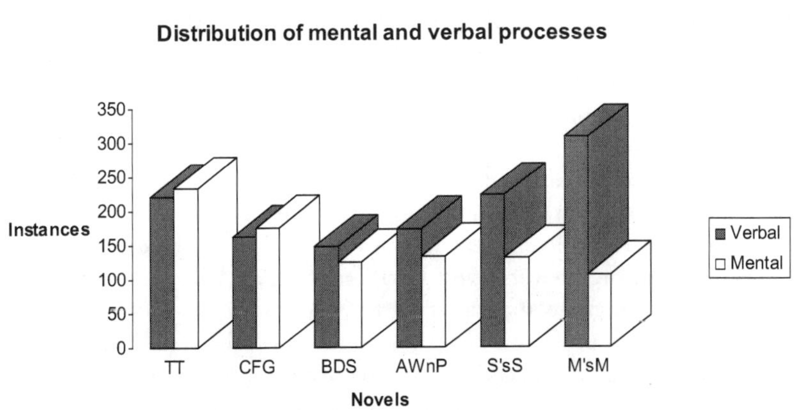

Fig 4.1 Distribution of mental and verbal processes.

The distribution of mental and verbal processes in Figure 4.1 shows that some preliminary pattern is emerging. On the one hand, the results suggest that a particular grouping of the novels is possible as in two of the works mental processes score higher than verbal processes (TT and CFG), whereas in the other four it is the verbal processes group which is preferred; on the other, and more importantly for this chapter, that grouping roughly correlates with the classificatory taxonomy used so far inasmuch as it sets Chick Lit (TT and CFG) apart from series-embedded (BDS and AWnP) and standalone romances (S'sS and M'sM). This suggests that the non-linguistic criterion (publication style) that I adopt to differentiate the various manifestations of popular romantic fiction (understood in its broadest sense) appears to have found an initial backing correspondence in some of the linguistic characteristics of the novels. Obviously, extrapolating the statistical significance of these differences to cases other than those studied here might be contentious given the relatively small scale of the samples I use, but the fact that Chick Lit works exploit mental and verbal processes differently from the standalone and series-embedded romances is, nonetheless, worth investigating further. For instance, consider how verbal processes are used in Cohen's *All Work and no Play*, one of the novels in the series-embedded romance category:

> 'Let them look,' **said** Jonny, but when he glanced back at Jane, her skin was white to the lips.
>
> 'You really care that much about what your colleagues think of you?' he **said**, more gently this time.
>
> 'My job is all I have left, Jonny,' she **whispered** [...]
>
> 'I didn't think Gary would **tell** anyone,' she **continued**, 'but now that he has it must be all over the agency. I hadn't even **told** people we'd broken up. And now they must think I –'
>
> 'Let's give them something to really think about,' **said** Jonny.
>
> (AWnP: 84)

In the above quotation, the emboldened verbs signal out the verbal processes; the various sayers are realized either by pronouns or nouns ('he, 'she' and 'Jonny') and the verbiage includes the propositional content of what was actually said ('we'd broken up', for instance). Cases such as this are prototypically illustrative of processes in which the essential components of the verbal act are incorporated, that is, readers learn about the fact that either 'Jonny', 'he' or 'she' performs a verbal activity (the process) as acts of 'saying', 'whispering' or 'telling', and that such a verbal activity is materialized in the message they convey, the verbiage ('Let them look', for instance). These cases, therefore, are indicative that a verbal activity has taken place because the verb signalling the process is present. However, as discussed before, fiction (especially, although not exclusively) is characteristically capable of signifying that some kind of communicative act has occurred among characters despite the possible absence of the inquit ('said', 'whispered', 'continued'). In order

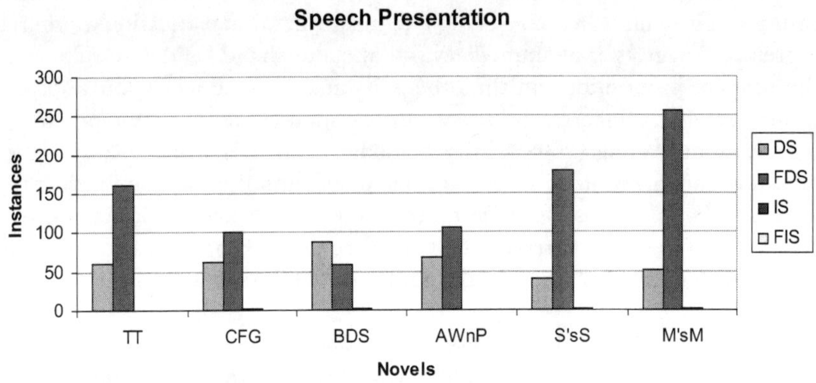

Fig 4.2 Speech presentation

to consider how those cases in which the process is expunged combine with others in which the verbal marker is purposefully kept, I look at the speech presentation patterns of the extracts, graphically displayed in Figure 4.2.

Section 4.2.2 above summarizes the differences between the various categories of speech realizations,[10] that is, the graphological, syntactic and deictic markers that distinguish the direct, indirect and free versions of speech presentation: for instance, the use of inverted commas, first-/second-person pronouns or proximal deictic markers for direct speech; absence of inverted commas, back-shifted tenses and distal deictic markers for the indirect version; the free forms are subsequently defined as those direct and indirect cases in which the introductory verb and/or the graphological markers are dispensed with, as well as further combinations of the above. Figure 4.2 shows that only four of the speech categories occur in my samples; furthermore, the indirect speech and free indirect speech forms play only a rather minor part as they score very low when compared to their direct speech counterparts. The fact that the indirect and free indirect versions of speech presentation are given a lesser role underscores that my samples discourage the presentation of speech via the mediating report of a teller who is made responsible for describing in her own words what other characters have allegedly said. The communicative exchanges between the characters happen, instead, as the result of verbal acts in which the immediacy resulting from the non-back-shifted forms and first-/second-personal pronouns, for instance, are preferred despite the introductory verb also being used in the case of direct speech. As this tendency is further reinforced by the higher scores of free direct speech that dispense with this introductory verb altogether in all but one of the novels (BDS), the immediacy I refer to is considerably marked and strengthened. Besides, as discussed earlier in relation to the functional criteria that Leech and Short (1981; 2007) originally, and Semino and Short (2004) more recently, have investigated, the choice of direct and free direct forms also underscores claims to a faithful representation with regard to the propositional content of the original message. The combination of formal and functional criteria, therefore, suggests that immediacy, on the one hand, and faithfulness to the original proposition, on the other, characterizes the way popular fiction women air their concerns and preoccupations, whichever these happen to be. As Ferriss and Young (2008: 4) discuss above, 'choice is individual – whether of family, career, cosmetic surgery, or nail color', and these women having the option of freely expressing that choice in their own voice via direct and free direct speech seems to corroborate that. My results in Figure 4.2 also appear to concur with some of the findings in Semino and Short (2004):

> Although IS is, after DS, the most well-known form of speech presentation, it is in fact slightly less frequent in our corpus than NRSA(p),[11] and less than half as frequent as (F)DS [...]. This provides quantitative support for the view expressed by Leech and Short (1981) and Halliday (1994) that IS is not the most prototypical way of representing speech. [...] More specifically, [...] IS is most frequent in the press section of the corpus.
>
> (Semino and Short, 2004: 78)

A preliminary assessment of my samples in comparison with the far more extensive, quantitative study in Semino and Short highlights that the three popular fictional forms under scrutiny abide by the general tendency suggested by Leech and Short (1981) and Halliday (1994) and empirically proven by Semino and Short (2004). The latter also comment on the low score that FIS displays in their corpus:

> Free indirect speech (FIS) is by far the least frequent category of speech presentation [...]. This may seem surprising, given the amount of attention that scholars have devoted to what is generally called 'free indirect discourse' or 'represented speech and thought'. [...] The free indirect form is much more central as far as thought presentation is concerned.
>
> (Semino and Short, 2004: 82)

As with their results, my own manual analysis also underscores that the free indirect speech category is not one that Chick Lit, standalone or series-embedded romance authors choose to signal out verbal activities. This tendency, as Semino and Short suggest and I discuss below, is turned on its head as far as the free indirect version of thought presentation is concerned.

The speech categories just considered, however, seem to come slightly short in their ability to provide a definitive characterization of Chick Lit as a genre separate from other cognate forms, although they seem to be more useful for a possible distinction between standalone and series-embedded romances. For instance, the Chick Lit novels (TT and CFG) and the standalone romances (S'sS and M'sM) concur as far as the more recurrent use of free direct speech forms. This should be viewed in light of the larger number of occurrences of verbal processes in the case of standalone romances with respect to series-embedded romances shown in Figure 4.1. The results of the combined analyses that I implement here seem to suggest that readers are allowed more immediate access to the actual voice of standalone romances women than those in series-embedded romances because, whatever message they convey to their readership, it is presented without the mediating voice of a narrator. As described in Section 4.1, series-embedded romances need to conform to the stricter narrative, topical and structural patterns that define the series in question (for instance, the Mills & Boon 'Blaze', 'Cherish', 'Desire', 'Historical', 'Intrigue', 'Medical' and 'Modern' series) so it can be argued that one way of marking that freedom for the standalone romances from the slightly corseted structure of series-embedded romances is by letting the female voice be heard without any intermediary. The results obtained from tallying the speech presentation markers in the series-embedded romances (BDS and AWnP) are, however, inconclusive, which shows that this is an aspect that requires more work. The analysis of verbal processes from the viewpoint of speech presentation models, thus, does not provide compelling evidence with regard to Chick Lit categorization as an independent genre but it does point out certain trends and indicate that further lines of investigation should be considered, which I now take on in relation to mental processes and thought presentation.

Mental processes, as explained above, refer to those linguistic forms that encode humans' cognitive abilities, that is, mental processes 'are concerned with our experience of the world of our own consciousness' (Halliday and Matthiesen, 2004: 197). Halliday and Matthiesen distinguish four processes capable of projecting that world of our consciousness: cognition, perception, desideration and emotion. Figure 4.3 contains the breakdown of the four processes types in the novels.

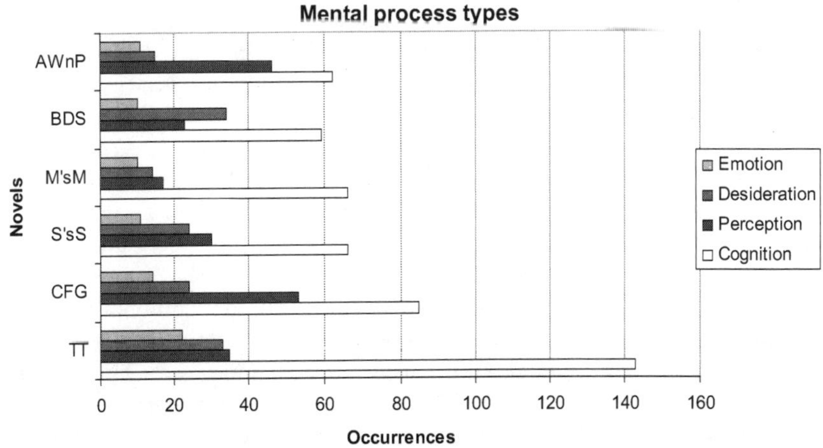

Fig 4.3 Mental process types

Figure 4.3 shows that, although in varying proportion, cognition processes are the preferred way to project linguistically the workings of characters' consciousness in all three versions of popular romantic fiction. Perception processes are the second highest scorers in Chick Lit, followed by desideration and emotion processes. Standalone romances follow a similar pattern to Chick Lit, whereas one of the novels of the series-embedded group (BDS) once more disturbs this regularity and shows desideration processes as the second most frequent mental type after cognition verbs. Because of the aim of this chapter, I do not pursue further the role of desideration, perception and emotion processes. Instead, I concentrate on the large number of occurrences of cognition verbs in all three popular fiction forms, as they can clearly tell us something about the way women's thinking activities are portrayed; thus, the results in Figure 4.3 should be considered in combination with those discussed above in Figure 4.1 where the ratio of mental versus verbal processes is graphically displayed. With regard to the distribution of mental and verbal processes, Chick Lit stands out from the two romance categories because mental verbs are more frequently used here than in the two romance types. This result, on its own, indicates that the thinking activities of the women in Chick Lit are underscored so that the reader is given the illusion of some kind of privileged and more frequent access to the Chick Lit woman's consciousness. Moreover, this emphasis on the mental activities of the women in Chick Lit is somehow augmented by the also higher ratio of those verbs that prototypically encode thinking activities, that is, cognition verbs. When these two circumstances are coupled together, Chick Lit novels seem more characteristically defined and segregated from the two romance categories; so, if the linguistic presentation of the characters' world of consciousness is the one parameter that could help separate Chick Lit from the two versions of romances, a thought presentation model can provide the kind of definitive linguistic proof that I am after here. The four thought presentation categories that feature in my extracts correspond closely to those previously described with regard to speech presentation: direct thought (DT), indirect thought (IT), free direct thought (FDT) and free indirect thought (FIT). The structural and formal features of thought presentation very much equal those of speech presentation, but the functional characteristics of the presentation of thought are based on narrators' hypothetical surmise concerning the actual propositional content of their characters' thoughts. To account for how this ontological impossibility takes linguistic shape in my samples I have tallied the various instances of the four thought categories mentioned above, as summarized in Figure 4.4.

Figure 4.4 seems to suggest that thought presentation techniques might be the linguistic dimension that, so far, more clearly justifies not simply a characterization of Chick Lit, but also a tripartite classification of popular romantic fiction into Chick Lit, series-embedded and standalone romances. On the one hand, the series-embedded romances (AWnP ad BDS) employ the prototypical free indirect thought technique for the linguistic encoding of the characters'

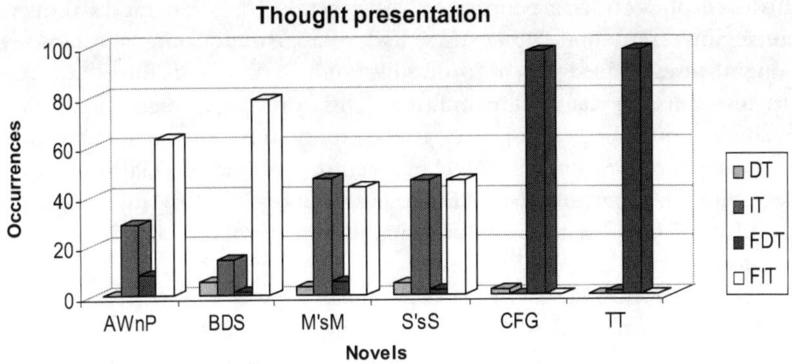

Fig 4.4 Thought presentation

world of consciousness. This outcome is in tune with Semino and Short's results, as they claim that:

> FIT is perhaps best regarded as the most frequent of the 'canonical' thought presentation categories. [...] [T]he vast majority of instances of FIT [...] are contained in the fiction section of the corpus. [...] This confirms the importance of FIT as a form of thought presentation in twentieth-century fiction. [...] The popular and serious sub-sections of the fiction section are almost exactly equal as far as FIT is concerned. [...] Our figures do not, however, suggest that the preponderance of FIT can be used to differentiate serious from popular fiction, even though this form of thought presentation has normally been discussed in relation to the writing of prestigious authors.
>
> (Semino and Short, 2004: 123)

The fact that Semino and Short consider the category-discerning potentiality of FIT with regard to serious and popular fiction is useful for my own endeavours here. However, they also confirm that this technique is not an exclusive prerogative of serious, prestigious and canonical literary fiction as it is the functional effect of FIT that authors of popular or serious literature find useful for thought presentation. For instance, consider how series-embedded romances exploit FIT:

> What was real here, and what was fake? Because you couldn't fake a kiss like that, could you? [...] Oh, what a mess.[12] [...] She really had no clue what men wanted, if Jonny could walk away from a kiss like that with nothing more than a reminder to her about what to call him [...] Were they all putting on a show, too? Or did they have something that Jane lacked, something that let them connect with others, stop being self-conscious, stop second-guessing and just *be*?
>
> (AWnP: 113)

This excerpt portrays a typical FIT construction; question marks return in interrogative sentences (after they had disappeared from typical indirect thought cases), third-person pronouns and back-shifted forms are kept, and introductory clauses are omitted. This form of thought presentation is characteristically capable of transmitting the propositional content of messages expressing the feelings, emotions and special nuances of the character's persona (the ontological impossibility of this happening notwithstanding), as well as filtering these through the lens of the narrator.

A second conclusion that can be drawn from the use of thought presentation techniques summarized in Figure 4.4 is the fact that standalone romances employ the IT and the FIT techniques in a more or less equal ratio so they do not dispense with the mediation of the narrator as freely as the series-embedded romances do. As an example of how IT is used in standalone romances, consider the following:

> Cool as an Atlantic breeze, he **decided**. A little frazzled and unnerved at the moment, he **thought**, but not willing to show it. [...] Nathaniel usually preferred women who were dark and sultry, but there was something to be said for all that rose and gold. She had blue eyes, the color of a calm sea at dawn. Stubborn mouth, he **mused**, though it softened nicely when she smiled at her son. A bit on the skinny side, he **thought** as he finished off his coffee.
>
> (M'sM: 270)

The emboldened verbs are used to allegedly introduce the verbalization of characters' thoughts in typical IT form. Obviously the ontological impossibility of reporting thoughts needs to be borne in mind too. FIT also features prominently especially because, as mentioned above, free indirect thought is particularly useful to merge, sometimes rather intricately, the reporting effort of the narrator with the alleged linguistic manifestation of the character's consciousness; the ontological impossibility of thought reporting also particularly highlights the fictionality of the reporting in free indirect thought instances. Because IT and FIT are combined roughly in the same ratio, sometimes it is not clear where the boundaries for each category lie. I use mainly formal criteria to distinguish among them but, functionally, they can be rather difficult to separate, especially in those cases where the introductory verb is missing:

> Odd she should remember the color of his eyes, she **mused**. But then again, the one time she had seen them up close and personal he'd all but burned her alive with them. He had probably forgotten the altercation, she **assured** herself. She hoped so. Altercations made her shaky and sweaty, and she'd had enough of them in her marriage to last a lifetime. Certainly Holt wouldn't still hold a grudge – it had been more than ten years. After all, he

> hadn't been hurt very much when he'd taken a header off his motorcycle. And it had been his fault, she **thought**, setting her chin.
>
> (S'sS: 18)

In sum, FIT seems to be prototypically employed by omniscient narrators who are aware of the thinking activities of their characters but report on them from their own vantage point. So far, therefore, it seems that the various ways in which thought presentation techniques are employed and combined might be the most likely tool to distinguish between Chick Lit and romances, on the one hand, and series-embedded and standalone romances, on the other.

Chick Lit appears to be at the other end of the thought presentation scale, as the considerable number of free direct thought instances suggests. According to Semino and Short:

> (F)DT is the least frequent category of thought presentation in our corpus. [...] Presenting thoughts in language involves 'translating' into words a phenomenon that might have consisted of non-verbal cognitive activities. This issue is particularly relevant to (F)DT, since, as Cohn puts it, the analogy with (F)DS 'creates the illusion that [it] render[s] what a character "really thinks" to himself' (Cohn, 1978: 76). [...] Not surprisingly, therefore, (F)DT often occurs at moments of heightened emotion or of sudden and momentous realization.
>
> (Semino and Short, 2004: 118)

The presence of FDT in Chick Lit seems to have, therefore, two significant consequences. As Cohn (1978: 76) explains, by using FDT the reader is allegedly allowed direct access into the character's way of thinking as if she could eavesdrop upon the content of the character's mind and learn about her stream of thoughts. As I develop below, Chick Lit presents an interesting case in relation to the use of FDT because of the high proportion of first-person narrators, and more specifically, because of the considerable number of novels which employ the confessional style of a diary format. For many Chick Lit females, diaries become the forums in which they can pour their hearts out, in which they can express their concerns and preoccupations; besides, because of the 'private' nature of the platform they choose to do so, these thoughts are, allegedly, meant to be faithfully rendered. Second, Semino and Short also highlight that the apparent intimacy that direct access to the characters' thoughts begets works particularly well in cases of heightened emotion. This statement also seems to ring true in Chick Lit, as these females take advantage of the freedom with which they can express themselves in diaries to put their most intimate, personal and emotionally significant secrets to paper. FDT, nevertheless, also features in other novels that eschew the diary format but still keep the first-person narrator, as in the following:

> 'No. No, she sure couldn't. I better get out there, you know Cole.' My stomach lurches.
>
> The rest of the day is a blur of downward spiralling and knocking my head against any hard surface. [...] This is classic Maggie – falling so hard and falling so fast and never asking any serious questions. It's me on the monkey bars again. I jump from an offhand glance in my direction to marriage and babies. [...] I should be spending my time finding someone more suitable for me. [...] Texas Steven.
>
> (CFG: 130)

In this quotation, the co-text helps identify the use of FDT. When the FDS instance in the first line ends, the conversation between Maggie, the protagonist of *Conversations with the Fat Girl* and Cristina, another waitress at the coffee shop where they both work, gives way to Maggie's sad realization that the guy she has been holding a torch for, Domenic, is not really interested in her. Emotionally, this is a marked moment for Maggie, so it seems appropriate that her thoughts are portrayed in the most direct way possible to let the reader in on her feelings of dispiritedness and sense of rejection. Linguistically, the lack of an introductory verb identifies this as free direct thought, but so do the lack of quotation marks and the first-person pronouns and present-tense perspective of the passage, despite the fact that Maggie is clearly recollecting some events from her childhood which seem also to bear the same signs of insecurity and unhappiness she is currently feeling. The noun phrase 'Texas Steven', which in the original is separated from the previous paragraph as a standing alone phrase or verbless clause, heightens the sense of apparent direct access to Maggie's thoughts conveyed by FDT because it suggests that the name of 'Texas Steven' has immediately followed her deep sense of unhappiness and has popped out in Maggie's mind as a possible male replacement for Domenic. Palmer's *Conversations with the Fat Girl* is typically representative of Chick Lit in the way appearance and weight matters are combined with emotional issues: the reason why Maggie is, in fact, rejected by the man she is in love with is because she is overweight. More importantly, it seems that Maggie, as also do many other Chick Lit women, chooses to disclose intimate and personal topics or instances of heightened emotion as thoughts, rather than as conversations with other characters in which any kind of speech presentation technique might be used.

As mentioned above, the presentation of women's intimate thoughts is intricately linked to the diary format that plenty of Chick Lit authors adopt. The original formula, famously established by Fielding's *Bridget Jones's Diary* (1996), seems fool-proof for the prototypical Chick Lit novel (notwithstanding the many off-shoots discussed in this book; see Chapter 1 for more on this), so much so that, failing the diary format, a homodiegetic narrator taking advantage of a variety of discourses such as emails or letters seems to be preferable to a third-person teller. This variety of discourses suggests that this formula is functionally rather than formally useful for Chick Lit authors, as it enables characters to provide their readership with a personal account of their own affairs irrespective of the kind of discourse employed to do so, that is, diary writing, emails or a first-person narrator. Therefore, although not all prototypical Chick Lit novels formally adopt a diary format, most aspire to the functional effect that this confessional style affords. As Ferriss and Young state:

> Fielding's novel suggested spontaneity and candor with its use of the diary form. Others exploit the confessional style of letters and e-mails, or simply employ first-person narration to craft the impression that the protagonist is speaking directly to readers. These narrative techniques not only appeal to readers but also link chick lit significantly with a large body of women's fiction from earlier generations.
>
> (Ferriss and Young, 2006: 4)

Ferriss and Young's observation concerning the alleged prevalence of the first-person perspective is echoed in a small survey of 40 prototypical Chick Lit novels (see Appendix 3 for the full list) that reveals that 75 per cent of those works use a female homodiegetic narrator. These homodiegetic narrators, thus, engage in diary writing, communicate via emails, send copious amounts of letters or simply relate their story via a first-person teller. As a result these character-narrators manage to create the illusion of a sense of closeness with their readership because they appear to be conveying their messages directly to them, something that, perhaps, is less easily achieved by reporting the 'saying' and 'thinking' processes of female protagonists via the intermediary telling voice of a third-person narrator. The considerably high score of FDT in the Chick Lit samples I analyse (Figure 4.4), which most clearly puts Chick Lit in a category of its own when compared to series-embedded and standalone romances, therefore, must also be analysed in light of the frequency with which first-person narrators become the enactors of those thinking processes. As Rochelle Mabry discusses:

> Like their forebears, chick lit [...] usually focus[es] on a female main character and use[s] a variety of strategies to make her desires and motivations the focus of the story. Bridget Jones and many of the chick novels [...] are written in first person, in the heroine's voice, conveying the notion that these novels, although fictional, are authentic, in-depth accounts of women's experiences. This move toward first-person narration is an especially significant change from the third-person narration employed in most traditional romance novels.
>
> (Rochelle Mabry, 2006: 195–6)

Rochelle Mabry argues that the use of first-person narrators projects a sense of (false) authenticity with regard to the messages and values that Chick Lit women communicate. This assessment indirectly echoes the ontological impossibility discussed above with regard to the presentation of the actual thoughts of the characters. However, because the presentation of these thinking processes is, allegedly, so convincingly portrayed from the perspective of the sensers in mental processes and subjects of the FDT instances, the readership appears to be invited to circumvent this impossibility and to consider the character's rendition of her thoughts as indeed authentic. Rochelle Mabry, furthermore, highlights that the plausibility of bypassing that impossibility is linguistically marked by shifting to first-person narration from the prototypical third-person perspective of traditional romances. The linguistic preference for third-person narration in the latter has been pointed out by some other scholars. Modleski, in her now classic monograph on romance, *Loving with a Vengeance. Mass-Produced Fantasies for Women* (1984; 2008), states that the third-person point of view in romances is, actually, a compulsory narrative feature: 'The publishers offer the following guidelines to prospective authors: Harlequins are well-plotted, strong romances with a happy ending. They are told from the heroine's point of view and in the third person' (Modleski, 2008: 28). Modleski's statement, nevertheless, needs to be contextualized, as this assessment corresponds to the first edition of her book published in the 1980s. Currently, though, the Harlequin website provides guidelines for authors wishing to write romances but they eschew any reference to the obligatoriness of a third-person narrator. More interestingly is Modleski's explanation concerning the functional role of the third-person narrator:

> It is easy to assume, and most popular culture critics have assumed, a large degree of identification between reader and protagonist, but the matter is not so simple. Since the reader knows the formula, she is superior in wisdom to the heroine and thus detached from her. The reader, then, achieves a very close emotional identification with the heroine partly because she is intellectually distanced from her and does not have to suffer the heroine's confusion.
>
> (Modleski, 2008: 33)

According to Modleski, therefore, the romance reader reacts to the third-person perspective in the romance novels in a twofold way because, despite her superiority towards the women in the books, this reader nevertheless still engages emotionally with her fictional counterparts.[13] The issue of reader identification and empathy in Chick Lit is amply discussed in Chapter 5. As far as whether the shift to first-person perspective from the most prototypical (although, in modern romances, by no means exclusive) third-person viewpoint, Rochelle Mabry concludes:

> The move toward first-person voice in most contemporary chick novels not only strengthens the heroine's voice and increases the reader's opportunities to identify with her but also offers at least a temporary escape from the feeling of constantly being watched or controlled by a male-dominated society. Of course, this doesn't mean that a female author or main character,

> or even the use of first-person narrative voice, guarantees that a particular [...] novel is a 'real' representation of female experience. More significant here is how hard these texts work to present themselves as authentic stories of women's lives and feelings.
>
> (Rochelle Mabry, 2006: 196)

I concur with Rochelle Mabry's honest recognition regarding the functional role of first-person narrators, as the use of this linguistic form does not unequivocally also sanction over-emphasizing the authenticity of the female experiences presented by this first-person teller. However, what the higher scores of FDT instances combined with the preference for homodiegetic narrators can confirm is the fact that the female voice in Chick Lit is allowed to express herself in ways that more traditional forms of popular fiction do not seem to contemplate. Unlike the prototypical omniscient narrator in standalone and series-embedded romances that use FIT or a combination of FIT and IT, Chick Lit characters are eager to air whatever concerns they may have (weight, appearance and emotional issues) and also let the readers in on their most intimate and personal thoughts by using FDT in which the mediating report of a narrator is minimized. This combination of linguistic parameters (FDT and first person narrators), therefore, backs up a characterization of Chick Lit as an independent and fully-fledged variety of popular fiction, connected but still separate from its sister genres.

Furthermore, the 'candor' in the presentation of Chick Lit females' desires and motivations, as discussed by Ferriss and Young (2006: 4), combined with the authenticity claims that, according to Rochelle Mabry (2006: 196), Chick Lit is characterized by, echoes a crucial issue that typifies Chick Lit in a way that does not seem so forcibly proven in romances; I am referring to the 'that's me' phenomenon discussed in Chapter 3:

> She [Bridget Jones] became an icon, a recognisable emblem of a particular kind of femininity, a constructed point of identification for women. Newspapers set out to find the 'real' Bridget Jones or sent 'genuine Bridget Joneses' to review the films. Bridget generated instant recognition among many young heterosexual women; as Imelda Whelehan (2002) has argued, part of the success of the book lay in the 'that's me' phenomenon whereby Bridget became regarded not as a fictional character but as a representative of the zeitgeist.
>
> (Gill and Herdieckerhoff, 2006: 489)

As discussed in the previous chapter, Gill and Herdieckerhoff (see also Smith, 2008; Bernard, 1999) maintain that the self-identification with which real-life women contemporaneous to the fictional Chick Lit women embraced the genre marked a kind of scission with other forms of modern romance. Also raised in Chapter 3 is the fact that the fictional Chick Lit women, unlike some prototypical heroines in romances, are more realistically portrayed because it is their own voices that candidly and unashamedly depict themselves in a kind of 'warts-and-all' attitude which emphasizes, for instance, their romantic aspirations to find the perfect match as much as their insecurities with regard to their bodies or their jobs, and do so by also underscoring the funny side of it all. In fact, for some, this attempt at some alleged authenticity concerning the rendition in fictional form of twentieth- and twenty-first-century women is the real secret of the genre's success.

All of the above, finally, can also be discussed in relation to the Chick Lit–feminism relationship also addressed in this chapter. Above, I attempt to provide a summary of how this relationship has been theoretically approached and argue that: (i) the notion of femaleness has been multifariously dealt with; (ii) the constant references to feminism in the novels seem to indicate that these women have not abandoned entirely all of the conventional feminist preoccupations; (iii) their newly formulated concerns are, nevertheless, symptomatic of twentieth- and twenty-first-century realities, not of the prototypical feminist involvement of the 1960s or 1970s. All of this suggests that their claims to feminism should be understood as anchored firmly on the authors' contemporary worldview of the reality that has begotten the genre and not as independent from it. Finally, the linguistic make-up of the novels underscores and facilitates that those concerns are presented to the readership in the heroine's own voice, not via the filtering lens of a third-person teller.

4.4 Conclusion

To conclude, I have attempted to show that a language-based analysis of the three variants of popular fiction discussed in this chapter can put Chick Lit in its appropriate literary context. The combination of a transitivity analysis and a speech and thought presentation framework has enabled me to highlight the relationship of these sub-genres to each other as well as point out how their structural, linguistic and functional characteristics might overlap but they do not completely coalesce. The main linguistic differences and commonalities between the three varieties can be summarized as follows:

- Chick Lit uses more mental processes than verbal processes; the latter are, instead, far more common in series-embedded and standalone romances.
- All three manifestations of popular romances present speech as FDS or DS and avoid the indirect and free indirect versions.
- In all three forms, mental processes are mainly realized by cognition verbs; perception, desideration and emotion verbs do not score so highly in any of the categories.
- The above result warrants a closer analysis of thought presentation techniques. These finally disclose that, not only does Chick Lit stand in a category of its own by eschewing most forms of thought presentation in favour of FDT, but also that standalone romances and series-embedded

romances appear to belong in categories of their own too, because of the way thought presentation techniques are employed: the former characteristically use a combination of IT and FIT in roughly the same ratio, whereas the latter overwhelmingly veer towards FIT.
- Finally, the defining use of FDT in Chick Lit is viewed in relation to the confessional style of personal writing and general first-person narration.

A description of the linguistic make-up of the genre, therefore, underscores that in Chick Lit the female protagonists do not shy away from airing their most intimate thoughts and concerns, captured in occurrences of FDT in which no voice but their own describes what those thoughts, motivations and desires are about. Although to a lesser extent because they do not solely characterize Chick Lit but also occur in series-embedded and standalone romances, instances of FDS similarly project a desire to free female protagonists from the mediating voice of a narrator. In sum, it seems that linguistic tools can help complement previous appraisals on Chick Lit and cognate popular forms in a way that most clearly contextualize the peculiarities, commonalities and points of discordance between the three manifestations of romantic fiction. The more marked freedom from any intermediary reporting allowed in Chick Lit, coupled with the apparent authenticity in these women's expression of inner concerns, underscores that these female characters are not ready to give up their, admittedly unorthodox, claims to feminism, albeit understood in the context of twenty-first-century circumstances.

Chapter 5

The Chick Lit Reader

5.1 Chick Lit and its Readers

In the previous chapters I have provided an account of some of Chick Lit's features, linguistic and otherwise, that, as a whole, embody the essence of the prototypical novel in the genre. Thus, I initially set out by considering in Chapter 2 the multimodal characteristics of Chick Lit book covers because effectively they are the first point of contact that Chick Lit consumers have with the works; I conclude that some of the general characteristics associated with the genre already materialize multimodally on the book jacket. In Chapter 3, I analyse key issues concerning characterization in Chick Lit, and then, in Chapter 4, I follow on with an analysis of transitivity and speech and thought presentation models to investigate how ideological meaning, among other concerns, is encoded in the novels. The present chapter rounds off the discussion of Chick Lit by focusing on the *reader*, who is, after all, the essential component of the reading act. It is important to highlight here that my concern is with the real Chick Lit reader, so I do not delve into the textual manifestation of implied or ideal readers (see Rimmon-Kenan, 2002, for a general view on the role of the reader). Instead, I look into the responses of Chick Lit readers because they are, in effect, the ultimate judges; that is, they cast the verdict on the success or possible downfall of any work or, as is the case here, any genre. As sales figures seem to indicate that the genre continues to be a hit with readers, it would be safe to assume that their engagement with Chick Lit is not, at least not at the moment of writing this chapter, waning. The responses of the Chick Lit readership are specifically investigated in relation to two main issues: the readers' emotive and evaluative response to the genre, for the reasons explained below. This interest in assessing how affective and evaluative concerns manifest translates into a twofold methodological perspective: on the one hand, I look at a series of theories of emotion and consider how they can help explicate readers' affective reaction to Chick Lit. One of the thematic traits of the prototypical Chick Lit novel that has been recurrently highlighted is the felicitous romantic resolution whereby the protagonist lives happily ever after with the modern equivalent of a 'prince charming'. My objective is to consider how readers, first, react, second, enjoy, and finally expect that the happy ending of their novels is forever present in the prototypical Chick Lit novel.[1] Pursuing this aim, I have gathered data that come from two main sources: on the one hand, I have conducted a small sample questionnaire in which readers are asked to reflect on their own Chick Lit reading experience. On the other, I look at the content of some blogs and online book-club forums specifically devoted to the discussion of Chick Lit novels. For the most part (that is, with the exception of the questionnaire), my choice of data illustrates my interest to consider unprompted contributions by readers; the open nature and availability of the blogs and online book-club forums I analyse has clear methodological advantages, as it frees these bloggers' contributions from some of the restrictions sometimes associated with experimental work on reader response, as I explain below. The qualitative slant of this first section is complemented by the quantitative approach adopted in the second part of the chapter, where I specifically focus on the linguistic input of a larger sample taken from Chick Lit blogs and from a selection of online book-club forums which has been run through the corpus-analysis tool Wmatrix (Rayson, 2009), as was employed in Chapter 3. The double perspective adopted here throws some interesting results and allows me to draw some solid conclusions regarding the readerly aspects of the genre. Mainly, this double take highlights that the linguistic expression of Chick Lit readers' reaction to the novels encompasses some crucial and fairly constant aspects that can be concretized by looking at the *language of emotion*, on the one hand, and the *language of evaluation*, on the other. The linguistic realization of these two components, consequently, acts as the backbone of the chapter. I discuss the way readers verbalize their feelings (language of emotion) in response to the genre, but also I consider how the readership, in the context provided by their contributions to blogs and online book-club forums, become avid critics of the novels. Such emotional and evaluative verbalizations are so fundamental that I have elsewhere (Montoro, 2003, 2007) coined a complementary label to refer to Chick Lit: *Cappuccino Fiction* (see Chapter 1 for an explanation concerning this label). Both the qualitative and the quantitative approaches seem to underscore that one of the main appeals of the genre is the 'feel-good' factor and general upbeat mood gained from reading these novels. As explained below, readers' expectations concerning the way the novels should be resolved become particularly strong; their constant references in my data to the way in which these novels should unfold suggest that they vehemently expect the genre to be manufactured in the 'happy-ending-novel' factory. That is, the novels' resolution should leave in the reader a 'sweet taste', as if they had just enjoyed a nice cup of their favourite cappuccino. *Cappuccino Fiction* also seems to encompass a view of the novels as being illustrative of certain middle-class aspirations and lifestyle (see Chapter 3 for more on characterization and its relation to genre and class); additionally, this label equally evokes an image of 'frothiness', of which Chick Lit has been occasionally accused. Despite the advantages of my own coined term, the intrinsic references to femaleness embodied in the original Chick Lit label seem somehow diluted in *Cappuccino Fiction*, so to avoid this I follow the now well-established and most widely-used label.

The two methodological approaches implemented in this chapter contribute to a confirmation that readers' expectations are characteristic of the Chick Lit readership. This twofold analysis is preceded by some theoretical considerations concerning how theories of emotion, on the one hand, and linguistic approaches to the verbal realization of emotion and evaluation, on the other, can shed light on who this typical Chick Lit consumer might be. Needless to say, and as has been the norm for the entire monograph, the choice of frameworks, theoretical principles and models is ultimately informed by the thirst for rigour associated with stylistic analyses of texts. As was also the case in Chapter 3, the tenets characterizing corpus stylistics will guide the quantitative analysis of my data. I, thus, move on to look at some theoretical considerations on both the language of emotion and evaluation first, to later take on the analysis of the novels proper.

5.2 What is Emotion?

Given the central role that expressions of emotion have in this chapter, it follows that we should set off by asking the basic question of what emotions are, a question which is here tentatively answered by Parkinson:

> The traditional and obvious way to begin a discussion of the present topic would be to attempt to answer the question 'What is emotion?'. Indeed, the modern psychological approach to emotional phenomena started with an article written over a hundred years ago which had as its title a very similar question (James, 1884). As yet no one has been able to come up with a completely satisfactory answer (one paper on this topic listed ninety-two distinct definitions organized in eleven separate categories; Kleinginna and Kleinginna, 1981).
>
> (Parkinson, 1995: 4–5)

Judging from this initial outline, coming up with a comprehensive and encompassing rendition of what constitutes an emotion is not child's play, especially if, as Kleinginna and Kleinginna (1981) suggest here, there are more than 90 possible variations of the term that can be subsequently arranged in 11 separate categories. Despite this initial, slightly overwhelming, assortment of possible approaches, Parkinson highlights that there are some 'central defining features' (Parkinson, 1995: 9) that might actually concretize the concept and that should, consequently, also help my task here in relation to Chick Lit reading:

> To summarize, although it is not easy to come up with a thoroughgoing definition which includes all the phenomena that laypeople might want to call emotion (and excludes all those that they would not), it is still true that certain characteristics are agreed to be fairly central defining features. The

> chances are that if someone is considered to be emotional, they will be seen as having a positive or a negative evaluative position with respect to some definite object (whether imagined or real), and this position will not be a constant or permanent one. In other words, emotions are conceptualized as evaluative, affective, intentional, and short-term states.
>
> (Parkinson, 1995: 9)

A couple of issues in this definition seem pertinent to my own endeavours. On the one hand, emotionality involves that a sentient being displays some kind of evaluation (positive or negative) in relation to some identified 'object (whether imagined or real)' (Parkinson, 1995: 9). The fact that emotions can emerge out of encounters with 'imaginary' objects confirms that investigating the role of emotion in literary contexts is an enterprise worth pursuing, notwithstanding the non-reality of that identified object. Second, Parkinson also conceives of emotions as 'evaluative' and 'affective', discerning the former from the latter state but acknowledging both as actual manifestations of emotional reactions. The results that my data throw confirm that the type of emotional engagement that Chick Lit readers display goes hand in hand with their desire to be evaluative of the novels; that is, readers express what and how they feel as well as 'critically' appraise the worth or otherwise of the novels they read. Thus, Chick Lit readers do not simply verbalize their happiness, sadness or indifference towards the novels but also engage fully in assessing why they feel that way. All of this gives rise to expectations in relation to what they hope to find in their Chick Lit books. Parkinson's assessment regarding what constitutes an emotion, though, is clearly informed by psychological concerns which, by no means and as described in the next section, exclusively cater for all the different ways in which to approach and analyse human emotion. Burke (2011), for instance, also echoes the intrinsic complexity of attempting to find a comprehensive definition of emotions. His assessment regarding what that role must be, moreover, is of more significance to this chapter as he specifically focuses on the literary reading process and on how emotional aspects shape and influence it. Pursuing that aim, Burke summarizes several central themes discussed by emotion theorists, such as, for instance, what can be classified as 'basic emotion' or how many different types of emotion can be identified (2011: 44–5). Burke quotes Oatley and Jenkins (1996), who attempt to discern the various emotion types as follows:

> Emotion: A state usually caused by an event of importance to the subject. It typically includes (a) a conscious mental state with recognisable quality of feeling and directed towards some object, (b) a bodily perturbation of some kind, (c) recognisable expressions of the face, and, (d) a readiness for certain kinds of action.
>
> Affect: A general term used to include emotions, moods and preferences.
>
> Mood: A maintained state of emotion or a disposition to respond emotionally

> in a particular way that may last for hours, days or even weeks, perhaps at a low level and perhaps without the person knowing what started the mood.
>
> (Oatley and Jenkins, 1996: 375–81)

This tripartite classification seems to suggest that the main difference between each type is one of intensity although arguably it fails to fully spell out whether there are further examples of discordance among them that justify the existence of this threefold taxonomy. For instance, the definition of 'affect' includes both the notions of 'emotion' and 'mood', whereas the latter also underscores intensity by prioritizing the fact that the affective response characterizing moods lasts longer than might be the case for the previous two. Further theoretical considerations discussed by Burke are those proposed by Damasio (1994), Frijda (1986), Hogan (2003) and Tan (1996) (among many more). Below, I recall the depth and breadth with which emotional issues are dealt from the multifarious perspectives of a variety of disciplines. I close off this section by highlighting one aspect which merits attention because of its practical applications with regard to Chick Lit; in fact, this aspect is more profitable to my own interests than simply attempting to come up with an all-encompassing definition of emotion which might, after all, become, if not a totally futile, certainly a slightly impractical task. Instead, following Burke (2011), I focus on one of the core components repetitively mentioned in those theories of emotion which specifically deal with the arts, in general, and literature, in particular: that is, I look at the incontrovertible factuality of the fictional work being capable of begetting emotional responses in the same way as non-fictive objects do. Burke lucidly summarizes this as follows:

> If film viewers have goals, which they clearly do, literary readers must have them too and [...] these start long before the reader engages with the text. Hogan engages in an insightful dialogue with Tan's work (2003: 149–50) and poses a probing question [...]: 'why do we formulate this "preferred final outcome" then care so much about it when the events are fictional and we have no egocentric involvement in them' (2003: 223). My provisional answer to this would be that even though the events are fictive, our commitment as readers to become emoted by the chosen literary work of art most definitely makes literary reading an egocentric process from the level of the reader's macro-goals.
>
> (Burke, 2011: 46)

The references to narrative films' capability to conjure up emotional responses come from Tan (1996); by focusing on the film narrative, Tan concludes that emotive expectations are inextricably linked to the film-watching experience, as cinema audiences, by the mere fact of deciding to engage in film-watching, have emotional goals they expect to be fulfilled (Tan, 1996: 98). Following on from this, Burke concludes that the literary experience must also give rise to a series of expectations on the part of the readership, and he (2011: 46) adds that these expectations necessarily come about prior to the actual engagement with the literary work. Burke concludes that, in spite of their fictional nature, literary accounts are fully capable of evoking emotional responses from the readership (see also Hakemulder, 2000; Oatley, 1994, 2003, 2011; van Peer, 1994, 1997) and is, thus, in agreement with Parkinson's initial definition, above. Therefore, the first conclusion agreed upon by most emotion theorists regarding the role of emotion in relation to fictional accounts is that the non-reality of the identified object does not preclude the emotional mechanisms in the human experiencer from being triggered.

Accepting the fact that emotional responses are part of the literary reading experience, however, still poses one further problem in relation to the genre that occupies me here. Most of the theoretical and empirical considerations emanating from the social sciences (psychology, cognitive psychology) concerning what role emotions play for the literature reader, and which have primarily fed subsequent critical appraisals from literary critics or stylisticians, tend openly to restrict their discussion of the literary experience to aspects of Literature with a capital 'L'. In fact, some of the conclusions drawn by some of these researchers (e.g. Hakemulder, 2000: 150) clearly distinguish between the emotional responses that highbrow fiction is capable of generating in contrast to the somewhat diminished experience afforded by genres labelled as popular fiction. Although my main aim in this chapter is not to contest the conclusions so far drawn by these scholars (more on this below), I still maintain that the existence of a 'diminished' experience in the sense discussed by some scholars does not equal a total 'absence' of any emotional response or engagement with the popular novel. For instance, authors such as Dixon (1999), Modleski (1984, 2008), Radway (1991) and Warhol (2003) focus on the engagement of female readers and audiences with forms of popular fiction, mostly, although not exclusively, the popular romance (for instance, Warhol (2003) also looks at the reactions of female audiences to soap operas). Their investigations are not, admittedly, directly concerned with the psychological, cognitive or linguistic tenets put forward by studies carried out in psychology, cognitive psychology or other cognate disciplines; however, their research distinctly confirms that the involvement of consumers of popular fictional forms is highly determined by an affective side. Because I have not directly dealt with other forms of popular fiction apart from Chick Lit, I will refrain from making any further claims in this respect. In relation to Chick Lit, however, and as I further elaborate in Section 5.5.2, the way Chick Lit readers react to the novels suggests that they partake in what I call the 'socio-emotional' function of Chick Lit which, in turn, might be otherwise absent in the reading experience of literary fiction. In sum, I examine to what extent reading popular fiction and, crucially, sharing its enjoyment in the way my informants do in the context of web-based book-clubs or in their own blogs, quenches a particular thirst for emotionally-satisfying novels in a way that might not prototypically characterize the reading of other fictional formats.

A second aspect that needs highlighting at this point concerns terminological issues. The attempt at a definition of the notion of emotion discussed above, together with the various approaches to emotional research introduced below, underscore that terminological variation is not only possible but is a somewhat uncomfortable reality that researchers have to face. In this chapter, the complex fluctuation in the use of terminology is heightened by the fact that my analysis is informed by the expertise of scholars coming from a variety of disciplines. In order to clarify my own use of terminology pertaining to the emotional aspects of the Chick Lit reading experience, I employ terms such as *emotion, affect* and *sentiment* interchangeably; contemplating fully the various nuances emanating from the variety of disciplines that utilize these terms differently might, in fact, hinder the core concern of this chapter which is, after all, a consideration of who the prototypical Chick Lit reader is and how she affectively relates to the reading of the novels, not the formulation of new perspectives on theories of emotion.

5.3 Approaches to Emotion

The previous section has highlighted some initial concerns regarding the complexities associated with attempting to formulate a definition of the concept of emotion. This section expands on such a tentative attempt by summarizing a few of the wealth of approaches and correspondent research that emotion issues have given rise to. To try to do justice to the myriad of publications on emotion is not only a mammoth task but also an endeavour that falls well outside the remit of this chapter. Instead, I present an overview of some of the theoretical perspectives that try to account for how emotional manifestations can be analysed, for whether emotions have a cognitive or a psychological origin, and for the social effects of emotion; in sum, for the relationship between emotional matters and the reading of literature. These theoretical positions can be initially distinguished by their linguistic or non-linguistic focus. Ultimately, because of the stylistic slant of this monograph, I am more concerned with the former than the latter. However, that does not imply that the vast array of research monographs, articles and journals that have dealt with emotional aspects in general, and more specifically in relation to the literary reading experience, can or should be overlooked. Because this is an overview and because presenting a totally encompassing account is not achievable, I focus on those scholarly accounts (linguistic and non-linguistic) that have contemplated the relationship between emotion and literature, with or without the capital 'L'.

For a long time, one contentious issue in emotion research has been that of ascertaining the origin of emotions. Recently, scholars seem to have come to an agreement regarding not only the cognitive origin of emotions but also their core role for human cognition. As Hogan states:

> For many years, affective psychology – the psychology of emotion – was widely seen as an entirely separate field from cognitive psychology. Feeling

> was viewed as something noncognitive. However, in the past decade or so, emotion has become an increasingly important topic in cognitive science. Far from being the opposite of thought, emotion is now viewed as intimately bound up with thought, to such an extent that one cannot fully understand cognition without understanding emotion, and one cannot fully understand emotion without understanding cognition.
>
> (Hogan, 2003: 140)

This same tenet is also held by Burke (2011), who has appropriately entitled his book *Literary Reading, Cognition and Emotion* and who tellingly combines affective-cognitive aspects (among others), mainly in his theoretical notion of 'disportation'.[2] Notwithstanding the relevance of Hogan's alignment of emotional and cognitive concerns, Oatley's (1992) argument about the cardinal significance of emotions also merits mentioning: 'emotions are not on the periphery but at the centre of human cognition' (1992: 3). Thus, although the centrality and cognitive dimension of emotions was not always accepted, it seems now a tenet endorsed by most scholars, as amply discussed in Oatley's innumerable publications; see, for instance, Oatley (1994; 2003; 2011), Oatley and Johnson-Laird (1987), Oatley and Jenkins (1996), and Djikic, Oatley *et al.* (2009).

A second, albeit closely connected line of research on emotional aspects and literary reading, is illustrated by the research of van Peer. In a similar light to Hogan, but focusing specifically on literary reading, van Peer underscores the cognitive basis of emotional reactions:

> Emotions, then, are intimately related to cognition. Thus, in assessing the emotional potential of literature, we shall have to take this relation into account. Reading literature is not an activity in which emotions have the upper hand. [...] Reading literature is [...] one such form in which our emotional involvement has clear cognitive overtones.
>
> (van Peer, 1997: 218)

Van Peer's research is informed by, but does not directly emerge from, cognitive psychology; instead, stylistic, linguistic and narratological (among many other) concerns contribute to his work on readers' emotional involvement with the literary work. The fact that the investigations of a researcher whose work is more akin to my own interests here echo, and concur with, findings coming from the social sciences highlights that identifying literature as capable of emotion-projection can shed light on aspects of human affect and cognition. As van Peer states, 'I wish to analyse one particular function literary texts may fulfil. Literature, so my central assumption runs, provides readers the possibility to learn about and to experience human emotion' (van Peer, 1994: 210). Van Peer's line of investigation is also taken on by others; see, for instance, Dutta and Kanungo (1975), Gilligan and Bower (1984), Laird et al. (1982), Lindauer (2009) and Martins (1982), whose empirically-driven methodologies and subsequent conclusions confirm the cognitive basis of emotional engagement.

The empirically-driven strand of the work above, however, is not absent from van Peer's research; on the contrary, his own work (van Peer, 1992) and plenty of his collaborative research (van Peer *et al.*, 2007a) underscore not simply the advantages of, but also the urging need to, examine emotion issues from the solid perspective afforded by empiricism. These empirical takes primarily emanate from the varied and ample testing of reader responses in a variety of environments,[3] as exemplified by Hakemulder (2000):

> Fictional narratives [...] have the same effect as narratives in general [...] . The fact that readers know that the events did not really happen does not impede their impact. [...] Therefore, literature can be considered a Moral Laboratory, in which plausible implications of human conduct and ideas can be studied in a relatively controlled and safe way. Readers can [...] mentally place themselves in the position of the character, so that their reading becomes an intense experience of the emotions, thoughts, and desires people are likely to have in certain situations.
>
> (Hakemulder, 2000: 150)

Hakemulder's label 'Moral Laboratory' appears to encompass rather befittingly and illustratively the various implications concerning the affective dimension of literary reading discussed so far, as it conceives of literature as a scenario where humans effectively emote (whatever that emotion might be), despite the fictive nature of the object triggering such an emotion. Furthermore, Hakemulder's primarily empirical methods solidly support and act as foundations for his claims on how readers can transport themselves mentally to the world of the characters so that 'their reading becomes an intense experience of [their] emotions, thoughts, and desires' (Hakemulder, 2000: 150). Interestingly, Hakemulder's research explicitly draws a distinction between those literary texts which can be trusted as a type of 'culture medium' and which aptly belong in his 'moral laboratory' because they can conjure up affective-cognitive reactions akin to those in real life, and those popular fiction works which are somehow incapable of generating such a heightened experience:

> These experiences are assumed to be of quite another order than the experiences one has in reading popular fiction. If we learn about the inner-lives of others through reading literary fiction, this may be expected to lead to more profound psychological insights, because literary characters are usually more complex than the stereotypical beings encountered in more popular genres.
>
> (Hakemulder, 2000: 150)

I stated above that it is not my concern to contest this conclusion here, mainly because to do so I would have had to carry out comparative studies of texts prototypically representing literary, canonical or highbrow fiction with forms associated with popular writing, which this chapter fails to do. I do, however, take on Hakemulder's statement above and develop it further in Section 5.5.2. If, as Hakemulder argues here, the kind of experience readers gain from consuming literary fiction differs from that obtained from popular novels, it might be interesting to consider which function might these popular forms, instead, fulfil. Tentatively, and in the context of the Chick Lit reading experience, on the one hand, and the contributions by bloggers and online book-club forums users, on the other, I claim in Section 5.5.2 that this function is related to socio-emotional concerns which are reminiscent of what Parkinson calls the 'interpersonal function of emotion' (Parkinson, 1995: 277), but this is further elaborated later on. Suffice it to say here that, whereas I do not contest Hakemulder's claims regarding the heightened sense of emotional intensity that ensues the reading of literary fiction,[4] the results of my own investigation suggest that the emotional gain involved in reading popular writing should not be discarded either.

The empirical-psychological basis of some of the research presented so far has found a particularly linguistic anchor in the work on foregrounding (Hakemulder, 2007; van Peer, 1986, 2007; van Peer *et al.*, 2007b; Zyngier *et al.*, 2007). The theory of foregrounding is obviously not new, reaching as it does back to the Greeks:

> The study of foregrounding has been around for a while now. Its roots reach into Greek Antiquity, but it is in the last century that it received its full-fledged status as a theory, first in the years 1916–17 with the Russian Formalists, then a second time in the 1960s and 1970s, mainly through the reception of the Formalists' principles and their further development in the West.
>
> (van Peer, 2007: 99)

The way foregrounding is now understood in stylistics research, however, is based primarily on the way it was formulated in the 1980s by van Peer (1986), although it has, since, received much theoretical and practical attention and re-evaluation. As a theory, foregrounding can be summarized as follows:

> It is a theory about the form of literature, about language, the raw material out of which literature is made [...] . Second, the more innovative aspect, it also refers to readers' reactions to such form, linking it to the functions of literary texts more generally.
>
> (van Peer, 2007: 99)

Several aspects concerning the formulation of a theory of foregrounding seem pertinent to this section and to the entire chapter: on the one hand, van Peer's focus on the linguistic aspects of the literary form as basis for the trigger of readers' emotional reaction is in tune with the general stylistic perspective of this monograph. Second, the conclusions so far drawn by theorists working on this theory have progressively been backed up by empirical studies on the effect of linguistic foregrounding for the reader of literary texts. As van Peer confirms, his original hypothetical proposals of the 1980s have been firmly substantiated by his own subsequent work (van Peer, 1992; 1994) and the work of others (Miall and Kuiken, 1994). But, most saliently, van Peer highlights that readers' emotional engagement with the literary piece is not restricted to the reading of the literary canon, highbrow fiction or, in fact, to any specific genre:[5]

> Wollheim (1980, 315) has pointed to a connection between emotions like mourning and the literary genre of the autobiography, but one need not restrict this view to particular genres, or indeed to 'high' literature. Similar processes are at work in the encounter with more popular genres.
>
> (van Peer, 1997: 223)

It seems, therefore, that, van Peer's conclusions differ from those propounded by Hakemulder (2000) in so far as literature, with or without the capital 'L', is characteristically defined by its capability to engage readers emotionally although, likewise, it might be cautionary to conclude that perhaps it is the type of, or the intensity of, such emotionality that distinguishes high from popular forms. As mentioned already and elaborated below, my argument concerns exclusively the Chick Lit reading experience so I refrain from extending any conclusions to genres other than the one that occupies me here. Having said that, behind the verbal realizations of Chick Lit readers' contributions in my data seems to be a clear sense of emotional engagement with the genre, which it would also be also erroneous to ignore.

Another discipline that has concerned itself with explaining readers' emotional engagement and that is taken on in Section 5.5.2 is that of narratology, especially the feminist narratological perspective adopted by Warhol (2003):

> A sentimental novel, a 'women's weepy' film, a narrative structured by the marriage plot, a serialized fiction all follow established conventions for inspiring certain feelings at particular junctures of the story. Such popular narrative forms are what I call *technologies of affect*, providing structures of feeling in the daily lives of their devotees.
>
> (Warhol, 2003: 7; italics mine)

Although not directly informed by the empiricism that characterizes some psychological accounts of the emotional responses by readers, Warhol, nonetheless, seems to have tapped into some fundamental aspects concerning the reception side of popular forms. Because her research is not restricted to written forms but also contemplates formats such as films and soap operas, her take on popular fiction is rather encompassing. Whether in the written, filmic or televisual version, the narrative forms she analyses are what she calls 'technologies of affect'. This label appears to embody several aspects that also ring true in the case of Chick Lit. On the one hand, the term 'technology' suggests that there is some kind of structuring and pattern in the way narratives of the kind Warhol studies are conceived. Second, this structuring appears to target specifically the affect-inducing capability of the narrative form. That is, there are certain thematic or stylistic features that promote a particular emotional reaction from the audience or reader, such as 'a narrative structured by the marriage plot' (Warhol, 2003: 7), for instance, which is, consequently, recurrently evoked by writers, film directors and television producers, and eagerly anticipated by readers and film and television audiences. Furthermore, this basic capability for emotionality seems crucially to emanate from the lengthy engagement of readers and viewers with the narratives in question, whether these are romantic novels or long-standing television soap operas. If, as a result of their long involvement with these narratives, these audiences and readers become clear 'devotees' of the genre, it follows that their emotional engagement with whichever technology of affect is their favourite operates, likewise, long-term. Warhol's suggestions regarding the long-term affective involvement with these forms and the fact that these emotional reactions are not random but, Warhol argues, prompted by particular narrative structures are issues worth taking up again, as I do in the qualitative analysis of my data in Section 5.5.2. Besides, it is interesting to compare how the slightly diminished sense of emotionality identified by scholars such as Hakemulder (2000) might be somewhat contradicted or, at least, called into question, if considered in the context of the long-term emotional investment discussed by Warhol.

Apart from the study of emotion emerging out of the theory of foregrounding, the rather brief summary of emotion research presented so far mainly illustrates approaches that are not specifically linguistic in nature. This theoretical introduction is still missing an overview of those approaches to the analysis of affective elements in language grounded on linguistic tenets, especially in the context of this monograph that has, so often now, highlighted its particularly strong linguistic bias. To start with, addressing the way language and emotion are related is a rather convoluted matter, as Bednarek (2008) points out:

> The relation between language and emotion is itself quite complex: we can express feelings that we have, we can have feelings that we do not express, and we can express feelings that we do not have. [...] The feelings may be expressed consciously or subconsciously, intentionally or unintentionally, spontaneously (automatically) or strategically [...] and may relate to various aspects of the communicative context.
>
> (Bednarek, 2008: 6–7)

Beside the fact that scholars have not always seen eye to eye with regard to the actual connection between affect and its linguistic realization, the multifarious ways in which linguistic and affective matters have been theoretically linked have essentially depended on, and emerged out of, the various linguistic branches that have accepted the challenge of studying the linguistic expression of emotion. Bednarek (2008: 7–10) identifies 11 possible strands, some of which can be split into further subcategories. The 11 approaches set apart by Bednarek are: the *cognitive* approach, the *cross-linguistic* approach, the *linguistic-anthropological* approach, the *diachronic* approach, the *functional* approach, the *syntactic* approach, the *conversation analytic* approach, the *stylistic/literary* approach, the *psycholinguistic* approach, the *pragmatic/textlinguistic* approach (including the sub-category of *intensity/ involvement* approach) and the *systemic-functional* approach. Needless to say, the way these branches address the affective-linguistic connection is not exclusive, as there are quite obvious overlaps; besides, the differences are, on occasions, mainly terminological or simply variations of focus on what constitutes the core and fundamental object of study of each analysis. For instance, the stylistic/literary approach to the language of emotion can and, as a matter of fact does, feed on most of the other branches mentioned by Bednarek because stylistics, by definition, tends to be a hybrid and interdisciplinary application of a diverse set of frameworks and models. Thus, commonalities between a traditional stylistic analysis of the linguistic manifestation of emotion in a literary text and a cognitive-stylistics approach, on the one hand, or, even, a systemic-functional approach to the same piece, on the other, are more than likely to be found. Further to these, it should be added that corpus tools are currently also being felicitously employed for some of the investigations carried out by researchers in the various branches and sub-branches above (with remarkable success, it should be added), so further macro-branches that would function as umbrella disciplines, or some micro-strands emerging from some of the disciplines above, could be added to the previous list, including that of emotion talk across corpora as implemented by Bednarek (2008) herself, or the phraseological orientation on evaluative language favoured by Hunston (2011). The linguistically-focused slant of the analysis of my own data is primarily taken on in Section 5.5.3; because the corpus-stylistic perspective of that section is informed by quantitative concerns but, also, intrinsically determined by the pre-established classification of emotion and evaluation terms set by the software programme employed for quantification, such computerized, pre-set taxonomy of linguistic emotionality also needs to be borne in mind. As was the case above concerning the discussion of non-linguistic approaches to the study of emotion, terminological matters are also an issue of contention here. Further nomenclature and its different uses concerning the language of evaluation are also discussed in Section 5.4, but I remind the reader that my own stance on the matter as far as the notion of 'emotion' is concerned is to use terms such as *emotion, affect, mood* and *sentiment* in more or less interchangeable ways to prevent further confusion.

To conclude this section, I have here attempted to synthesize some theories of emotion that will later be summoned again, as they can shed light on Chick Lit readers' verbalization of their emotions in blogs and web-based book-club forums. As I have mentioned previously, this summary does not, by any means, claim to be exhaustive or fully comprehensive. Instead, I have simply selected those theoretical positions that can reveal some fundamental aspects of the emotional involvement of the readers in my data with the novels they read. I now move on to introduce some theoretical tenets concerning the language of evaluation as the second axis on which this chapter is based.

5.4 The Language of Evaluation

As has been the case with my previous account concerning the way emotion research, and more specifically, the emotional implications of the reading of literature, is pursued, issues related to the language of evaluation are also discussed in some distinctive and manifold ways, basically conditioned by, and subject to, the main tenets of the discipline that directly informs each take on the concept of evaluation. One important difference between the approaches to emotion research discussed in Section 5.3, and the theoretical principles behind a general definition of the concept of evaluation introduced here, is the fully-linguistic bias (obviously, with a variety of nuances) of the studies on evaluation I go on to oversee. Notwithstanding the primarily linguistic nature of the various takes on evaluation I discuss, an attempt at defining this concept still gives rise to a series of different terminological and structural interpretations as to how to conceptualize it, the first one of which is here illustrated by the work of van Peer (2008):

> The evaluation of literary texts is something that readers almost always, automatically, and spontaneously, engage in. They judge the development of a plot and generate feelings of pleasure or dislike at particular events, they feel that the text does not yield what they had expected, or they find the author's style rewarding or awkward. All of this evaluation usually takes place as an integral part of the reading process. [...] Evaluating a literary text is an instinctive practice in which we engage both routinely and with fervor.
>
> (van Peer, 2008: 1)

Van Peer's work has already been discussed, especially as far as aspects of the affective psychology of literature and the theory of foregrounding are concerned. The quotation above illustrates yet another endeavour van Peer embarks on to cater for the relationship between literary forms and their readers, this time in connection with the notion of evaluation. Because it is viewed as a constitutive and instinctive part of the reading process, it appears that evaluative moves are inexorably associated to reading. In relation to how this unavoidable act of assessment on the reader's part is to be understood, van Peer defines it initially as akin to 'judgement', 'appraisal',[6] or 'interpretation' of the literary work. A consequential result of such appraisal or interpretation, however, is the generation of 'feelings of pleasure or dislike at particular events' (van Peer, 2008: 1) which seems to indicate that evaluation might also encompass the sense of emotion, affect or sentiment discussed earlier. If this is the case, thus, attempting to combine a close analysis of the emotional reactions to the reading of Chick Lit novels with the open evaluation, judgement or appraisal that readers engage in, should be a task worth looking into, hence my interest in investigating jointly these two phenomena. The collection of articles in van Peer's book (2008), nevertheless, does not fully implement the double perspective I am concerned with; instead, most of the articles in that collection look into how the linguistic aspects of the literary text guide and determine the evaluative processes that readers consequentially engage in. This focus on the linguistic side results in the detriment of two other elements that van Peer (2008: 1) also identifies as integral to the evaluative activity: the readers themselves and the context. Other examples of how the linguistic aspects of the literary text generate readers' evaluative concerns are those of Barney (2008), Miall (2008), and Short and Semino (2008).

A second way in which scholars have shown an interest on the concept of evaluation is amply illustrated in what is known as Appraisal Theory. Firmly anchored within and influenced by Systemic Functional Linguistics, Appraisal Theory is fundamentally the progeny of Martin and White (2005). The tenets and principles of Systemic Functional Linguistics have already been called for and employed rather profitably in previous chapters of this monograph. For instance, the multimodal take of Chapter 2 is solidly grounded, among other aspects, on the three metafunctions which jointly support Systemic Functional Linguistics as a theoretical framework; Chapter 4, on the other hand, expanded on the linguistic realization of the ideational metafunction and investigated how the grammatical system of transitivity can shed light on some of the feminist claims associated with Chick Lit novels. Now, Systemic Functional Linguistics can also aid in characterizing the way evaluation is linguistically encoded, in particular as it relates to the interpersonal metafunction. Martin and White introduce evaluative meanings as follows:

> This book [Martin and White, *The Language of Evaluation: Appraisal in English* (2005)] is concerned with the interpersonal in language, with the subjective presence of writers/speakers in texts as they adopt stances towards both the material they present and those with whom they communicate. It is concerned with how writers/speakers approve and disapprove, enthuse and abhor, applaud and criticise, and with how they position their readers/listeners to do likewise. It is concerned with the construction by texts of communities of shared feelings and values, and with the linguistic mechanisms for the sharing of emotions, tastes and normative assessments.
>
> (Martin and White, 2005: 1)

According to this introductory theoretical positioning by the authors, evaluative meanings intrinsically permeate the interpersonal aspect of communication as speakers and writers, on the one hand, and listeners and readers, on the other, cannot avoid participating in both encoding and the mutual interchange of judgements, attitudes, emotions and evaluations.

Interpersonal meanings in Systemic Functional Linguistics are generally seen to be realized in the grammatical systems of mood and modality (see Chapter 2 for more on this), but Martin and White (2005) propose to include the language of evaluation as a further instance of the linguistic projection of the interpersonal metafunction. In fact, as Hunston (2011: 20) states, 'dealing with evaluative meaning is a relatively recent development in SFL'. The take on evaluation developed in Appraisal Theory suggests that appraisal (Martin and White's term of choice) belongs in discourse semantics, that is, it functions at levels higher than the sentence. Second, Martin and White (2005) view appraisal as subdivided into three distinctive, albeit interrelated, categories:

> Appraisal itself is regionalised as three interacting domains – 'attitude', 'engagement' and 'graduation'. Attitude is concerned with our feelings, including emotional reactions, judgements of behaviour and evaluation of things. Engagement deals with sourcing attitudes and the play of voices around opinions in discourse. Graduation attends to grading phenomena whereby feelings are amplified and categories blurred.
>
> (Martin and White, 2005: 34–5)

Each of these domains is, itself, further subdivided; for the purposes that occupy me here, however, I am merely focusing on the notion of 'attitude' as it is concerned with the expression of feelings and judgements, which echo the emotion and evaluation categories I am interested in learning about further. Martin and White define attitude as follows:

> Attitude is itself divided into three regions of feeling, 'affect', 'judgement' and 'appreciation'. Affect deals with resources for construing emotional reactions. [...] Judgement is concerned with resources for assessing behaviour according to various normative principles. [...] Appreciation looks at resources for construing the value of things, including natural phenomena and semiosis (as either product or process).
>
> (Martin and White, 2005: 35–6)

Martin and White's tripartite taxonomy is useful for my own endeavour because the three categories seem in agreement, although not in complete alignment, with the way the readers in my data express their own attitudinal meanings. As a way of illustration, Hunston (2011) exemplifies the three types of 'feeling' with the following made-up sentences:

> 'I loved the film' (Affect – expressing attitude by construing an emotional response).
>
> 'The film is carefully balanced' (Appreciation – expressing attitude by construing an aesthetic view of the film as an object).

> 'This director really knows what she is doing' (Judgement – expressing attitude by construing a view of the behaviour of the director as a social being).
>
> (Hunston, 2011: 20)

Notwithstanding Martin and White's discrete categorization of the three possible linguistic realizations of attitude, claiming exclusivity concerning where the boundaries of the three sub-categories actually lie might not be an easy, judicious or fruitful task. In fact, further to the examples above which are meant to illustrate not just the three possible ways in which attitude can be linguistically materialized but also the fact that this plurality of meanings allows speakers to emphasize one discourse-semantic aspect over another by simply opting for the affect, judgement or appreciation category on each occasion, Hunston (2011) expresses some qualms regarding this tripartite distinction:

> Although Martin and White present the three kinds of meaning as equidistant from each other in terms of system choice, it seems to me that Affect is different in kind from the other two. If evaluation is both 'expression of a subjective reaction to something' and 'expression of the social value of something', [...], then Affect relates to the first of these and both Judgement and Appreciation to the second.
>
> (Hunston, 2011: 21)

Hunston may have hit the nail on the head here with regard to how to conceive of the notions of emotion and evaluation/appraisal as interrelated but certainly distinctive of one another. Whereas affect in Systemic Functional Linguistics seems to encode the 'expression of a subjective reaction to something', the emphasis being on the subjective nature of that reaction, judgement and appreciation project, instead, attitudinal meanings linked to the 'social value of something'. Both sets of meanings have a role to play at the interpersonal level of communication, although what seems to vary is the domain of operation, from the personal and subjective, to the shared and social. The Systemic Functional Linguistics approach undertaken in Appraisal Theory together with the more fine-grained comments on the theory suggested by Hunston, thus, seem to confirm that investigating the two notions (emotion and evaluation) as separate phenomena might be beneficial for the practical applications to the analysis of texts.

Evaluative language has, nonetheless, received much more attention from the viewpoint of other linguists, not least in connection with the concept of stance. Stance is mainly associated with the work of Biber and Finnegan (1989; see also Beach and Anson, 1992; Conrad and Biber, 2000; Levorato, 2009; Simon-Vandenbergen, 2008) who define it as 'the lexical and grammatical expression of attitudes, feelings, judgments, or commitment concerning the propositional content of a message' (Biber and Finnegan, 1989: 93). Most studies on stance coincide in correlating the use of stance markers to different types of register (academic writing or conversation, for instance). Biber and Finnegan (1989) originally identify 12 linguistic categories[7] selected according to semantic and grammatical criteria as stance-encoding; subsequently, those categories have been applied by many other scholars to the study of a variety of texts (see Opas and Tweedie, 1999 and Opas-Hänninen and Seppänen, 2010). Conrad and Biber (2000) expand on the original definition by Biber and Finnegan (1989) and describe three possible senses associated with the use of the term: 'epistemic stance', 'attitudinal stance' and 'style stance'. The first deals with 'the certainty (or doubt), reliability, or limitations of a proposition, including comments on the source of information' (Conrad and Biber, 2000: 57); attitudinal stance, on the other hand, projects 'the speaker's attitudes, feelings, or value judgements' (Conrad and Biber, 2000: 57); style stance, finally, looks closely into 'the manner in which the information is being presented' (Conrad and Biber, 2000: 57). Because of the manifold and rather encompassing way in which Conrad and Biber construe the notion of stance, the closest sense to the kind of evaluative/appraisal meanings I am trying to account for in this chapter is their rendition of attitudinal stance which conveys the speakers' attitudes, feelings and their value judgements. Epistemic stance is reminiscent of the concept of modality, whereas style stance could be likened to the textual metafunction identified in Systemic Functional Linguistics (see Chapter 2 for a more detailed description). Narrowing down Conrad and Biber's tripartite classification to attitudinal stance as the sense most in accordance with the cognate notions of appraisal or evaluation, nonetheless, does not fully explicate either how stance categorically and discriminatorily differs from the notions of evaluation, appraisal, affect, judgement or appreciation, as despite all the terms apparently partaking in some core aspects, they do not seem to be full synonyms either. As pointed out at the beginning of the chapter, because of the wealth and variety of disciplines I borrow and feed from for the analysis of my own data, terminological variation is a rather difficult reality to be faced with and virtually impossible to elude. For the sake of clarity, an executive decision concerning terminology must be made at some point in scholarly research, as I also did in relation to terms relating to the notion of emotion; thus, I concur with Thompson and Hunston (2000) below in adopting the term *evaluation* as an umbrella word to encompass nuances sometimes accounted for by the concepts of appraisal, attitude, judgement and stance, and reserve the terms *affect, emotion* and *mood* to discuss emotionality:

> We take a combining approach, and therefore need a superordinate term. [...] For us (and see also e.g. Georgakopoulou and Goutsos 1997), evaluation is the broad cover term for the expression of the speaker or writer's attitude or stance towards, viewpoint on, or feelings about the entities or propositions that he or she is talking about. That attitude may relate to certainty or obligation or desirability or any of a number of other sets of values. [...] The term evaluation is, admittedly, as slippery as any of the others in this

> field: [...] it is also sometimes used [...] more or less equivalent to Martin's appraisal or Conrad and Biber's attitudinal stance.
>
> (Thompson and Hunston, 2000: 5)

Despite the admission that choosing this term over others might bring in a different set of problems to those generated by the use of any other label, it seems that evaluation, as a term, is more comprehensive, slightly less connotatively-charged, and its meaning can fan out in a way that can include senses related to appraisal or stance. Admittedly, this does not imply that there will not be occasions when the more fine-grained distinctions conveyed by any of the other two concepts will need to be brought to the fore. However, for the purposes of this chapter, there is an added terminological advantage in abiding by this choice of term, which is related to the fact that the software employed for the analysis of Chick Lit readers' contributions in blogs and online book-club forums distinguishes clearly between emotion and evaluation terms as belonging in two distinct domains differentiated by the semantic criteria on which each domain is based. As mentioned already, I emphasize that I do not discard the concepts of appraisal or stance on any basis other than the added ease that doing so brings about in the execution of my own analysis.

5.5 Emotion and Evaluation: Chick Lit Readers

Once theoretical considerations have been introduced, the rest of the chapter deals with the analysis proper of the contributions by Chick Lit readers. This analysis is based, as explained, on two different but complementary methodological approaches: a qualitative analysis of a small sample questionnaire and some purposefully selected contributions by bloggers, on the one hand, followed by a quantitative analysis of a much larger sample from blogs and online book-club forums selected according to a set of criteria described in the appropriate section below, on the other. An initial premise to bear in mind is the series of claims that I refrain from making based on the data I have gathered. For instance, I stay away from drawing theoretical conclusions concerning the act of reading in genres other than Chick Lit. The results emanating from my data are, thus, not fully extensible to other literary or popular genres without further investigation, something which is outside the realm of this chapter or, indeed, the monograph. Second, because of the small number of informants in my questionnaire, I also abstain from aligning my analysis with the most purist examples of empirical research on the readerly aspects of literature undertaken in cognate disciplines such as cognitive psychology or the like. Thus, the large-scale experimental objectives of the empirical research on the psychology of literature implemented by scholars such as van Peer or Hakemulder, for instance, are not pursued here. Note, however, that by the previous statement I do not intend to undermine, nor totally invalidate, the results of my own empirical work as my questionnaire presents some methodological advantages missing from larger-scale studies on the psychology of literature, as I spell out below. What I am trying to avoid is the fallacy of making unsubstantiated claims based on insufficient data. Unfortunately, I also leave out a study of some of the multimodal realizations that accompany the verbal mode in the online book-club forums and blogs because of lack of space, despite the increasingly fundamental role played by modes other than the verbal in these relatively new forms of human communication. For an overview of how the multimodal aspects of blogs and online communication can and do influence the emotional perception of the verbal component see Derks *et al.* (2008), Picard (1997), Walther and D'Addario (2001), and Westerman *et al.* (2007).

A second important preliminary to pay heed to is a clarification concerning how I exploit some of the frameworks, models and tools that I borrow from the disciplines mentioned so far, as I employ them in a slightly different way to the one that they might have originally been conceived for. For instance, some of the theories of emotion discussed above are generally characterized by their focus on readerly rather than writerly aspects of literature. That is, the various researchers observe, investigate and analyse how readers react to their encounters with the literary product. Experts on the affective psychology of literature, for instance, undertake this task, so their research is characterized by a top-down focus (see Chapter 3 for more on this), with which I concur and which I also adopt. On the other hand, scholars interested in viewing how the literary text actually guides and somewhat predetermines what the response of the reader is likely to be opt for a bottom-up analysis, which implies that their primary data emanate from the linguistic component of the literary text. Those concerned with investigating the theory of foregrounding, for instance, can be situated in this camp although they are ultimately also interested in observing the effects that such textual devices have on the reader. The various approaches concerning the notions of emotion and evaluation based on linguistic tenets (stylistic approach to emotion, Systemic Functional Linguistics approach to emotion, Appraisal Theory, analysis of stance, for instance) are, obviously, also involved with the analysis of bottom-up processes. Besides, when these approaches are used to look at the language of emotion or evaluation, most often, the raw data are the novels themselves rather than the contributions by readers, and this is where my approach differs from some others. Instead, I use the various frameworks and models which propose different lines of research on emotion and evaluation (including that of the software Wmatrix) to look into the responses of the readers themselves (that is, the initial top-down process), which means that I am using their linguistic input as data (hence, a bottom-up process) rather than the novels themselves. At the risk of sounding repetitive or over-simplistic, because the tools I choose to implement here have been employed elsewhere for a variety of investigative purposes other than the analysis of literary texts, I reiterate that it is the application of well-known models to the *unprompted contributions* by Chick Lit readers that endows my approach with some novel focus not attempted by other scholars before. In this connection, my analysis differs from others, first, because the top-down analysis of readers' linguistic input is investigated in the light shed by the application of rigorous and solid frameworks; second, because the data emanating from the top-down approach are, for the most part, spontaneously produced, that is, informants have freely generated those contributions without the restrictions and somewhat artificial conditions under which they sometimes verbalize the linguistic input subsequently analysed by scholars in empirical research; finally, the bottom-up analysis is backed up by the solid support of computerized methods so the conclusions eventually drawn should, at least to some degree, be free from the excessive intervention of the analyst. Next, I move on to explain in a bit more detail how the gathering of the data has been carried out.

5.5.1 Methodological considerations

The nature of the data I have collected raises a series of methodological questions that also need addressing. For instance, I have gathered contributions from blogs and online book-club forums but these also require some terminological clarification. A very basic definition of the notion of blog is provided by Blood (2002) who states that 'the influx of blogs has changed the definition of weblog from "a list of links with commentaries and personal asides" to "a website that is updated frequently with new material posted at the top of the page"' (Blood, 2002: 12). A slightly more elaborate account is that of Yang *et al.* (2007) who state:

> Weblog (blog) is one of the most widely used cybermedia in our internet lives that captures and shares moments of our day-to-day experiences, anytime and anywhere. Blogs are web sites that timestamp posts from an individual or a group of people, called bloggers. Bloggers may not follow formal writing styles to express emotional states. In some cases, they must post in pure text, so they add printable characters, such as ':-)' (happy) and ':-(' (sad), to express their feelings. [...] Different kinds of emoticons are introduced into text expressions to convey bloggers' emotions.[8]
>
> (Yang *et al.*, 2007: 133)

Two aspects of this definition interest me. On the one hand, blogs tend to be associated with the personal expression of people's thoughts, ideas or concerns, in the shared arena of the cyber-world. Blogs can be as much made up of real as fictive accounts on any aspect that the blogger wishes to write about, the only common thread among such a distinctively varying assortment of topics and themes being the desirability on the part of the person posting such comments to do so. The most immediate corollary deriving from the freedom with which bloggers post online is the marked 'naturalness' of these contributions when used as data for analysis that liberates them from the restrictions or impositions that scholarly research on reader response has sometimes been accused of. Second, and mostly because of the freedom associated with this medium, emotionality (and also evaluation) features prominently in the wording of people's posts (those that I analyse, at least). That is, personal opinions, judgements, assessments and the speaker's attitudes on whichever topic the blogger is discussing are more than likely to feature. These two characteristics turn bloggers' entries into rather attractive data for linguistic analysis, especially, although not exclusively, in connection with reader response analysis.

A second issue that needs mentioning is that of the online book-club forums used as data-generating sources. In a similar, although not totally equivalent, fashion to blogs, these forums are characterized for their open availability and also present some methodological advantages for the study of unprompted readers' opinions on their reading experiences. There is, however, a major difference to blogs regarding the protected nature of some of the content in these forums. Some of the forums discussed in this chapter are password-protected but, importantly, password protection only comes into operation in those cases in which the forum visitor wants to become a more active participant and contribute to the various threads or, indeed, initiate threads of their own.[9] That is, the content is open to all, but the possibility of contributions is restricted to members only. I did join some of these online book-clubs but, since I do not disclose any password-protected content which is not fully available to the internet community as a whole, I do not feel that basic principles of ethical research have been contravened.

Face-to-face book-clubs are actually generating quite a lot of interest among scholars as plausible laboratories where the actual reader's role can be observed without too much intervention from the analyst. For instance, Swann and Allington (2009; see also Myers, 2009) highlight where the advantages of these book-clubs as sources of data lie:

> Reading groups provide an example of how 'ordinary readers' – i.e. readers other than academic critics and professional reviewers – interpret and evaluate literary texts. While the reader is routinely appealed to in many forms of literary study, including literary stylistics, this is usually an ideal or implied reader [...]. Interest in 'real readers' has given rise to an increasing amount of 'extra-textual' research on literary reading [...]. Much of this, however, has been experimental, or quasi-experimental. Research such as our own shares an interest in real readers and a commitment to empirical methods, but seeks to provide evidence of reading activity outside of the artificial environment of a reading experiment.
>
> (Swann and Allington, 2009: 247–8)

Swann and Allington take issue here with the 'artificiality' that seems to largely characterize research on reader responses, as, despite the best efforts of researchers, it could be argued that informants provide data in their role as 'informants' rather than as 'real readers'. A second aspect that Swann and Allington strongly dispute is also who those informants, for the most part, end up being, especially in the humanities where funding grants are scarce and scholars do not have access to ample demographics:

> Experimental studies often take as their subjects students enrolled at the experimenter's institution and sometimes participating for course credits [...]. In all cases, however, the need for experimental control leads to rather artificial reading behaviour being investigated, with readers interacting with atypical texts and with discussion of the activity, if there is any, being limited to talk with a researcher.
>
> (Swann and Allington, 2009: 248)

My data circumvents, at least, some of the problems underscored by Swann and Allington. First, contributors to blogs and online book-club forums are not 'students enrolled at the experimenter's institution' (see Burke, 2011, and Mar *et al.*, 2006). They might actually be students in real life, of course, but that has no bearing on the data as they are posting irrespective of what their professional dedication might be in real life. They are, first and foremost, readers. Second, informants do not 'talk' directly to the researcher; their reactions to the novels appear online when, and as, the contributor feels appropriate. This freedom should ensure that informants are not providing the answers that they, somehow, might consider the researcher wants to hear; for instance, sometimes contributors are 'rewarded' for their time with small payments, a practice that already introduces an element of artificiality not present in the real life of a reader. Also, and this is an aspect which might be considered an advantage over traditional face-to-face book-clubs, bloggers and online book-clubbers do not tend to read a previously decided work. They, of course, post recommendations on, enquiries about, or requests for specific novels to be discussed, but the act of choosing one novel over another tends to be entirely personal, rather than agreed upon by the club. All of the above suggests that the ever-present conundrum of the *observer's paradox* might be, if not totally eliminated, certainly diminished to some degree.

Equally, it must be acknowledged that using this type of data is not free from problems of its own, especially as far the lack of control that the researcher is left with. Ironically, the vastness of blogs and online forums existing on the web that, in itself, could be seen as a neverending source of research material, might also pose serious problems because of the difficulty of monitoring the variety of factors associated with it. In my case, and in order to allow for consistency in the collection of data and to impose some kind of delimiting parameters, the chosen blogs and online book-club forums have been selected in accordance with a series of criteria. The main criterion concerns the predetermined tagging of the various pages used: I have selected contributions only from those pages already tagged under the label 'chick lit'. On occasions, the title of the webpage includes the label itself, *Chick Lit books*, for instance; some other times the webpage advertises itself as a site where matters related to Chick Lit can be discussed, as in *Chick Lit.co.uk*. This means that my material, as much as possible, has been kept neutral of the analyst's subjective perspective in choosing which pages to use. Second, I have also stayed clear of any webpage with professional undertones on the evaluation of chick lit novels. Therefore, despite the fact that a general search on the web for Chick Lit will bring up references to articles in newspapers or journals, I have not included these in my corpus for they do not contain the kind of unprompted reaction to the novels I am looking for. Third, there is some variation in the number of words collected from the various webpages, which is due to a number of reasons. Some of the pages were temporarily partially down at the time of data collection, which meant that they were only allowing access to some parts. As the material in those parts fitted the rest of the criteria mentioned above, it was accepted for inclusion. Others have stopped being operational, although they were still up on the web until further notice at the moment of data collection. The posts that still remain available fit the criteria above so they have also been included in the final tally. In the case of active blogs, I have followed a 50,000-word threshold so that there is not an overwhelming discrepancy between sites. That being said, however, total equality in the number of words of the various pages should not necessarily be seen as an imperative premise; due to the fact that blogs and threads in the forums are made up of the posts of the original blogger or person posting followed by those of the several contributors who react to and comment on the initial prompt, such variation in the number of words should not skew results. There is no danger of over-representing the writing of one particular blogger or book-club contributor, therefore, because the wording used for analysis incorporates the added text from all the contributions to the original post uploaded at the time of data collection. Finally, the corpus has required a certain amount of editing. In order to avoid skewed scores, some of the temporal references of the posts have been deleted, especially in the cases of responses to the initial post; some typos have been amended and some acronyms (LOL, 'laughing out loud') have been spelled out. My corpus[10] contains in excess of 200,000 words extracted from the following sites (blogs and book-club forums):

About.com (+10,000)
Bookseller Chick (+5200)
Chick Lit Books (+20,000)
Chick Lit Club (+40,000)
Chick Lit.co.uk (+3,000)
Chick Literate (+900)
ChickLITchick (870)
Melissa Senate (+6325)
PalmBeachPress.chick lit (+11,000)
Pop goes fiction (+1,500)
Trashionista (+20,000)
Wordpress (+20,000)
Write Meg (+6,000)
Book-club forum (+50,755).

The qualitative component of my investigation emerges primarily from the questionnaire I distributed among some Chick Lit readers. The questionnaire contains 16 items and is closely based on the original Novel Reading Questionnaire (NRQ) formulated by Burke (2011), whose work has already been discussed above in relation to theories of emotion and the literary reading experience; the original questions in Burke's NRQ, however, have been reformulated to suit my needs in relation to Chick Lit. Informants were asked to provide basic details about themselves first, before they were requested to appraise and comment on their Chick Lit reading experience. The questionnaire was sent out to various web-based book-clubs, academic distribution lists, university students and lecturers; admittedly, the number of returned filled-in responses was much lower than I had envisaged and hoped for, but this is always an aspect that needs factoring in when people are requested to participate in surveys that need some investment of time on their parts. On a more positive note, it is important to bear in mind that the students and lecturers who were invited to participate and who finally took part in the survey were not enrolled in the investigator's institution, so, as discussed above, their responses have research value because informants did not respond as students but as actual readers. In fact, the varied geographical background of the informants vouches for a particular lack of intervention on the part of the researcher, as responses came in from Hungary, the UK, the US and Pakistan.[11] My anonymity as well as that of the informants was compromised because of the medium utilized, that is, email. The aim was to gather data from an ample mixture of readers, with varied backgrounds, geographical and social, diverse ages, possibly even different gender.[12] The electronic format of the questionnaire, as well as the absence of a specifically allotted time in which to complete it, allowed informants to answer the questions in their own time and in as detailed a way as they deemed appropriate. Such an open way of eliciting information allows the researcher to minimize the effects of the *observer's paradox* whilst maintaining a certain level of control as to which issues to question the informants about. In a further attempt not to overlook the objectivity issue, informants were always encouraged to elaborate on their responses as much, or as little, as they wished to do, so that the inescapable danger of leading questions was not too over-imposing. The difficulties and possible controversial nature of some data-gathering methods used in the social sciences and humanities whilst trying to maintain a certain level of objectivity are discussed by Long (2003). From the perspective of sociological concerns, Long investigates the social role of book-clubs for women readers but, more interestingly for my own analysis here, she initially considers the problematics of data-collection:

> Objectivity has been a vexed issue in sociology since its emergence as a discipline. [...] This discussion has highly politicized and 'metatheorized' the issue of objectivity, which is not always useful for scholars who are trying to generate fair and accurate knowledge of the social world.
>
> (Long, 2003: 84–5)

I concur with Long's assessment on two fronts: academic endeavours must undeniably remain methodologically rigorous but, similarly, hindering research by excessively problematizing whether some research tools are capable of throwing results which are irrefutably valid might not be beneficial to the whole academic exercise either. Therefore despite the controversial aspects associated to surveys containing questions that might be deemed leading or slightly biased, I still maintain the usefulness of the methodology chosen as a whole, because of the complementary tools that I have also adopted.

As far as the questions themselves are concerned, the fundamental focus of the survey is to try to elicit answers that could shed light on readers' emotional engagement with the novels, so enquiries on that particular aspect feature more than once. For instance, Question 7 requests readers to consider the following:

> Try to recall the moment when you had just finished reading a/some much-enjoyed novel/s. Can you remember the feeling you had at that moment? If so, can you say something about that feeling? You can name the novel/novels if you want to and elaborate on how each particular book made you feel; otherwise you can simply say something about your impressions, ideas or general sentiment after finishing your Chick Lit books.

Question 11 similarly intends to elicit any possible aspects of the emotional state of the reader:

> Can you explain what mood you find yourself in after finishing a Chick Lit novel? Does your mood tend to vary depending on the novel itself? Or are you disappointed if you don't end up being emoted in the way you expected to be? Please expand below.

As tends to be the case with surveys, questionnaires and data-eliciting exercises in general, not all the responses provided by my informants were equally illuminating as far as the Chick Lit reading experience is concerned, and hence, not especially useful for my investigation here. But this does not imply, either, that the whole exercise lacked qualitative worth. In order to see that merit in detail, I start with the discussion of the qualitative aspects of my research in relation to readers' emotional response to Chick Lit in the next section. To my knowledge, so far there is no other study dealing with the reception aspects of Chick Lit reading from such first-hand material, nor is there much work focusing on how those first-hand reading responses convey the affective side of Chick Lit.

5.5.2 Qualitative analysis

This section investigates the role of emotive aspects in the reading experience of Chick Lit consumers based on the responses that readers themselves have provided in my questionnaire and in some blogs and online book-club forums from which I also extract some data. Besides the information regarding the nature and characteristics of the questionnaire already provided, some further clarifications regarding the informants are still needed. For instance, the varied geographical location of the contributors has been established in the previous section. On top of that, the age group of the survey-respondents also illustrates some welcome variation, as their ages range from the youngest participant at 18 years old to the oldest contributor at 59. A third issue to highlight is the fact that the number of informants was eventually narrowed down to 13 despite the fact that many more showed an initial interest in contributing with their opinions on Chick Lit. As I mention before, surveys and questionnaires that require some investment of time on the part of the interviewee pose some risk for researchers, as this request is not always met with the collaborative enthusiasm that the investigator would wish to find.[13] Despite the small sample of contributors, their responses still provide insightful qualitative data on the emotional aspects associated with Chick Lit books. For instance, there is one aspect with which most informants seem to agree: my respondents all share firm opinions and expectations concerning how they consider the prototypical Chick Lit novel should unfold and conclude, and this ending always involves the happy resolution of the various vicissitudes the main protagonist has lived through in the story. That the prototypical novel does abide by such a principle suggests that the continuous success of the genre is, indeed, linked to the feel-good factor and positive emotions gained from such an ending and which the prototypical Chick Lit author is more than happy to help generate through her work. Alongside all of the above, this qualitative analysis also highlights that blogs and web-based book-clubs fulfil a socio-emotional function that reinforces the positive affective component generally expected of Chick Lit novels. Before getting on with the analysis proper, I remind the reader that any consideration regarding how emotional aspects are linguistically and narratively conveyed in the novels themselves falls outside the remit of this chapter.

In order to contextualize some of the responses provided by Chick Lit readers, it is worth revisiting some of the theoretical aspects on emotion research introduced in Section 5.3. For instance, as already mentioned, describing the part that affect plays in human experience is a task undertaken by scholars from a broad range of disciplines and schools of thought. Philosophers, neuroscientists, psychologists and stylisticians, among others, have all tried to incorporate emotional concerns in their description of our relationship to the world, in general, and in particular, to the nature of reading. Johnson (2007), for instance, specifically refers to recent discoveries made in the field of neuroscience that underscore the fundamental function of emotions for human experience:

> The major neuroscientists agree that emotions play a central role in an organism's assessment of its internal milieu – its bodily states and processes that are tied to its ongoing interactions with its environment, thereby

> motivating both internal body-state adjustments and outwardly directed actions in the world.
>
> (Johnson, 2007: 54)

Although the investigative efforts of neuroscientists (neurolinguists and neuropsychologists, for instance) have not been dealt with in detail in this chapter, it is interesting to observe that research emanating from clinical sciences is in agreement with the various other positions that also underscore the core role that emotion plays for human experience. The same goes for some philosophical perspectives on emotion, such as that of Yanal (1994, 1999), who accounts for how emotional considerations affect the way we process fiction in what he calls the 'fiction paradox':

> 1. Some people (we'll call them emoters) on occasion experience emotions toward characters or situations they take to be fictions.
> 2. Any person experiences an emotion only if he believes that the object of his emotion both exists and exhibits at least some of the emotion inducing properties specific to that emotion.
> 3. No emoter who takes the object of his emotion to be fiction believes that the object of his emotion exists and exhibits any emotion inducing properties.
>
> Propositions 2 and 3 logically imply that emotion toward fiction is an impossibility, and yet proposition 1 claims emotions toward fiction to be an occasional occurrence. We thus have yet cannot have emotions toward fiction.
>
> (Yanal, 1999: 11–12)

Irrespective of the various possible ways in which the paradox has been dissolved, resolved or dismissed by several other thinkers (see also Boruah, 1988; Currie, 1997; Lamarque, 1981), my initial interest in Yanal's work is in the presupposition included in the formulation of the paradox itself, according to which, the paradox exists because there is unequivocally an affective side to the reading of fiction. As Yanal states:

> This is a book about how emotions toward fiction are paradoxical, and how something called 'thought theory' solves the paradox. But where is the paradox? Isn't having a good cry over a sad movie a simple fact of life? On the surface it is, but we'll find on probing deeper that there are good reasons to wonder how the good cry is even possible.
>
> (Yanal, 1999: 2)

Yanal's philosophical perspective is, thus, in accordance with the varied accounts of emotion research presented so far regarding the actuality of the emotions experienced by readers.[14]

The feminist narratological perspective on emotion and popular culture already introduced above and discussed by Warhol (2003) is also worth revisiting. Although Warhol's work does not belong to the same school of thought as the cognitive or philosophical takes of Johnson (2007) or Yanal (1999) respectively, interestingly, she seems to bring to the fore some aspects specifically pertinent to popular genres that are still in tune with some of the conclusions drawn by the previous scholars. In fact, Warhol's *Having a Good Cry* (2003) does not simply confirm the actuality of popular forms' emotion-inducing capability, but also underscores that popular forms are particularly and especially apt to elicit emotional responses from its consumers. As Warhol states:

> Certain pop-cultural formulas can be astonishingly effective in evoking predictable patterns of feeling, even (perhaps especially) when their origins are the very antithesis of authenticity. I have been thinking about these formulas, about how texts make audiences cry.
>
> (Warhol, 2003: xvi)

Warhol, thus, believes in the power of popular culture to stimulate the generation of emotions among its audience, but she also shares commonalities with all those scholars who point out the non-essential nature of actual, grounded referents attached to emotionality. Having said that, there is a fundamental difference between the type of emotional response on which her work is based and the kind of emotional reaction that Chick Lit, for the most part, generates:

> My focus will be upon [...] [the] study of the physical experience of reading: that is, the somatic, bodily aspect of a selection of reactions – crying, hope and worry, interest and boredom, suspense and relief – that reading can invoke.
>
> (Warhol, 2003: 13)

My data on the emotional responses of Chick Lit readers contrast with Warhol's because her work investigates mainly 'crying, hope and worry, interest and boredom, suspense and relief'. Conversely, she seems to disregard the positive emotions that either humour and comedic components, on the one hand, or the felicitous resolution of the novel, on the other, might beget. Contrary to the 'good cry' that Warhol underscores as inherently characteristic of the popular forms she looks into, my respondents and the online contributors highlight that their expectations regarding which affective outcome they mostly desire to gain concern the feel-good factor that only a pleasurable, agreeable and congenial resolution of the novels can provide them with.

In order to analyse how the theoretical proposals put forward by the various disciplines dealing with emotion research can help explicate the way in which my informants emotionally react to Chick Lit novels, I now move on to discuss in detail the various responses to the questionnaire as well as to complement some of their responses with posts from the online Chick Lit readers' community. For instance, after a request for some personal details, the survey sets off by encouraging informants to provide what they would deem to be a definition of the genre.[15] Chapter 1 amply discusses the manifold components of the prototypical Chick Lit novel; Yardley's account of the genre (2006) neatly summarizes some of what those components tend to be:

> Chick Lit is a subgenre of the larger classification of women's fiction, generally a coming-of-age or 'coming-of-consciousness' story where a woman's life is transformed by the events of the story [...]. They're usually fairly upbeat, too [...]. For those writers who take offense at reviewers and critics who call Chick Lit 'fluffy,' 'frothy,' or 'dumb' and who want to counter by making Chick Lit novels literary heavyweights, I have one piece of advice: *switch to decaf.* Seriously. As Chick Lit authors, we'll have messages, themes, and insights, of course. But our primary job is to entertain.
>
> (Yardley, 2006: 4, 5)

Besides aspects such as the age group (20s or 30s), ethnicity (mainly white), sexual orientation (predominantly heterosexual), social class (middle class) and professional occupation of the female protagonist (services, public relations, editorial jobs) (Gormley, 2009) already outlined in Chapters 1 and 3 as illustrative of the prototypical chick in Chick Lit, two other elements in Yardley's definition above merit discussion. These two aspects suitably fit the focus of this chapter because they indicate that readers' emotional response is triggered by certain thematic and structural characteristics of the novels themselves: 'they are fairly upbeat' and 'our primary job is to entertain'. On the one hand, it seems that the cheerful and optimistic undertones of Chick Lit works have become nothing short of a trademark for the genre. Second, Yardley seems adamant that entertaining, that is, focusing on the amusing and ludic, is the main function of Chick Lit novels irrespective of whether this focus might detract from the literary merit of the works. The way my respondents portray their own version of what the genre seems to be about is quite enlightening, as they also echo, among other things, both the optimistic and the amusing aspects of the prototypical Chick Lit novel. For instance, of all the informants, only two failed to characterize Chick Lit in some shape or form; the rest volunteered definitions that suggest that, for them at least, Chick Lit has come of age and is not to be understood as a trendy, transitory fad, but as a genre that displays instantly recognizable traits clear and distinct from other manifestations of what could be categorized as women's fiction.[16] As an illustration, consider the following comments:

4) I would say that Chick Lit usually encompasses a few different things, romance, some type of a bitchy woman, and they're fun to read.
10) A novel written for an audience of females in their 20s and 30s that centers around one (or occasionally more) female protagonist in her 20s or early 30s struggling with relationship and work issues, usually in an urban setting. These issues are resolved within the course of the

novel, leaving the protagonist in a committed heterosexual relationship and in an exciting and promising career situation. The writing is straightforward and simple [...]

13) Good chick lit: strong, funny, assured narrative voice with a bit of comedy-of-manners social analysis; breezy, witty dialogue; engaging, intelligent, funny, genuinely nice characters (mostly in their mid-twenties through their mid-thirties) who care too much about brand names and shopping for my taste; an actual plot; some amusing superficial relationships among minor characters and a romance with more to it than chemistry alone for the main characters.

Online book-club members are also eager to facilitate their own definition of the genre:

> I think chick-lit has its place, it [sic] fun to read and not to be taking too seriously and the beauty part is that anyone can read it. I go through phases of just light reading which for me is chick lit.
>
> (Gyre, http://www.bookclubforum.co.uk/forums/index.php [posted 23/03/2008])

The numbers in the questionnaire examples above are used exclusively for informant-identification and simply indicate the order in which the questionnaires were received. Judging from these responses, it could be argued that these readers are more than capable of coming forward with a thoroughly elaborated definition. For a start, they seem to pick out characterization as a key strategy in the genre as illustrated by the contributions of informants 10 and 13 who provide a well sketched-out account of what kind of female protagonist is meant to feature in these novels. Second, informants 4 and 13 underscore the ludic aspects of the novel as also intrinsically illustrative of Chick Lit, so they are in agreement with Yardley's evaluation above. Additionally, it is important to highlight that these incipient attempts at a definition are solidly supported by the fact that the survey-respondents describe themselves as accomplished Chick Lit readers in the information they provide for Question two,[17] which requests that contributors state roughly the number of novels they have read. Although informant 9 fails to provide a figure, the rest seem well acquainted with the genre, as only one has read between 0 and 5 Chick Lit novels; three ticked the 5-to-10 box, four the 10-to-15, two went for the 20-to-25 option, and a further two acknowledged that they have read in excess of 25 novels. Online book-club users also comment on how well acquainted they are with the novels in terms of numbers:

> I have an awful lot of chick-lit books. My mum usually buys those [sic] kind and then I get them. They're good in the summertime or if you're after a light read :)
>
> (Stephanie2008, http://www.bookclubforum.co.uk/forums/index.php [posted 14/05/2009])

> well i [sic] have all of Sophie Kinsella's novels even the latest one, I have 2 Gossip Girl novels, I have 2 Monica McCaffertys, 4 Meg Cabots [...] . I choose my novels by the blurb, although I have this strange habit to look at the last sentence of the ending of the novel, some people find it ruins the novel, but I don't see it as a form of spoiler.
>
> (bubbleprincess, http://www.bookclubforum.co.uk/forums/index.php [posted 1/05/2009])

The questionnaire responses and the comments on the web, therefore, seem grounded on the knowledge gained from being very familiar with works that they, themselves, have selected, in their own time and free from the meddling of an investigator, which highlights the 'naturalness' of the results. Question 3 was, in fact, formulated to test and verify such naturalness, on the one hand, possibly the probity of the responses provided by informants, on the other, and to monitor what eventually prompts readers to opt for a particular choice of novel over another: 'How do you choose your novels? Word of mouth? Friends' tips? Book-clubs? Websites recommendations? Please elaborate below.' The responses were varied:

3) I mainly just read Marian Keyes because I like her books. The rest I find a bit 'too' trashy.
5) Word of mouth, book groups, websites, blogs, Publisher's Weekly and the publishing houses first look lists.
8) All of the above! I prefer once a year to send an email out to everyone in my address book requesting that they recommend one book for me to read that year. I generally compile a list of about 20 books and make a commitment to read those titles (in addition to anything else that catches my eye) by the end of the year.

Admittedly the kind of dedication shown by informant 8 is not necessarily the norm for all readers; however, these responses illustrate that my informants go to some lengths to learn about Chick Lit novels and authors prior to the act of reading itself. The intrinsic value of their responses, therefore, is the way they show that involvement with the genre for these readers starts well before they hold the selected book in their hands, which echoes some of Burke's (2011: 46) suggestions regarding the reading experience discussed above: 'If film viewers have goals, which they clearly do, literary readers must have them too and [...] these start long before the reader engages with the text.' Whereas Burke discusses primarily literary fiction, my data appear to suggest that, by engaging with popular forms, readers also entertain certain goals and expectations. Moreover, combining this sense of anticipation and eagerness to learn about the novels before reading them with the avidness in relation to the amount of books that at least some of the readers confess to have pored over confirms that the genre has undoubtedly gripped the imagination and emotional involvement of readers. Plus, it also gives some countenance to the qualitative value of their feedback for my endeavours here.

For ease of explanation, the rest of the questions in the questionnaire are divided into two sections: those that more directly address the issue of emotionality and the novels, and those that delve into some other concerns, not all of which are fully usable for the objectives of this chapter. In the latter group are Questions 6, 8, 9, 12, 14, 15 and 16 which are dealt with here first. For instance, Question 6 is formulated so that it directly follows on from Question 5, but whereas the latter specifically attempts to elicit information on the reader's emotional reactions, the former, in the context of the rest of the survey, acts as a kind of dummy request. Question 6 is formulated as follows:

> Question 6:
> Do you think that any of the above themes can be evoked in a reader's mind even if they are not mentioned directly in the text? (For example, is it possible that a novel can invoke in you memories of your childhood, past relationships, friendship, illness, etc. even if the passage you are reading is not specifically dealing with such events?)
> a. Yes b. No
> If you have answered [a] why do you think that this is the case? i.e. how do you think it works?

The thematic components of the novels that this question refers to are evaluated in Question 5 in connection with their potentiality for emotion-activation:

> Question 5:
> Do you think that certain themes that may appear throughout a novel can affect your emotional mood during the actual reading process itself?
> a. Yes b. No
> If you have answered [a], could you please expand on this below. For instance, which themes are you most affected by?

The responses provided for Question 5 are analysed below. As far as Question 6 is concerned, though, results are not particularly illuminating or useful for my purposes. In fact, a similar dummy request is introduced in Question 8,[18] which also invites respondents to think of their reading experience in light of any previous memories or recollections from the past. Although all but one of the informants indicated that retrospection into times past did occur, with a further one failing to respond at all, the issue of how memories influence the reading process is not one that I develop in this chapter. For more information on this matter see Burke (2011).

Question 9[19] was initially included because I hypothesized that one of the possible consequences of the emotional attachment and pleasurable experience gained from looking at some much-enjoyed novel could be that readers would want to rekindle the same type of positive sentiments originally entertained by rereading some pages or paragraphs. This hypothesis, however, was met by some mixed responses as five informants categorically answered in the negative, whereas the rest did indicate a few of the reasons why they would revisit some previously-read novel. For instance, for informant 8, the reason for going over some pages of a finished novel again is a desire to relive the affective sentiment originally felt which, according to her, can be achieved by rereading the writer's words: 'The feelings from a novel don't stay. You need the words to bring you back to it.' Informant 11, on the other hand, finds emotional solace in the clarification that comes from verifying all aspects of the storyline, which also helps instigate again the initial sentiments: 'To re-enjoy the experience, if possible, and also to clarify questions about the sequence of events or aspects of character.' My hypothesis, therefore, was not sufficiently borne out by the responses provided as a relatively high proportion of the respondents simply confirmed that rereading was not part of their individual routine. The inclusion of item 12[20] was similarly motivated by my prior hypothesizing on how the ludic component of the novels yields itself particularly well to having specific physical surroundings in which to enjoy the novels. This question, therefore, wanted to delve into the physical aspects of the reading process itself and requested readers to describe whether the actual location in which reading takes place has an effect on the reading experience at all. Although my initial incline was that informants would indicate a preference for surroundings that would improve and intensify comfortableness so that the positive sentiments accompanying the reading process would, subsequently, be enhanced, the results greatly differed from my original expectations. Nine informants categorically responded negatively and another one provided no answer at all. The online contributors, however, did show a clearer sense of preferential physicality. For instance:

> I have a favourite chair where I love to read, ideally with chocolate at hand but I usually carry one book with me and will read anywhere.
>
> (Lorelei, http://www.bookclubforum.co.uk/forums/index.php [posted 10/06/2009])

Despite the above, to prove or disprove my intuitively formulated assumption concerning the way physical surroundings affect the emotive reaction of readers would, obviously, require a much larger-scale study of these aspects. As it stands at the moment, it appears that the enjoyment experienced by Chick Lit readers occurs irrespective of the location where reading takes place.

The running thread linking Questions 14, 15 and 16 is my interest in investigating how readers react to the linguistic and stylistic aspects of the novels. In particular, Question 15 tries to elicit whether readers correlate the stylistic aspects of writing with their own sense of emotionality. Question 15, thus, addresses the language-emotionality connection as follows:

Question 15:
Do you think that a well-structured literary style can as much as alter or affect your emotions?
a. Yes b. No
If you have answered [a], could you say how?

Question 14[21] does not straightforwardly mention emotionality; still, I urge readers to elaborate on whether stylistic aspects influence the way they read. I discuss the responses to Questions 14 and 15 below. Prior to that, item number 16 requires some attention as, for the most part, it failed to provide the results I had predicted. Thinking about my request in retrospection, I realize now that this item presented too much of an imposition on my informants. Item 16[22] (see also Burke, 2011) was more of a case study than an actual question, as it asked informants to choose a particular passage from any Chick Lit novel they would have enjoyed and to select lexical items, expressions, or any sentence structure that might have had a particularly salient emotional effect for them. In sum, I wanted my informants to do some analysing as well as introspecting. The demands on the respondents were, simply, too high, so most of them declined the request. Only informant 3 took on the challenge and produced both an extract from Marian Keyes's *Lucy Sullivan is Getting Married* (1997), and the corresponding analysis prompted by my own questions. Nevertheless it is interesting that, despite the fact that her responses did not feasibly enlighten the connection between linguistic or stylistic aspects and her sense of emotionality, they did underscore the crucial role of the novel's entertaining value for the reader: 'The piece didn't really touch me – I just found the novel as a whole, quite entertaining and a good form of relaxation and escapism.' Informants were far more enthusiastic and eager to answer item 14, which asked them to discuss whether the style of a particular novel influenced their reading experience in general, without any mention of emotionality. All of the informants answered affirmatively and resolutely confirmed that the way a novel is linguistically and stylistically constructed, even in the case of popular genres which are not necessarily always praised for their literary merits, becomes a factor that can decidedly influence, positively or negatively, the opinion of the readership. Some of the rather lucidly spelled-out opinions put forward by my informants are the following:

3) I think some styles people find more natural to read than others; some styles are effortless to read and the story just filters through, whereas other styles you have to make more of an effort. I think Chick Lit books should be quite 'effortless' to read.
6) Poorly executed metaphors enrage me. The abuse of adverbs enrages me. The excessive (more than one per page) use of italics really enrages me. When an author repeats a word instead of finding a good synonym, and this is done out of laziness rather than for effect, it disgusts me.
10) One of the things I like about chick lit is that its generally simple style allows me to read it quickly and purely for plot.

Informants three and ten coincide in drawing parallels between effortlessness, simplicity of style and Chick Lit novels; in fact, that correlation seems to be precisely the appeal of the genre for these two readers. Informant six, on the other hand, is far more eloquent concerning what exact linguistic and even typographic aspects of the text are capable of triggering some rather strong emotional reactions that, in her case, can tellingly range from irateness to pure disgust. Question 15[23] is similarly met by the positive endorsement of my informants who, with the exception of two, overwhelmingly confirm that the literary style of a novel can indeed alter or affect their emotions:

2) Yes, you can enjoy a book better or it can touch you deeper if it is well-written.
8) Yes, of course! The words chosen and how they are presented can add so much flavour and realism to the story, and therefore make a bigger impact on me emotionally.
9) Yes: if something is well-written, it is able to really get its point across, which can alter the way the reader feels because it can evoke emotion that was not previously present.
10) Yes. I respond differently to language that is crafted carefully or self-consciously – I start to pay attention to the language itself, the way it sounds and looks, etc. The more beautiful the language, the more likely I am to respond emotionally to individual moments in a text.

One caveat needs to be added to the solid way in which respondents assess the connection between style and emotionality. Besides the examples above, all the other occurrences in the questionnaire also discuss 'well-written books', 'beautiful language' and 'good quality writing', but they fail to spell out what 'well-written' or 'beautiful language' mean. That my informants provide answers in their capacity as readers, unfortunately, also highlights their role as non-specialists, so their lack of a sophisticated linguistic description regarding what style is, for instance, renders their evaluation rather subjective and personal. Question 16 was intended to try to thwart this bias by asking informants to specifically pinpoint the linguistic components that generate emotionality, but, as discussed, there was a lack of response to my petition, so clearly there is more work to be done to investigate these matters further. What does stand out in the responses to Questions 14 and 15, though, is that the linguistic material of which novels are made is not something that Chick Lit readers disregard as secondary, even though Chick Lit is one of those genres that might be associated more clearly with plot development, storyline and dénouement than with the way in which the novel is linguistically and stylistically construed. This awareness of linguistic aspects and the subsequent effect on the emotionality of readers seems to be in agreement with what van Peer (1986; 1997) describes as the theory of foregrounding: 'It is a theory about the form of literature, about language, the raw material out of which literature is made [...]. Second, the more innovative aspect, it also refers to readers' reactions to such form' (van Peer, 2007: 99). Although the number of my respondents can offer only limited confirmation, nor can it empirically validate fully the tenets of the theory, it does not contravene the basic principle according to which the raw material of literature, that is, language and readers' emotional reactions to it, are inextricably linked.

The final group of questions focuses more specifically on affect, with regard to both the sentiments that readers feel and the expectations concerning what they desire to, and envisage, they would feel. Questions 4[24] and 10[25] deal with the latter and respectively investigate what elements readers presume they would find in the novels and how they expect a novel to end, plus, readers were also requested to introspect on whether having those expectations fulfilled mattered to them. Expectations seem to be a rather strong component in the Chick Lit reading experience, not only in relation to the themes, issues or elements that readers hanker after in each book, but also with regard to the ending and resolution of the storyline; this seems to be confirmed in my survey, as 11 informants responded positively to Question 4 and ten to Question 10. This is how they describe (in their answer to Question 4) their desire to come across specific elements in Chick Lit:

4) Yes. If i [sic] read a chick lit novel … and I found it difficult to follow the plot and there were none of the classic 'girl' elements in it, I would definitely be disappointed.
5) Yes. I expect the main character to be strong and to take care of herself. I expect the book to be funny. I expect [sic] connect with the characters. I expect a satisfying ending (she gets the job she wants/the boyfriend/ whatever.) And, I do feel cheated when one or more of these elements are missing. In particular, I feel cheated when I don't connect with the character, or if I end up hating her because she's overly whiny or helpless.
10) I expect to have a happy ending. I also expect for the problems that the protagonist faces to be relatively superficial. I am disappointed if the book turns out to be too serious – if it's about mental illness, for example.

According to these responses, readers keep coming back to the genre because of a sense of familiarity with the 'classic "girl" elements' in Chick Lit, but also because of the comforting effect that this familiarity and total absence or, at least, small presence of, unexpected events, generates in them. For respondent 5, for instance, not encountering some of those elements means that she even feels 'cheated', as if the author had not kept her end of the bargain. Informant 10, on the other hand, anticipates an answer to the query I put to the readers later on in item 10, and confirms that the felicitous resolution of the novel is not just another component but it is integral to the genre. In the words of the informants when answering Question 10:

2) a. Yes. I expect a happy ending. Usually these novels have a happy ending anyway. I think that's why people read them. They are not at all realistic and that's also partly why people read them. They just want a nice, romantic story with a good ending – no sadness. (If they expected realism they'd read proper literature! ;))))
5) a. Yes. I expect a positive outcome for the heroine, definitely.
9) a. Yes. Happily ever after.
10) a. Yes. I expect the protagonist to have a boyfriend that I like and who treats her well at the end. I also expect her to be employed at something she loves to do and not stuck in a dead-end job.

Respondent 2 highlights two important aspects concerning expectations towards the genre: on the one hand, happy endings are an asset sought after by readers because they allow them to enjoy a sense of escapism. This reader seems to suggest that novels that emphasize realism instead of the happy-ever-after formula more prototypically employed in Chick Lit might not facilitate or particularly encourage the same sense of evasion from reality that appears so enthralling in Chick Lit. On the other hand, respondent 2 is also assessing the high–low literature dichotomy of which Chick Lit readers are not totally unaware.[26] Informant 10 tellingly combines some of the elements typically associated with the genre (boyfriend, enjoyable job) with her own affectivity, as the fact that the female protagonist ends up having a boyfriend that the reader likes is important to her.

Finally, Questions 5, 7, 11 and 13 require that readers introspect and elaborate on the affective aspects of their reading experience; each question refers to a different stage of this reading process, from the moments before engaging with the books, to the feelings after completion, via the affective states and moods during the act of reading itself. As has been the case in the rest of the survey, so that respondents did not anticipate what the investigator required of them, these requests were mixed in with the rest of the questions. Thus, Question 13[27] tackles the issue of whether the mood prior to engaging with the novels affects the subsequent reading experience; seven informants ratified that their pre-reading mood impinged upon the way they approached the books:

3) Yes. I think what you are thinking and feeling can become part of what you visualise as you are reading, and can affect the things you notice and perceive.
8) Yes. Of course ... how I feel when I go into the book will color my reactions to the book, and the actual process of reading it.
9) Yes. If I am in a bad mood, it is unlikely I would ever choose to read a chick lit novel.

Their pre-reading mood, thus, might even determine whether these readers actually engage in the act of reading at all; furthermore, according to subject number 3, that pre-reading affective state might eventually be responsible for whether a reader is capable of noticing all the various nuances in the text. Once readers have decided to engage with a novel, nevertheless, the affective component seems especially influenced by the themes raised in each work, as examined in Question 5[28] (nine informants answered in the affirmative):

8) Yes. Isn't that the point of reading ... to be affected and to change? The tone of the book will reflect in my own emotional mood ... within reason. I'm not going to turn into a homicidal maniac because I'm reading about one. I'm just going to feel a shadow of the feelings presented in a book. (Empathy, I believe they call it).
9) Yes. Some novels designed for females employ extremely emotional situations [...] and when these situations come about, if the writing is good enough, I'll probably wind up crying due to the fact that I get very involved in what I am reading. Themes of death and divorce especially affect me emotionally.

The responses above leave little doubt concerning informants' opinion on the affective effect that certain themes are capable of raising. Needless to say, it is clear that some of the answers provided in the survey can lead to some conclusions that are not, by any means, to be understood as exclusively applicable to Chick Lit. However, because I clearly state at the beginning of the survey that my interests are concerned simply with the Chick Lit reading experience, I must assume that the responses in the survey are, for the most part, illustrating my informants' impressions on the former. Equally interesting, though, are the responses that informants 3 and 10 provide for Question 5:

3) No; I think the whole thing about Chick Lit is that it doesn't really affect you emotionally.
10) No (I read these to avoid having intense feelings – most book [sic] do provoke this response, but these are comfortingly formulaic).

In the context of the strong emotional reactions that other respondents acknowledge, the information above stands out because it seemingly contradicts that emotionality and Chick Lit have anything to do with each other. It certainly highlights that this issue is in need of further investigation. For instance, whereas informant 3 is adamant that Chick Lit, as a genre, is not capable of evoking affective reactions in its readers, respondent 10 indicates that, although she approaches these novels to escape 'intense feelings' she, nevertheless, still gains some 'comfort' from the repetitive and nearly mechanic nature of these books. It could be argued, therefore, that finding solace in such formulaic conventionality is, in itself, a kind of affective reaction to the novels, so emotionality would not be completely absent from her Chick Lit reading experience. As mentioned, this issue needs further investigation and perhaps only a much larger-scale sample will throw significant and conclusive results.

Finally, Questions 7[29] and 11[30] attempt to elicit what kind of mood readers find themselves in after coming to the end of the novel. The aims pursued by including these two items are not all that dissimilar; in fact, Questions 7 and 11 were formulated as two separate queries for cross-referencing. So, whereas in the former informants are asked for details concerning the 'feeling' ensuing from the end of a novel, the latter invites comments on the 'mood' she found herself in at the novel's closure. Discussing the various interpretations of the concepts of 'feeling' and 'mood' falls outside the scope of this chapter; besides, I have already indicated that I use them synonymously here. In the survey, my intention was to try to elicit as much information regarding the affective response from the readers at novel closure, so I opted for doubling up the request as two separate items. The following are some of the survey responses for Question 7:

3) I can remember feeling quite positive after reading Marian Keyes – she is a good story-teller. [...] it's therapeutic as the themes are always quite basic and humorous and centred around women together and what they go through in day to day life.
4) I'm always a bit sad when I finish a book I find to be particularly enjoyable, [...] But, I get very emotionally attached to novels and the characters in them, and most end on a happier note, therefore leaving me happy.
5) [...] When I finish reading a novel which I very much enjoyed, I feel a huge rush of adrenaline, tinged with sadness because the book is over.

Only two respondents failed to provide details to this question; the rest of the subjects did elaborate on their responses relatively amply. The feedback on Question 11 is also illustrative of emotional engagement with the novels:

3) I tend to feel positive after reading Chick Lit, as I said earlier that I find it quite therapeutic.
5) If the novel ended well, I usually feel pleased. If it didn't, I feel disappointed. Chick Lit is typically the sort of thing that gets stuck in my craw and I have to mull over. I read it as an escape, so if it did bother me for days or seriously adversely, I'd stop reading it.
6) My general expectation before I begin reading a Chick Lit novel is that it will not be great literature but that it will be light entertainment which has some funny moments. So far, I have not been let down. I guess I would call my mood upon finishing a Chick Lit novel as 'amused' or 'slightly entertained,' but mostly I just feel the same sense of accomplishment I feel upon finishing any book.

At this stage, and to recap on how the various questions have been answered, it is interesting to bring in some further comments posted in web-based book-club forums which also report on the kind of emotional involvement that the subjects in my survey have drawn attention to. For instance:

> Well I loved this book! I was gripped from the word go. This is pure chick-lit – with a cheesy storyline, which was quite unbelievable and predictable, but did that effect [sic] the book? Nope. I was excited about reading it – I didn't want to stop, I didn't want the book to finish.
>
> (Kate, http://bookclubforum.co.uk/forum/ [posted 18/01/09])

> I want to be left satesfied [sic] or just wishing it had went [sic] on a little longer, just read that back and it sounds very rude! :smile2: But that is how I want to be at the end of any book.
>
> (shaka1909, http://bookclubforum.co.uk/forum/ [posted 22/04/09])

Because of space constraints I do not discuss here any other examples taken from the online book-club forums consulted, especially as these are developed further in Section 5.5.3[31]. However, as suggested by some of the examples quoted, many of the issues brought to the fore by the answers to my questions are also dealt with in the posts left on websites. The next step, therefore, is to take stock and review what kind of theoretical tenets can be inferred from all of this material. The small-scale sample I have used only allows me to draw preliminary conclusions but some tendencies and trends in the reading pattern of Chick Lit enthusiasts seems to be emerging. For instance, as introduced above, Warhol (2003) tackles emotionality in popular forms in a way that encompasses some of the aspects already described in my questionnaire and the online posts. Warhol borrows the term 'metaemotion' from Oliver's work (1993) (see also Oliver *et al.*, 2000; and Schramm and Wirth, 2010) although Oliver focuses mainly on the sad film, and applies it successfully to her own investigations of the 'good cry'. The notion of metaemotion can also shed light on the way the Chick Lit readership discloses the emotional reactions that accompany their reading experience, both in my questionnaire and websites:

> Oliver makes a useful distinction between 'emotional reactions' and 'feelings about emotional reactions,' which she calls 'metaemotions.' Her detailed, quantitative study shows that feminine subjects report positive feelings about crying, finding pleasure and even satisfaction in the experience of textually induced tears.
>
> (Warhol, 2003: 31)

The main difference between Warhol's work and my own investigation is the fact that Warhol is primarily concerned with examining the emotional and cultural aspects of what she calls the 'good cry', that is, shedding tears over popular forms such as soap operas and romances. Considering the responses of the survey, such physical reaction is not something that Chick Lit is particularly characterized by; although I am not denying the possibility of a good cry ever taking place after reading Chick Lit, there have been no instances pointing at such bodily response to the novels. The notion of metaemotion, however, refers not so much to the bodily reaction itself but to the somehow contradictory reporting of happiness and pleasure on the crying act. In my case, the subjects who took part in the questionnaire and those posting online also report on the emotionality attached to the genre, but their reports do not clash with the positive affective reaction initially felt. Second, the unprompted nature of the online posts needs to be brought to the fore once again to underscore the naturalness of the data. As a result of the combination of all these factors, the term metaemotion in this chapter takes on a slightly different sense, so that what emotionality means for Chick Lit readers can be properly accounted for. Although I borrow the term itself from Oliver via Warhol, I use it to mean primarily the kind of unprompted reporting on affective matters that online book-club members and bloggers report. I recover the basic sense of the prefix 'meta' to mean 'about', so I focus on the fact that bloggers and online book-clubbers are more than happy to disclose their own affectivity in websites and online book-club forums rather openly and candidly; their online contributions, thus, become frank and genuine commentaries about their own emotionality. This definition of metaemotion, hence, applies in particular to the more naturalistic contributions of my data. The questionnaire responses, nonetheless, complement and support the lack of artificiality offered by the online posts because, despite the fact that respondents react to the triggers in the shape of questions that I pose to them, they are Chick Lit readers all the same.

The notion of metaemotion needs developing on a second but fundamental plane too. It seems that the online format utilized by Chick Lit bloggers and online book-club members allows these readers not only to verbalize openly the affective side of their reading experience, but also, crucially, to share those emotions and their linguistic manifestations with the rest of the online community. The entries on blogs and forums enable the channelling of these emotions onto a different medium, one that is clearly publicizing and circulating affective reactions in a rather flagrant way. I would suggest that the concept of metaemotion might be better served if understood in conjunction with what I would like to call the 'socio-emotional function' of these novels. The responses by Chick Lit bloggers and the entries in my questionnaire seem to amply endorse the emotional gain that Chick Lit readers experience; crucially, though, the verbalization of these emotions and their subsequent sharing on the various online platforms is also flavoured with a social component, as these bloggers and online contributors have, in fact, become part of a community of practice where affectivity is shared. Studies on more traditional forms of book discussion have already pointed out the blending of the social and emotional aspects of reading in the discourse of book-clubs. Long's work (2003), for instance, highlights that these gatherings are not exclusively devoted to the critical appreciation of literature:

> They can become much more than a class or a solitary reading. It is as if the discussion is a lens that reveals the books under discussion and the inner lives of coparticipants and, through this process, allows participants to reflect

> back on their own interior lives as well [...]. In that sense, reading group discussions perform creative cultural work, for they enable participants to articulate or even discover who they are: their values, their aspirations, and their stance toward the dilemmas of their worlds.
>
> (Long, 2003: 145)

Long's concept of 'intersubjective accomplishment' (2003: 145) among book-club attendants, offered as explanation for the experience-sharing exercise initially prompted by the reading of novels, also resonates with the social qualities of web-based reports. Long concludes that participants in these discussions end up sharing much more than their opinions on the novels because part of who they are as people also permeates their discussion. The crucial difference with the online contributions I deal with, however, lies in the compelling immediacy allowed by new media, as bloggers and online book-clubbers' narratives, unlike those of face-to-face book-club contributions, can reach their audience almost instantly. Furthermore, the community of practice in which web-based forums are integrated allows the reinforcement of social links in a way not possible in the case of traditional book-clubs. Doing away with the boundaries of 'physically' meeting up frees members as to when and where they can contribute to discussions, all the while still maintaining the cohesion of the group.

Further support for my suggestion that the metaemotional aspects of Chick Lit readers' feedback on the web are possible because of the socio-emotional function of the genre emerges from the field of psychology:

> My claim in this chapter, however, is not just that social factors influence and are influenced by emotion, but that emotions are socially constituted [...] over the course of our on-line[32] interpersonal encounters. Not only does the idea of emotion emerge from social and cultural discourses and related practices, but also, and more fundamentally, the true nature of emotion is in many cases as a form of communication.
>
> (Parkinson, 1995: 170)

Parkinson's assessment on the actual nature of emotions opens up very interesting possibilities to account both for how affectivity and fiction relate to each other and for the subsequent interpersonal consequences of that affectivity. If emotions, as Parkinson claims, emerge from social and cultural discourses, surely one major discourse that would give rise to emotionality must be fiction that also fulfils the proviso of being a form of communication. Parkinson elaborates on this premise as follows:

> A basic social effect of emotions is that they often make us seek out company. [...] Why do we share our emotional experiences with other people? [...] From the point of view of the present analysis, talking about an emotion afterwards restates the evaluative claim it contains and assesses consensus for

it. We want to feel justified in our emotional attitudes, and the only possible authorization is an interpersonal one.

(Parkinson, 1995: 194)

Bloggers and online book-club contributors certainly seem to seek out the company of other like-minded individuals for the ratification of their evaluative and affective viewpoints on Chick Lit. Unlike the type of physical company that Parkinson refers to above, online Chick Lit enthusiasts opt for the advantages of the cyber-world, although the same need for confirmation and validation of their emotional responses appears to be sought after. The fact that analyses emanating from psychology confirm that emotionality also includes a rather strong social component gives some countenance to my own assessment in relation to the socio-emotional function of Chick Lit readers' affectivity-sharing tendencies. As Parkinson *et al.* (2005: 20) state, 'we want to draw attention to how emotions are always produced in particular contexts that give them their meaning and shape the ways in which they unfold.' Thus, bearing in mind that different contexts will generate different emotions, the claims I make here in relation to Chick Lit novels and the websites containing readers' emotional reactions to them pertain exclusively to this specific genre and its readers and would probably need reassessing if dealing with discourses other than Chick Lit.

To recap, it appears that the qualitative aspects of the data I have gathered allow me to draw some solid conclusions. Based on the questionnaire responses, it can be argued that Chick Lit readers are part of a community that is capable of discerning what counts as Chick Lit and is, hence, constantly on the lookout for new additions to the genre. The immediate consequence of this eager search for new titles is the fact that Chick Lit readers have become faithful and avid consumers of the genre. Warhol (2003: 7) describes weepy films, soap operas and romances as 'technologies of affect' (see above) because they are capable of providing 'structures of feeling in the daily lives of their devotees'. In my case, Chick Lit readers seem to profess the same devotion to the novels they read but, in addition, that enjoyment is eagerly shared with other Chick-Lit-appreciative women. Their judgements and assessments, therefore, are backed up by the solid knowledge that these enthusiasts have for the novels. Third, the data I have looked at confirms that readers' affective reactions to the genre can be explicated via the concepts of metaemotion, on the one hand, and the socio-emotional role that characterizes the way they share information on their own affectivity, on the other. In sum, it appears that the qualitative analysis I implement provides enough evidence to support the claims made throughout this section. I now move on to investigate Chick Lit readers' emotional reactions from a different perspective, for which I use a larger-scale sample which should not just expand on the aspects raised here but also confirm that the study of emotionality in relation to the Chick Lit readership is an enterprise worth taking on.

5.5.3 Quantitative analysis

The qualitative slant of Section 5.5.2 has allowed me to discuss some key aspects concerning the emotional involvement of the Chick Lit reader with the novels. I complement this qualitative perspective with the quantitative focus I adopt in the present section, which is informed by the principles and general interests of corpus stylistics, as described more amply in Chapter 3. As I also do there, I take advantage of the software programme Wmatrix (Rayson, 2009) to test empirically the linguistic manifestation of emotionality and evaluation in my Chick Lit readers' blog and online book-club forums corpus. As explained above, this blog contains in excess of 200,000 words extracted from a variety of sites. For ease of reference, I refer to it as the *Chick Lit Readers Corpus.* In this quantitative analysis, thus, I do not compute the responses provided by readers in the questionnaire. By taking on a quantitative perspective, I can delve into both the language of emotion and the language of evaluation in ways that the qualitative approach fails to do, especially as far as the language of evaluation is concerned. A sense of complementarity, therefore, motivates this second take on the verbalization of emotionality and evaluation by Chick Lit readers.

As explained in Chapter 3, Wmatrix (Rayson, 2009) works on the premise of comparison between two corpora: the target corpus, in my case the *Chick Lit Readers Corpus,* and one of the various sub-sections of the British National Corpus on which Wmatrix is based.[33] As also explained, The British National Corpus (BNC) contains data from both written and spoken language from a variety of discourse types. Because a quantitative and computerized way of measuring data relies on the actual comparability of the two corpora chosen, the first decision that needs making to assess faithfully the linguistic components of the target corpus is to select the appropriate sub-section in light of which to evaluate the *Chick Lit Readers Corpus.* Chapter 3 contains a more detailed account of the various sub-divisions and the number of words that make up the BNC Sampler, a sub-corpus containing approximately one-fiftieth of the parent corpus (that is, about 2,000,000 words). Interestingly, this software offers investigators the option of analysing data by comparing the target corpus to either the whole of the Spoken or the Written sub-sections of the BNC Sampler or, alternatively, by viewing it in relation to one of the two major sub-divisions in each category. Therefore, researchers need to decide, first of all, whether the target corpus is considered to be representative of prototypical spoken or written language varieties. Next, the data can be assessed in relation to the Spoken Context-Governed or the Spoken Demographic sub-categories, and the Written Imaginative or Written Informative, respectively. For ease of reference I reprise below the summarizing table first shown in Chapter 3.

Needless to say, the comparability of the corpora is something that the investigator needs to decide upon beforehand, especially because putting together unmatchable sets would throw skewed results; besides, because of the special nature of blogs, the choice of reference corpus gains special significance. On the one hand, blogs and entries in book-club forums can be seen as written

Spoken (990,704 words)		*Written (1,010,690 words)*	
Context-governed (496,852)	Demographic (493,852) [by socio-economic class]	Imaginative (231,663)	Informative (779,027)
Leisure (136,606)	I (AB) (164,933)	Drama (23,786)	Pure science (32,974)
Educational (80,463)	II (C1) (98,700)	Poetry (30,144)	Applied science (117,685)
Business (134,275)	III (C2) (137,686)	Prose fiction (177,733)	Social science (29,868)
Public/Institutional (145,508)	IV (DE) (92,533)		World affairs (277,128)
			Commerce & finance (92,057)
			Arts (51,645)
			Belief & thought (43,626)
			Leisure (134,044)

Table 3.2 BNC Sampler Corpus (2,001,394 words) (Rayson, 2009; available online at http://ucrel.lancs.ac.uk/bnc2sampler/sampler.htm)

narratives in which individuals provide personal accounts, so the most logical conclusion would be to analyse the *Chick Lit Readers Corpus* alongside the Written sub-section of the BNC Sampler (or any of its sub-categories). However, the primarily interactive and changeable nature of these online accounts as well as the special features of the medium itself turn these narratives into more 'unstable' categories than other forms of personal writing such as, for instance, written diaries or private journals. Moreover, as already explained, my data are made up of material which includes, not just the original input by the blogger or the book-club forum contributors initiating a thread, but also the web-narratives of other people who have reacted to the initial prompts. Finally, the rather informal tone that bloggers tend to use when composing their narratives, not least because of the leisure, entertainment and ludic aspects behind these readers' decision to post their accounts on-line, needs mentioning too. As a result, my corpus illustrates a kind of multi-directional communicative interaction which echoes some of the characteristics of spoken language, in particular face-to-face conversations, but which does not totally eschew some linguistic features that would marshal these forms as written language either. Consequently, in order to analyse my corpus in as rigorous a way as possible, I have compared it to two different sub-corpora: the Leisure texts, a group of texts which, together with three other groups, forms the Context-Governed sub-section of the Spoken corpus, and the Informative texts which, together with the Imaginative category, makes up the Written Informative sub-corpus. The reason for choosing these two sub-groups is the discourse type that each variety is representative of, in the case of the Leisure texts, and part of, in the case of the Written Informative sub-corpus; that is, they both include what the software classifies as *leisure* texts. Whereas the spoken half of the BNC Sampler separates the Leisure texts from 'Educational', 'Business' and 'Public/Institutional' so that each discourse type can be used to measure other corpora against them, the Informative sub-category does not permit exclusive use of the leisure part. It is important to remember that my readers post online as non-specialist critics who volunteer contributions to book-club forums or upload their opinions on the novels through blogs in their spare time. Hence, I draw upon the linguistic features of the two selected categories as the most illustrative for comparison with my own data. Doing so, I intend to shed light on the linguistic make-up of my own corpus in as a comprehensive and exhaustive way as possible.

Chick Lit Readers Corpus compared to BNC Sampler Spoken Context-Governed Leisure							
	Item	O1	%1	O2	%2	LL	
1.	Z99	1049	3.52	17906	12.36	**–2299.18**	Unmatched
2.	Z4	190	0.64	8104	5.59	**–1893.84**	Discourse Bin
3.	Q4.1	655	2.20	105	0.07	**+1745.20**	The Media: Books
4.	Q3	435	1.46	65	0.04	**+1176.27**	Language, speech and grammar
5.	T1.2	302	1.01	130	0.09	**+588.18**	Time: Momentary
7.	Q1.2	274	0.92	212	0.15	**+382.50**	Paper documents and writing
8.	E2+	266	0.89	247	0.17	**+322.65**	Like
9.	E4.1+	148	0.50	68	0.05	**+279.74**	Happy
17.	A5.2+	85	0.29	67	0.05	**+117.09**	Evaluation: True
20.	E4.1-	78	0.26	77	0.05	**+89.78**	Sad
26.	A5.1+++	62	0.21	55	0.04	**+78.06**	Evaluation: Good
27.	X2.6+	49	0.16	32	0.02	**+76.56**	Expected
28.	E1	42	0.14	21	0.01	**+76.19**	Emotional Actions, States and Processes General
31.	E2+++	24	0.08	2	0.00	**+71.52**	Like
35.	A13.3	289	0.97	797	0.55	**+61.90**	Degree: Boosters
43.	A5.2-	35	0.12	24	0.02	**+53.03**	Evaluation: False
49.	E4.2-	25	0.08	11	0.01	**+48.21**	Discontent
77.	E2-	25	0.08	24	0.02	**+29.48**	Dislike
78.	X2.1	293	0.98	985	0.68	**+28.64**	Thought, belief
89.	E3-	54	0.18	110	0.08	**+24.29**	Violent/Angry
96.	O4.2+	88	0.30	230	0.16	**+22.13**	Judgement of appearance: Beautiful
109.	A5.3-	18	0.06	20	0.01	**+18.57**	Evaluation: Inaccurate

Fig 5.1 Chick Lit Readers Corpus compared to BNC Sampler Spoken Context-Governed Leisure sub-section[34]

As I also explain in Chapter 3, because of my interest in how emotion and evaluation are verbalized in Chick Lit readers' contributions to online sites, I mainly focus on the semantic aspects of their narratives, despite the fact that Wmatrix is also capable of tagging parts of speech and further grammatical and lexical elements. The semantic tagging of the software is organized in 21 major domains, expanding into 232 semantic field tags. Due to the focus of this chapter, I aim my attention mainly at two of those 21 domains because they also correspond to the two semantic categories on which the chapter pivots: 'E = Emotional Actions, States and Processes' and 'A5 = Evaluation'.[35] Wmatrix uses the log-likelihood (LL) statistical method to compare different corpora (see Chapter 3 for more on this). In order to diminish the possibility of error or chance I have applied the highest log-likelihood cut-off value offered by the software, 15.13, which provides a 99.99th percentile degree of confidence in relation to the significance of the comparison results. Running the *Chick Lit Readers Corpus* through the software by comparing it first with the BNC Sampler Spoken Context-Governed Leisure sub-corpus throws the following results, summarized in Figure 5.1 (note that I only include 22 out of the 119 categories over the pre-set LL of 15.13 that Wmatrix comes up with).

The number in the far left column indicates the position each item occupies in relation to the entire set of categories; several aspects can be highlighted from the results in Figure 5.1. The positive or negative value of each LL score indicates respectively the over-use or under-representation in relation to the reference corpus. Line 8, for instance, clearly shows that the results of the 'E2+ = Like' category are over-represented in the *Chick Lit Readers Corpus* as the LL score of +322.65 suggests. Second, and most interestingly, some of these results do not simply underscore the over-use of some items in relation to the reference data but also the under-use of some other categories. Of the latter, the 'Z99 = Unmatched' (line 1) category groups together those items that the system is unable to recognize; unfortunately, there were quite a few expressions such as bloggers' aliases and terms typically used in computer jargon that the software could not categorize properly.[36] More interesting is the negative score for the 'Z4 category = Discourse Bin' (line 2) which stands out with an LL of –1893.84. Some examples from this category are given in Figure 5.2.

2. Z4 = Discourse Bin	LL = –1893.84
al with romance, friendship	**or whatever** as the plot Michelle
rightly coloured cover too .	**I mean** how many people would have be
stuff was called 'Git-Lit':D	**Oooh** I like that one: laugh out l
Purple Poppy 28th March 2008	**Oh** my goodness, chick-lit, git
d I let him have me . "This	**kind of** spoiled the story for me. Be
) . Pros Same characters and	**sort of** plot that Shopaholic fans hav
ve a life everlasting . Then	**wow!** This book did the trick. T

Fig 5.2

The Z4 category includes linguistic markers prototypically associated with spoken versions of language and comprises emphatic terms, fillers or hedges such as 'or whatever', 'I mean' or 'kind of'. The rather overwhelming under-use of these forms in the *Chick Lit Readers Corpus* provides food for thought regarding a possible classification of the online contributions as spoken language. Characterizing the corpus as a kind of multi-directional interactive form of communication, as I do above, does not imply that all of the typical linguistic realizations of spoken language occur in the corpus too; so, online multi-directional interactive communication should not be fully likened to prototypical spoken varieties of language. This is a really interesting result which would be worth pursing as further research but which I cannot afford to develop here. As explained below, some other linguistic markers seem to also underscore that, despite the interactivity and informality of my corpus, its various entries should not be put on a par with prototypical manifestations of spoken language such as face-to-face interaction. Suffice it to say that comparing my corpus to both the spoken and written sub-sections of the BNC Sampler should result in a more accurate assessment of the linguistic make-up of my data, but the actual nature of the corpus as either prototypically spoken or written is an aspect which still requires much more work.

One additional applicability of the software besides contrasting different corpora is bringing to the fore the key semantic domains that most characteristically feature in any given corpus. Figure 5.3 shows the top five key domains in the *Chick Lit Readers Corpus*.

<u>Top 5 key domains</u>:
Q4.1 The Media: Books
Q3 Language, speech and grammar
Z8 Pronouns
T1.2 Time: Momentary
E2+ Like

Fig 5.3 Top Key Semantic Domains

These figures can be profitably exploited on two different planes: on the one hand, these domains highlight the 'aboutness' (Philips, 1989) of the corpus and, on the other, the E2+ category validates my claims on the crucial role of emotionality and the affective aspects of reading. Because of the topic and subject matter of the data, it should come as no surprise that the top semantic category identified by the software is that of 'Q4.1 = The Media: Books', but this is further supported by the semantic units included in the next semantic tag, 'Q3 = Language, speech and grammar'. Examples from both are illustrated in Figures 5.4 and 5.5 respectively.

These concordances illustrate that when these readers become 'cyber-world critics' they do so to discuss different aspects of the novels, so the corpus's aboutness is rather coherent and focused.[37]The third top semantic category in Figure 5.3 is 'Z8 = Pronouns',[38] but the significance of this grouping might

3. Q4.1 = The Media: Books	LL = +1745.20
what you want from a romance	**novel.** On the other hand, the
vel. On the other hand, the	**love story** and sex slowed down the
rn as quickly as in a typical	**thriller.** I would rate Angels Fa
e and wait until it is out in	**paperback.** Pros Angels Fall has
cenes (stereotypical romance	**novel** material) Description N

Fig 5.4

4. Q.3 = Language, speech and grammar	LL = +1176.27
I don't think you need to have	**read** any previous Shopaholic
s skilled writing . Pros Lovely	**prose** and a gripping, roman
17; s writes with short, choppy	**sentences** that break up the na
y baby product you can imagine?	**Read** Shopaholic &; Baby to
Can takes a similar approach but	**translates** it to the world

Fig 5.5

be best viewed in relation to the two reference corpora than isolated as a top key domain. As stated above, I have employed a 15.13 LL cut-off point that means that any semantic category scoring below that value is not included in the results provided by the software. Interestingly, when the 'Z8 = Pronouns' category is compared against the Spoken Leisure texts sub-corpus, this group fails to score. Most illuminating is the statistical significance of the same semantic category when measured against the Written Informative sub-corpus as, this time, it is over-represented with a score of +2039.22. From such significant figure, it can be concluded that the *Chick Lit Readers Corpus* does use certain pronominal forms that are not found in the Written Informative sub-corpus which, besides Leisure texts, groups together data representative of 'Pure Science', 'Applied Science', 'World Affairs', and 'Arts' discourses, among some others. And yet, the 'Z8 = Pronouns' category fails to feature in the comparison with the spoken Leisure sub-section. It is clear that viewing my data in light of the two selected reference corpora does not fully explain this disparate outcome. In order to clarify things, I also ran a comparison of the *Chick Lit Readers Corpus* and the entire Spoken Context-Governed sub-corpus; that is, I incorporated 'Educational', 'Business' and 'Public/Institutional' texts to the Leisure variety. This time, the 'Z8 = Pronouns' semantic tag did feature, with a negative score of –78.56, which again highlights an under-representation when measured against prototypical forms of spoken language. As was the case above in relation to the 'Discourse Bin' category, this under-representation would appear to point at the fact that some of the prototypical linguistic realizations of spoken forms of language are absent from blogs and book-club forums. Needless to say, the results are currently inconclusive, so this particular linguistic feature is clearly in need of more research which, because of space constraints, cannot be undertaken here.

Next, the fourth key domain of the corpus also characterizes it rather tellingly for it illustrates the timestamp that structures blog and book-club forums entries. However, it is to the final key concept that I turn my attention to for it most distinctively sums up what have been the main claims of this chapter. The high score for the 'E2+ = Liking' semantic tag, on the one hand, suggests that the aboutness of my data incorporates a rather strong affective component so that Chick Lit readers do not simply write about and discuss books but also like, enjoy or love them.[39] Second, these statistics seem to endorse empirically some of the conclusions that the qualitative analysis above has already allowed me to draw, although in order to give extra countenance to these results I delve into the issue of emotionality and evaluation further below. I conclude the discussion of the aboutness of the corpus by pointing out that other semantic categories that also score highly further confirm the subject matter of the corpus, such as the 'Q1.2 = Paper documents and writing' with an LL score of +95.17 (Figure 5.6).

7. Q1.2 = Paper documents and writing	LL = +382.50
sewives Eating Bon Bons is well	**written** and thoroughly enjoyabl
Keyes? other light-hearted but	**well-written** chick-lit novel
, and will keep you turning the	**pages.** The members of
those looking for a purely fun	**read** Description The novel
nally. The reader is a hundred	**pages** into the story before
one and the accessible, breezy	**writing** that characterized her
and makes her books such quick	**reads**. The other Walsh

Fig 5.6

One of the advantages of using a computerized method for the analysis of data is the possibility of contextualization at a much larger scale than by using the investigator's intuition alone. For instance, these concordances point out two issues of the semantic category 'Q1.2 = Paper documents and writing' that merit discussion: on the one hand, the semantic units that form this group support the aboutness of the corpus, but, on the other, they also confirm that the way in which readers talk about their data involves an element of evaluation; that is, they do not simply summarize the novel's plot, for instance, but they are keen to point out that the work is 'well-written and thoroughly enjoyable', that it uses 'accessible and breezy writing', or that it is a 'quick read'. It is to all of these aspects that I now turn my attention.

Emotionality in the *Chick Lit Readers Corpus* can be most clearly identified by looking at the general semantic category identified by the software, 'E: Emotional Actions, States and Processes', as well as its various fine-grained sub-divisions. Figure 5.1 above contains 22 semantic categories (selected from those 119 with an LL score higher than 15.13 in addition to the 'Unmatched' and 'Discourse Bin' categories) of which eight belong to the 'E: Emotional Actions, States and Processes' domain. Examples that illustrate readers' emotional engagement with the novels are, thus, not hard to find (Figure 5.7).

28. E1 = Emotional Actions, States and Processes General LL = +76.19	
sters Keeper both made me cry:	**blush**: House Rules made me
really bugged me – sparking an	**emotional** reaction is important
tant for me because it makes me	**feel like** I have connected
at book, leaving you with many	**emotions**. It has been walking
was well well written and quite	**emotional**. Her 2nd book
was passionate and romantic and	**emotional** everything good chick

Fig 5.7

The high proportion of cases in which emotionality is marked serves a double purpose, as illustrated in the concordances of Figure 5.7. On the one hand, readers are capable of singling out the emotion-inducing capabilities of some novels which are 'passionate and romantic and emotional'; but, also, the linguistic encoding of emotionality sometimes indicates that readers can diagnose their own affective reaction to the books which can '[make them] cry and blush', or can 'spark an emotional reaction'. Various other sub-categories within the general 'E: Emotional Actions, States and Processes' also feature prominently, as summarized in Table 5.1:

Tag-set	LL	Semantic categories
E2+	+322.65	Like
E4.1+	+279.74	Happy
E4.1–	+89.78	Sad
E1	+76.19	Emotional Actions, States and Processes General
E2+++	+71.52	Like
E4.2–	+48.21	Discontent
E2–	+29.48	Dislike
E3–	+24.29	Violent/Angry

Table 5.1 E (Emotional Actions, States and Processes) categories[40]

The scores for these eight categories (especially if viewed as combined rather than as isolated groups) demonstrate that emotionality is far more relevant in the *Chick Lit Readers Corpus* than in the Leisure sub-corpus. The verbalization of affectivity, however, is not restricted to cases in which readers report on their sentiment in positive terms, as there are also instances in which they declare negative affectivity. For instance, some examples of how the former are verbalized are illustrated by the 'E2+ = Like' and 'E4.1+ = Happy' categories (Figures 5.8 and 5.9).

8. E2+ = Like	LL = +322.65
couldn't put these books down.	**Loved** them! "Book-club forum
And, by the way, I used to	**love** the Bridget Jones column
hat Shopaholic fans have come to	**love** Easy to read Cons Shallow
and/or depressing . In fact, I	**like** the way they do keep the
hings to different people . I'm	**enjoying** my present read becau
vant to my experience, but I do	**enjoy** some of the stories on yo

Fig 5.8

9. E4.1+ = Happy	LL = +279.74
the rest of her books, but I am	**enjoying** it to the point
6 LAUGH OUT LOUD well I hope you	**enjoy** it, though I 'm sure you
yet … Louiseog 11th May 2006 I	**love** her books but have to
I joined any book forums!), I	**loved** it and the style of wri
haracters from The Pact. Really	**loved** My Sister's Keeper and
and shopping isn't something I	**enjoy**. However, if other wom
chick-lit reader is unlikely to	**enjoy** some of these books.

Fig 5.9

The verbalization of readers' emotions in negative terms can be found in the 'E4.1 = Sad' and 'E4.2– = Discontent' groupings (Figures 5.10 and 5.11).

20. E4.1– = Sad	LL = +89.78
e novel is unevenly paced:	**sad** and slow at the beginning an
Sold Separately is sort of	**depressing** (just as the title im
t is a quick read, it is a	**downer**, so it is heavier than some
tely was, however, a very	**sad** book with only a little rede
ces readers to grapple with	**suffering** and evil–and something
ese books are gritty and/or	**depressing**. In fact, I like the way t
vember 2009 Read 19 minutes	**sad** book I found but liked it Bo

Fig 5.10

49. E4.2– = Discontent	LL = +48.21
rrative purpose, but might be	**frustrating** for some readers. Keyes
lot that were still absurd and	**frustrating** to me, but overall I
sed on very much, it was very	**disappointing**, and an example of bad c
as a struggle in itself, very	**disappointing**. I hate to not finish bo
metimes produce an ending that	**disappoints** her readers, she is pr
hing my head … I was really	**disappointed**, I had such high hopes f

Fig 5.11

The last one of these categories, in particular, underscores an aspect of emotionality that has already cropped up in my discussion of the survey responses as well as some blog entries. The discontent felt by most readers emanates from a sense of frustration at having their expectations on the novels unmet (I come back to this matter below). Finally, the 'E2– = Dislike' and 'E3– = Violent/Angry' categories are also represented in the corpus although not as prominently as those above. Concordances from the former, for instance are illustrated in Figure 5.12.

77. E2– = Dislike	LL = +29.48
characters were surprisingly	**unlikable** and under-developed.
few readers uncomfortable or	**unsympathetic**. Finishing Touches is D
ocean Cons Underdeveloped or	**unlikeable** main characters
ot find the central character	**unlikeable** or shallow and I
ular, but I think it's just	**not for me** . When I 'm in the mood

Fig 5.12

In sum, the above categories empirically support that emotionality and affectivity lie at the core of the Chick Lit reading experience. The somehow limited proof offered by the questionnaire, that only allowed me to draw tentative conclusions, is now amply backed up by the data of a much larger sample of informants.

I now move on to discuss the linguistic manifestation of evaluation quantitatively as the qualitative slant of the previous section somehow falls short of providing the convincing argument I am in search of. Figure 5.1 contains the 22 semantic domains that most significantly characterize the linguistic make-up of the corpus; of those, four belong in the 'A5 = Evaluation' category, summarized in Table 5.2.

Although these semantic units do not score as highly as emotion terms, nonetheless they still feature more recurrently than the same categories in the reference corpus as proven by their positive scores; thus, the Chick Lit

Tag-set	LL	Semantic categories
A5.2+	+117.09	Evaluation: True
A5.1+++	+78.06	Evaluation: Good
A5.2–	+53.03	Evaluation: False
A5.3–	+18.57	Evaluation: Inaccurate

Table 5.2 Evaluation categories

readers in my data engage in some evaluative enterprises not characteristically featuring in the Leisure texts. For instance, the sub-group with the highest score is 'A5.2+ = Evaluation: True' which comprises lexical items capable of appraising an event in relation to its truth status (Figure 5.13).

Unlike the double take on emotionality discussed above, whereby readers are capable of assessing the emotion-inducing potentiality of books as much as their own level of affective involvement with the works, the concordances provided by the Evaluation domain focus almost exclusively on the appraisal of several narrative, structural or stylistic aspects of the novels, albeit still

17. A5.2+ = Evaluation: True	LL = +117.09
As a narrative technique, this	**proves** quite effective, and Jo
I expect their arguments to be a	**credible** representation of a c
it happened would have much more	**credibility** than someone claim
an's Cross, it does not have a	**true** ending. It does, howeve
ppointed. Pros 'Dune Road' is a	**compelling** read, nuanced but

Fig 5.13

exercised as lay people rather than specialists. For instance, in Figure 5.13 one reader seems capable of ascertaining what an effective narrative technique is, whereas a second one judges what a 'true ending' for a novel should be. It is, therefore, the assessment of the novels that is at stake in their verbalization of evaluation. Novel appraisal also operates as far as the quality (or lack of it) of the writing is concerned, as seen in the 'A5.1+++ = Evaluation: Good' category (Figure 5.14).

26. A5.1+++ = Evaluation: Good	LL = +78.06
erious pasts. Dune Road is the	**perfect** book for a beach read,
bble is a quick and easy read,	**perfect** for an afternoon at the
sh air . I think it would be an	**absolute** best seller if only we
are fluffy and light-hearted -	**perfect** for me to read after a
it" books I've read have been	**brilliantly** and have to be re
locally. Certainly up with my	**top** 5 authors! steffee 20

Fig 5.14

The LL score of +78.06 suggests that evaluating what is deemed 'good' as far as this genre is concerned is an exercise that Chick Lit readers are not afraid to undertake fully. However, analysing what aspects of Chick Lit readers appraise in a positive light merits further attention, for which fleshing out some of the concordances in Figure 5.14 can help:

a) *Dune Road* is the *perfect* book for a beach read, though I don't mean to suggest that it is fluffy or Manolo-focused. [...] Complex characters and shifting narrative perspectives make this a [...]
b) *Queen of Babble* is a quick and easy read, *perfect* for an afternoon at the beach. Pros Likable characters and a brisk narrative pace make this a fun read. The narrative is punctuated with short pieces on fashion history and quotes about gossip. Cons Cabot doesn't break new ground.
c) I have to admit to being a chick-lit fan and I'm proud of it. I know they're not the most intellectual books on the market but I like them because they're easy to read and more often than not are fluffy and light-hearted – *perfect* for me to read after a hard and quite often stressful day at work. Don't get me wrong I like a good thriller or whatever too but I don't necessarily want anything too heavy in the evenings and want something that I don't have to [...]

One of the core issues that this chapter has highlighted on several occasions is the fact that readers expect an entertainment component in their novels, so discovering that this desired element is present makes them evaluate works positively. Informants above seem to hanker after some kind of frolicsomeness and light-heartedness in their novels because that turns these books into the 'perfect' accompaniment when the objective is reading for pleasure. Quality, therefore, is viewed in terms of entertainment value. Moreover, the comments above also highlight an issue that the questionnaire informants failed to develop in the way I had anticipated, namely the fact that the particular physical location chosen by readers to pore over their novels does, indeed, matter. That particular physical bearings and the quality of the reading experience are discussed concurrently does not seem to be coincidental either. Although two of the subjects mention a very specific location, the beach, in which the pleasure they are after can be achieved, it could be argued that it is not so much a specific place (whether it is the beach or your favourite armchair), but the fact that readers are aware that some physical environments will facilitate, and perhaps also heighten, the general quality of their reading encounter that counts. Thus, although the qualitative analysis failed to confirm my own intuitive assessment on whether the location where the reading act takes place can affect the Chick Lit reading experience, the closer inspection afforded by using computing methods appears to vindicate that hypothesis. In order to be firmly conclusive, however, this matter would require much more empirical research.

Other semantic categories illustrating the way Chick Lit readers appraise their novels are 'A5.2– = Evaluation: False' and 'A5.3– = Evaluation: Inaccurate'. The former scores rather convincingly but, on closer inspection, the results are somehow skewed by the way the word 'fiction' is likened to falsehood (Figure 5.15).

43. A5.2– = Evaluation: False	LL = +53.03
ous experts make inaccurate and	**misleading** statements about
t " is by no offence, complete	**nonsense**. Change of Heart was p
nts. This is not deep literary	**fiction**, and those who expect
rst novel, and it's a work of	**fiction** drawn from the author
he gloss and fluff of chick-lit	**fiction**, but the meat of the

Fig 5.15

Finally, the category 'A5.3– = Evaluation: Inaccurate', although still over the pre-set LL cut-off point, scores significantly lower than the rest of the tags (Figure 5.16).

109. A5.3– = Evaluation: Inaccurate	LL = + 18.57
s your loss. It would'nt be my	**fault**. Hope You Read It!!
was delighted to find out I was	**wrong**. I did not want to put An
g with that, but it would be a	**mistake** to assume that's all Fi
lection. Some, though, might	**miss** the lengthy, slow devel
ying, and I felt like Kinsella	**missed** an opportunity to deal
c as well . If my definition is	**wrong**, then what is chick-lit?

Fig 5.16

The tenets and principles that guide corpus stylistics, as described in Chapter 3, underscore that the role of the analyst is to take advantage of computerized methods without being restricted by them. This criterion has led me to look beyond the pre-established semantic categories of Emotion and Evaluation identified by Wmatrix, as several other domains which, likewise, score positively seem capable of shedding light on the way affectivity and evaluation are linguistically formulated in the corpus too. The first of these categories is 'A13.3 = Degree: Boosters'; for this category, the software clumps together linguistic units capable of amplifying the meaning of a particular semantic item to a high degree (Figure 5.17).

35. A13.3 = Degree: Boosters	LL = +61.90
and sex slowed down the mystery	**so** much that the pages didn't t
thoroughly enjoyable to read. I	**highly** recommend it, especially
vik, I did not expect it to be	**very** good. I was afraid it wou
ike made-for-TV movies that are	**ridiculously** sad and were ob
ifer Weiner, is a charming and	**deeply** satisfying read about th
icatures For a book that relies	**so** heavily on voice to keep the
t is talking about, making you	**extremely** emotional about it,
n't as her books are generally	**very** humorous with dark moments
! And this is why I dislike her	**so** vehemently. She's a woman in

Fig 5.17

The linguistic units realizing these intensifiers tend to be adverbs. In my corpus, these adverbs are awarded with the specific task of heightening the affective and evaluative content of the readers' appraisal of novels that is highly reminiscent of the way in which Conrad and Biber (2000) define the notion of adverbial marking of stance. As discussed in Section 5.4, of the three possible ways in which stance can manifest (epistemic, attitudinal and style), attitudinal stance can be recalled here to account for the meaning-boosting role of these adverbs: 'attitudinal stance, conveying the speaker's attitudes, feelings, or value judgements' (Conrad and Biber, 2000: 57). For instance, consider the following:

a) I did not expect it to be **very** good. I was afraid it would be too gimmicky or feel like a Ya-Ya Sisterhood rip off. I was delighted to find out I was wrong.

b) *Best Friends Forever*, a new novel written by bestselling author Jennifer Weiner, is a charming and **deeply** satisfying read about the unexpected reunion of two estranged best friends. Like Weiner's other novels, *Best Friends Forever* is an absorbing book that's perfect for beach reading, but it's also emotionally resonant and takes unexpected turns.

c) The content itself makes you so intrigued about the subject it is talking about, making you **extremely** emotional about it, no matter what your views are of the subject. Let alone the attachment you develop for all of the characters, making the characters seem extremely real, as if you had known them forever. With all my heart, I recommend [...]

These concordances prove that the expression of emotionality is closely intertwined with the verbalization of evaluation and they are both emphasized by the presence of adverbial markers of attitudinal stance. This allows informant 'a' to underscore the evaluative content of her opinion by stating that her expectations regarding the quality of a particular book are quite low; informant 'b' confirms that her choice of novel has turned out to be 'deeply satisfying' and 'absorbing'; and informant 'c' openly admits that the novel makes her feel 'extremely emotional'.

A second category outside the pre-set Emotion and Evaluation groupings which is likewise inclusive of aspects related to some of the questions in the survey is 'X2.6+ = Expected'. My discussion of the Emotion categories, in particular the 'E4.2– = Discontent' sub-group above, has already pointed out the strong sense of disappointment that readers tend to experience when the expectations they have built up towards the novels are not happily resolved. Some of the questionnaire responses also highlighted that readers desire to find, above all, a specific happy ending for their novels. This aspect seems to be empirically confirmed by the positive scores of the 'X2.6 = Expected' category which contains terms depicting levels of expectation (Figure 5.18).

27. X2.6+ = Expected	LL = 176.56
n't fluctuate, as one might	**expect**, particularly since some of th
d setting. Unfortunately, my	**hopes** were dashed like waves against
s market paperback made me not	**expect** much from the story. I was, h
e up to the show, so maybe my	**expectations** were too high, but I sti
r the Posh Club 's next book.	**Looking forward to** getting to it very s
y i 'm enjoying it much. I 'm	**looking forward to** finishing it so I c

Fig 5.18

Finally, the same sense of general appraisal and judgement can be illustrated by the last category to consider in relation to the Leisure texts reference corpus, 'X2.1 = Thought, belief'. The terms gathered under this label pertain to aspects of reasoning or thinking, as well as different levels of belief or scepticism. When we delve into this category, it is clear that the 'thinking' and 'reasoning' of the *Chick Lit Readers Corpus* is undertaken, to a great extent, to assess and judge different aspects of the novels. This category is, thus, also exploited in an evaluative manner (Figure 5.19).

78. X2.1 = Thought, belief	LL = +28.64
aws the reader's interest, I	**found** it unrealistic as an example of
interesting story), I don't	**think** it was too plausible from Sydne
sthand account today. While I	**think** a plot that encourages readers
sensitive male characters. My	**imagination** was pleasantly surprised a
was pleasantly surprised as I	**found** myself being there right beside
is still fun to listen to. I	**feel** that chick-lit, like lots of S

Fig 5.19

The analysis of the last three categories, 'A13.3 = Degree: Boosters', 'X2.6+ = Expected' and 'X2.1 = Thought, belief', proves that even semantic groupings which at first glance would not necessarily have suggested connections with evaluation or affectivity can be explored to investigate how Chick Lit readers verbalize their opinions on the novels.

I conclude this section with the empirical assessment of the *Chick Lit Readers Corpus* measured against the written data of the Written Informative sub-corpus.

Chick Lit Readers Corpus compared to BNC Sampler Written Informative							
	Item	O1	%1	O2	%2	LL	
1.	Z8	3754	12.59	39487	5.30	**+2039.22**	Pronouns
2.	Q4.1	655	2.20	1538	0.21	**+1714.85**	The Media: Books
3.	Q3	435	1.46	1286	0.17	**+989.77**	Language, speech and grammar
4.	T1.2	302	1.01	1014	0.14	**+629.89**	Time: Momentary
5.	E2+	266	0.89	813	0.11	**+592.04**	Like
8.	E4.1+	148	0.50	545	0.07	**+288.40**	Happy
14.	X2.1	293	0.98	2560	0.34	**+221.66**	Thought, belief
22.	Q1.2	274	0.92	3039	0.41	**+133.36**	Paper documents and writing
27.	A5.1+	205	0.69	2095	0.28	**+117.84**	Evaluation: Good
30.	A13.3	289	0.97	3552	0.48	**+110.90**	Degree: Boosters
32.	A5.2+	85	0.29	543	0.07	**+98.60**	Evaluation: True
36.	E4.1–	78	0.26	489	0.07	**+92.47**	Sad
50.	E2+++	24	0.08	57	0.01	**+62.43**	Like
66.	E4.2–	25	0.08	110	0.01	**+42.17**	Discontent
69.	A13.6	64	0.21	620	0.08	**+40.64**	Degree: Diminishers
74.	A5.2–	35	0.12	232	0.03	**+38.85**	Evaluation: False
77.	A5.1+++	62	0.21	628	0.08	**+36.25**	Evaluation: Good
101.	E6+	23	0.08	154	0.02	**+25.22**	Confident
108.	A13.5	45	0.15	509	0.07	**+20.99**	Degree: Compromisers
122.	E4.2+	26	0.09	231	0.03	**+19.15**	Content
126.	X2.6+	49	0.16	613	0.08	**+17.98**	Expected

Fig 5.20 Chick Lit Readers Corpus compared to BNC Sampler Written Informative sub-section

The figures resulting from the comparison with this sub-corpus concur, for the most part, with the over-representation of emotion and evaluation terms in the *Chick Lit Readers Corpus* so, to avoid repetition, I do not discuss in detail all the categories. Figure 5.20 includes 21 of the 134 semantic categories with an LL score over the 15.13 cut-off value presented by the software.

This new set of statistics proves that running the *Chick Lit Readers Corpus* through different reference corpora does not contravene the fact that emotionality and evaluation are core components of the way these readers spontaneously evaluate the genre on websites. For ease of reference, Tables 5.3 and 5.4 summarize the scores for the Emotion and Evaluation categories respectively:

Tag-set	LL	Semantic categories
E2+	+592.04	Like
E4.1+	+288.40	Happy
E4.1–	+92.47	Sad
E2+++	+62.43	Like
E4.2–	+42.17	Discontent
E6+	+25.22	Confident
E4.2+	+19.15	Content

Table 5.3 Emotion categories

Tag-set	LL	Semantic categories
A5.1+	+117.84	Evaluation: Good
A5.2+	+98.60	Evaluation: True
A5.2–	+38.85	Evaluation: False
A5.1+++	+36.25	Evaluation: Good

Table 5.4 Evaluation categories

The category 'E2+ = Like' is overwhelmingly more recurrent in the *Chick Lit Readers Corpus* than in the Written Informative sub-corpus, with an LL score of +592.04. The top Evaluation category is 'A5.1+ = Evaluation: Good' which also has a rather convincing LL score of +117.84. Finally, attitudinal stance is also projected via adverbials, not just in relation to the 'A13.3 = Degree: Boosters' category, as was the case above, but also with regard to the 'A13.6 = Degree: Diminishers' and the 'A13.5 = Degree: Compromisers' categories. The former grouping clusters together lexical items acting as 'downtoners that express only part of the potential force of X, or seek to imply that the force of X is limited in some way' (Archer *et al.*, 2002: 8). As the examples below illustrate (Figures 5.21 and 5.22), the semantic potentiality of these diminishers still allows for a distinctively marked sense of evaluation or appraisal.

Further occurrences of adverbs also displaying characteristics closely related to the notion of stance are those in the 'A13.5 = Degree: Compromisers' category.

69. A13.6 = Degree: Diminishers	LL = +40.64
genre, which may be why I got	a **little** impatient with some of
vealed right away, which feels	**slightly** gimmicky Some parts a
beach house, etc.), this is	**slightly** out of sync with the t
hair more if the sub-plots were	**a little** more prominent . The e
you find yourself wishing for a	**less** pigeon-holed life, restri
se, romance . At times it was	a **little** hard for me to get thr

Fig 5.21

108. A13.5 = Degree: Compromisers	LL = +20.99
lightly gimmicky Some parts are	**quite** sad, which might not
light hearted, but also can be	**quite** heart breaking and sad
rrative technique, this proves	**quite** effective, and Joy 's
y, he doesn't turn out to be	**quite** who she remembered
ound, these books are actually	**rather** enjoyable. Roberts wri
er women, they also tend to be	**quite** aspirational with roman

Fig 5.22

Whether the kind of appraisal being exercised is more related to the Emotion or the Evaluative categories does not appear to have any bearing on the fact that these stance adverbs allow readers to constantly enact their right to appraise, evaluate, judge or assess.

5.6 Conclusion

The combination of qualitative and quantitative analyses of Chick Lit readers' involvement with the genre seems to have proven quite a fruitful enterprise because the slightly tentative conclusions based on the acknowledged shortcomings of the former have been carefully accounted for by the latter. For instance, as far as the qualitative analysis is concerned, the small number of informants responding to the questionnaire has been a drawback that, initially, only allowed me to make cautious claims. A second ever-present and unavoidable quandary when research relies on the responses to surveys and questionnaires is the actual wording of the questions. Despite the best efforts of the researcher, some of the items in the survey might be deemed to be slightly leading as, after all, there is an element of error to be factored in when empiricism involves the analysis of human contributions analysed by a human investigator. On the other hand, the fact that my methodological basis has veered away from the prototypical experiment which, far too often, uses specifically targeted subjects, informants involved, one way or the other, in academia, or simply individuals 'versed' in the art of participating in questionnaires, has given extra scientific support to my responses which were produced in a more independent environment.

The second part of the chapter has tried to accommodate some of these shortcomings with some encouraging results. For instance, studying the *Chick Lit Readers Corpus* in relation to two different reference corpora strengthens the validity of the claims that can be made on the results which, as discussed, concur in singling out the linguistic manifestations of emotion and evaluation as highly recurrent semantic categories in both sets of comparisons. Chick Lit readers, therefore, enjoy the genre and openly verbalize the pleasure that reading novels offers them. They are not afraid either of judging and criticizing aspects of the novels which they may deem uncharacteristic of, or not conforming to, what they have come to expect in a prototypical Chick Lit book, as that might not generate the satisfaction they yearn for. Finally, the various results obtained from measuring my corpus against various sub-corpora have also highlighted an aspect which only the perspective afforded by this double take on my data has brought to the fore in a discernible and noticeable way: because of the high scores of the various Evaluation and Emotion categories (among others), linguistic aspects of emotionality and evaluation should be viewed as *cumulatively* enriching the unprompted contributions of Chick Lit readers rather than as isolated features. That is, because emotionality and evaluation are, first of all, realized by more than one single semantic tag as Tables 5.1, 5.2, 5.3 and 5.4 above demonstrate, but also manifest as categories not even labelled as Emotion or Evaluation by the software (for instance, 'A13.3 = Degree: Boosters', 'X2.6+ = Expected', or 'X2.1 = Thought, belief'), their actual significance emerges from their accruing presence, something that the qualitative analysis is not capable of accounting for in such an apparent way. To sum up, the combination of qualitative and quantitative approaches has corroborated the initial intuitions of the investigator via the responses to the questionnaire and the online contributions by bloggers and book-club forums members.

Chapter 6

Concluding Remarks

6.1 Chick Lit

It has been my objective in this monograph to try to account for those features that, as a whole, characterize Chick Lit as a genre for which I have taken advantage of frameworks of analysis commonly used in stylistics. The motivation that prompted this particular focus was the realization that the wealth of research that by now has devoted time and effort to define Chick Lit, to describe its main traits, and to place it in its context of production and reception, among many other concerns, has, nevertheless, eschewed looking at how those characteristics may be mirrored, encoded and embodied in the linguistic make-up of the novels. I emphasize that my work feeds from those other previous and contemporaneous non-linguistic assessments of the genre, but I also underscore that stylistics has a lot to offer as it can augment them by confirming, contesting or criticising some of that other scholarly work on the basis of conclusions drawn mainly from an analysis of the language of the novels. As the manifold approaches I implement in this book demonstrate, the way the 'language of' the genre is understood in stylistics is also rather varied, ranging from non-verbal, multimodal aspects, readerly and interpretative, or cumulative and quantitative. Because that understanding of how the language of Chick Lit can be approached is so varied, it also attempts to be encompassing; a stylistic analysis of Chick Lit is, additionally, falsifiable because it purports to be verifiable; in sum, it is open to further appraisals. The insights that can be gained from a stylistics perspective are, therefore, not at odds with other approaches, nor do stylisticians claim to analyse literature in a way that will unveil some 'hidden truths' that a non-linguistic critical appraisal would be unable to disclose. On the contrary, my intention has been to find whether the language of the genre, which is, after all, the raw material of literary discourse, can inform us in a more objective and impartial way of the significations that lie in the Chick Lit texts.

For instance, one aspect which a number of researchers working from the non-linguistic camp have rightly and frequently pointed out is the scathing anti-Chick Lit attitude of some writers and critics who use British and American newspapers as platforms for the dissemination of their disdainful comments, especially in the 2000s when the genre had gained 'sufficient airtime' and had become a force to contend with on the back of its phenomenal sales figures.

Modleski (2008) is one of those authors who highlight the pejorative way in which Chick Lit has been described. She is mainly known for her analysis of the romance but, in the second edition of *Loving with a Vengeance. Mass-Produced Fantasies for Women*, Modleski also deals with its sister genre. In her description of Chick Lit, she observes the way some critics have highlighted Chick Lit's apparent lack of literary worth:

> Not only is chick lit bad, according to Merrick [...], it is, from a woman artist's point of view, the *most* pernicious form of women's popular art: the 'chick-lit deluge has helped to obscure the literary fiction being written by some of our country's most gifted women.' Therefore, Merrick maintains that chick lit is far worse than 'rags like *Us Weekly*' or 'detective novels and superhero comics,' which she confesses to enjoying [Merrick, 2006a].
>
> (Modleski, 2008: xxiii)

The issue of literary quality in Chick Lit novels was famously raised by Bainbridge (2001) whose description of Chick Lit as 'froth' subsequently spurred countless pro- and anti-Chick Lit reactions in the culture sections of the British and American newspapers. The issue of quality, however, goes far beyond the possible calibre of the novels and extends to the saleability potential of Chick Lit, Modleski argues. In the quotation above, Modleski is, in fact, reacting to one of those articles, '*This is not Chick Lit:* What's in a title' by Elizabeth Merrick (2006a). According to Merrick, the reason why many talented women writers are simply not allowed to have the place they deserve in the literary world is because of the avalanche of Chick Lit books that has taken over the market as well as, apparently, the weekly/monthly/annual book-purchasing allowance of women all over the world, who are, therefore, forced to choose between Chick Lit and the rest of women's fiction production. Modleski concludes that:

> The reasoning here strikes me as incredible. Are we to believe that 'serious' women writers would achieve greater notice by publishers and the public if chick-lit authors were to lay down their pens? Rather than berating chick-lit authors, its female detractors – the authors and editors of literary fiction – would do well to stop blaming other women for their misfortunes in the publishing world and to redirect their anger to its true source, briefly alluded to by Merrick herself: the male-dominated literary establishment that, she notes, supports and awards the 'big boy books' that get much more 'airtime' than 'women writers of literary fiction' [Merrick, 2006a].
>
> (Modleski, 2008: xxiii)

Rather than blaming the suffocation of non-Chick Lit female writing on the seeming barrage of Chick Lit publications, Modleski suggests that the attention should be redirected at the male-dominated literary world because not just serious but also popular fiction is awarded much more credibility and kudos if written by male authors:

> And maybe the anti-chick-lit critics could distribute the blame to include the big-boy blockbusters (rooster lit) – the novels of white men like Grisham, Clancy, and others – for cluttering up the literary landscape and preventing male and female readers from turning to literary fiction to expand their minds and imaginations.
>
> (Modleski, 2008: xxiii–xxiv)

The debate concerning the literary merit of Chick Lit, especially with regard to who is voicing those comments, is also amply discussed by Knowles (2008) who, because of the perspective afforded by time, writes not so much on the actual worth, or lack of it, that characterizes Chick Lit, but on the parallel industry begotten by the amount of reactions to the genre, as illustrated by Merrick's (2006a) remarks above:

> Considering not only the nature of the commentaries produced about chick-lit, but the identities of those writing them, allows us to develop a sense of an alternative chick-lit industry, in which the nature of writing and reading, the politics of publishing and selling fiction, and the way women are represented in contemporary popular media, are debated by those who are themselves stakeholders in these debates. A meta-industry of commentary and debate has thus developed alongside the industry of chick-lit production, resulting in an ironically parasitic relationship between the two, in which the production of commentary flourishes by propagating criticism of the genre on which its existence depends.
>
> (Knowles, 2008: 219)

Knowles argues here that what started as a similar 'deluge' of critics addressing the Chick Lit debate, more often than not in an attempt to paint the genre in some unflattering light, has evolved into a parallel industry which, in Knowles's words, displays a 'parasitic relationship' with those works they are apparently trying to discredit and do away with. More interesting still, Knowles points out that this meta-industry is very often motivated by a somewhat veiled exercise of self-promotion:

> Secondly, the final line of the piece is an advertisement for the author: 'Scarlett Thomas's new novel, *Going Out,* is published by Fourth Estate', declaring something of a personal interest in the fortunes of those less commercial novels that Thomas presents as being 'obscured by piles of pastel-covered chick-lit'. [...] It also represents one of the interesting outcomes of the chick-lit debate: that those entering it as chick-lit critics are often gaining from its high-profile media presence in the same way as the novelists they criticise so fiercely. [...] In some cases self-interest is evident

> and stated, but in others it is not, and as a result a debate about the value and nature of reading takes place which is presented with only partial admission of what is at stake for some of those feeding the interest in chick-lit by the act of scorning it.
>
> (Knowles, 2008: 220)

Knowles refers here to Thomas's (2002a) 'The great chick lit conspiracy' published in *The Independent* newspaper, but a similar case is that of Elizabeth Merrick's (2006a) '*This is not Chick Lit:* What's in a title' discussed above, as both articles end up including subtle allusions to the writers' own publications, the novel *Going Out* (2002b) and the short-stories collection, *This is not Chick Lit. Original Stories by America's Best Women Writers* (2006b), respectively. According to Knowles, therefore, behind some of the dismissive attitudes professed by some critics with respect to Chick Lit can be found some kind of invested interest which should not be overlooked either. Knowles also refers to the 'proof' that some of these critics base their criticisms on, and by alluding to Thomas's article again, she states:

> Thomas's argument is evidenced from the reader perspective by quoting a single chick-lit reader to represent the masses of ashamed readers of the genre: 'Rosie, a 27-year-old receptionist, says that although she reads a lot of chick lit, she throws the books away afterwards. "It's embarrassing," she says. "You just feel ashamed of yourself after you've read something like that"' (Thomas, 2002a).
>
> (Knowles, 2008: 219)

To be fair to Thomas, in the context of a newspaper article she would not have had the space to fully develop her argument with regard to Chick Lit readership, nor was she obliged to produce an academic-style piece of research for the journalistic discourse in which she published and which did not require that kind of exactness. Having said that, I also sympathize with Knowles's criticism regarding the extrapolation of the opinion of one single reader to a mass of apparently embarrassed readers, as proven by the results of my own research in Chapter 5; the readers whose opinions I analyse would, in the main, disagree with the embarrassment felt by 'Rosie'. In fact, it is comments of this sort that suggests that the rigour of stylistics is, indeed, necessary.

A second group of comments feeding the Chick Lit debate emanates from the novelists themselves who, occasionally, also react to the disdainful way in which their works have been presented in the press. For instance, Helen Fielding famously voices her surprise at the way people reacted to *Bridget Jones's Diary*:

> It's good for women to be able to be funny about women and not to be afraid to be funny. [...] Sometimes I've had people getting their knickers in a twist about Bridget Jones being a disgrace to feminism and so on. But the point is,

> it's good to be able to represent women as they actually are in the age you're living when you're a writer.
>
> (Fielding, quoted in Jones, 2001)

One of the most widely-discussed criticisms addressed at the genre, as has been developed amply in Chapters 3 and 4, is the seemingly reactionary – for some critics, plain shameful – treatment of feminist issues in Chick Lit. Fielding, however, shields her novel from those criticisms by emphasizing that *Bridget Jones's Diary* aspires to depict women 'as they actually are in the age you're living when you're a writer'; so, in Chick Lit, contemporaneity and current-ness are promoted over some feminist demands of previous times. As Smith (2008) also discusses, a telltale sign of this focus on the present is the consumerism typically pervading most of the novels. Finally, to this favouritism for current-ness, Fielding also adds the playful and comedic presentation of the various subject matters because, she claims, 'it's good for women to be able to be funny about women and not to be afraid to be funny', an aspect upon which, perhaps, critics do not see eye-to-eye with Chick Lit authors.

Another Chick Lit author who picks up the gauntlet thrown at her by critics is Jenny Colgan (2001) who, by reacting to Bainbridge's definition of the genre as 'froth', also raises some issues that might explain the negative comments addressed at the genre. She starts her article by stating:

> No! Not Auntie Beryl! This, from the woman who taught us it was fun to fall over at literary parties! But yes, someone else, in this case Booker Bridesmaid Beryl Bainbridge, has come out and added her voice to the polemic that says young women are too: ditzy/fizzy/stupid/drunken/man-crazed to a) write books and b) read them.
>
> (Colgan, 2001)

These comments were published when the negative assessment of the genre was, perhaps, at its peak. More interestingly, Colgan defends Chick Lit as follows:

> In fact, many chick lit novels are genuinely very funny, and comedy as a genre has never had the respect it deserves, either in films or literature. As for the idea that we are writing these books simply to get a publisher's attention, well, writing a book isn't exactly like knitting a jumper: it's rather harder to do it to a pattern, as the thousands of people whose books get rejected every day – chick lit or not – can testify to. There is good stuff and bad stuff, just as there is in any other genre – Helen Fielding, in fact, has written a comedy classic as far as I am concerned.
>
> (Colgan, 2001)

Two aspects stand out from Colgan's comments above: on the one hand, the fact that Chick Lit authors seem to have purposefully decided to dress their novels in comedic garbs might have provided critics with the final ammunition they were in search of; the reason, according to Colgan, is that, as a rule, comedy is always meant to come short if compared to serious fiction. Second, Colgan does not shy away either from acknowledging that Chick Lit is by no means exempt from the odd (or, perhaps not so odd) instance of bad writing, but this should not become a justification to trash the whole genre either. Finally, Colgan also defends Chick Lit readers:

> Young women aren't stupid. We do actually know the difference between literature and popular fiction. We know the difference between foie gras and Hula Hoops, but, you know, sometimes we just want Hula Hoops. And they work better on trains.
>
> (Colgan, 2001)

The analogy established between food and fictional accounts is not accidental, as the very many references in this book to cooking, restaurants and drinks followed by the inevitable diets and weight issues can prove. But more importantly, Colgan also highlights one fundamental aspect associated with Chick Lit, its readers and femaleness in general: choice. It seems appropriate to end this monograph by summarizing that most of the many issues discussed with regard to the novels seem motivated by a desire to have alternatives and not be constricted by any pre-established, default preconception of what contemporary femaleness is about. In this monograph, for instance, I have used multimodal stylistics to suggest that the choice of pastel-shaded book jackets, despite its repetitiveness or seeming predictability, has paid off for the genre as the spill of those multimodal features over non-fictional publications using similar book cover lay-outs demonstrates. Second, a combination of socio-cognitive analyses and corpus stylistics in Chapter 3 delves into the identity of the Chick Lit protagonist and also underscores the many choices available to her in terms of her relationship to feminism, her decision to abide by the latest fashion trend, or her discussing some more serious matters in a less frivolous way. In Chapter 4, a manual analysis of a sample of novels highlights that, despite the closeness between Chick Lit and its sister genres, Chick Lit authors choose to demarcate themselves by highlighting the voice of the protagonist via thought presentation techniques or a first person perspective, for instance. Finally, the readers in my questionnaire and the online book-club forums certainly claim their right to choose Chick Lit because of the emotional satisfaction they gain from doing so, but equally opt for a negative evaluation if in their capacity as non-professional but still avid critics they deem that to be a valid option.

As I have indicated throughout, there have been some stylistic and linguistic aspects that have not been addressed fully because of lack of space; this means, nonetheless, that there is still plenty of scope for further investigation on the genre, and the fact that Chick Lit keeps evolving attests to its health and the need for further research on it.

Notes

Notes to Chapter 1

1 During an interview broadcast on British television in the GMTV programme 'Lorraine' (29 October 2009; available online at http://www.youtube.com/watch?v=_yH5qIEDHBo, date accessed 17 November 2011), Marian Keyes claims that her books are read by men as well as women. The interviewer highlights the fact that she has sold 23 million copies of her works, which they use as justification for the fact that her followers must, necessarily, be male as well as female.

2 Nielsen Bookscan provide the following lifetime sales statistics for some of the most characteristic Chick Lit authors, (see over).
I thank David Walter, Research and Development Analyst for Nielsen Bookscan, for his generosity in supplying this information.

3 Whelehan (2004: 29), however, suggests that Kathy Lette's *Foetal Attraction* (1993) is a clear precursor to *Bridget Jones's Diary*. Whelehan also points out, though, that in her 1998 novel *Altar Ego*, Lette makes one of her characters, who is portrayed as being in search of a man, read *Bridget Jones's Diary*. As a result of such a connection between reading preferences and a particular romantic predisposition, Whelehan claims that this character is depicted as lacking much intellectual potential and simply reliant on the accomplishment of a romantic liaison. Whelehan considers that, perhaps, Lette wanted to distance herself from prototypical Chick Lit writing by doing so.

4 Selinger (2007) reviews five publications on romance: Flesch (2004), Goade (2007), Lutz (2006), Lynn (2006), and Regis (2003).

5 Note that I am not implying that there are no female authors exploring any of the genres here mentioned. What I am emphasizing is the fact that these three manifestations of popular writing (sci-fi, thrillers and crime fiction) are not, virtually exclusively, as is the case for romantic fiction and Chick Lit, targeted at a female readership.

6 Providing a fair comparison of how the work of Nick Hornby differs from the rest of the authors mentioned here would require space that I do not have. Suffice it to say that Hornby's work fails to abide by some of those tenets I am arguing for as being prototypically characteristic of Chick Lit, such as the gender of writer and reader, the concerns with body and appearance issues, or the urban locations in which most of the novels take place.

ISBN	*Title*	*Author*	*RRP*	*Binding*	*Publ. Date*	*Volume*	*Value*	*ASP*
9780330367356	*Bridget Jones: The Edge of Reason*	Fielding, Helen	£7.99	Paperback	15 Jun 2000	923,713	£5,497,912.15	£5.95
9780330332774	*Bridget Jones's Diary: A Novel*	Fielding, Helen	£7.99	Paperback	20 Jun 1997	859,056	£5,315,690.49	£6.19
9780007156108	*Devil Wears Prada, The*	Weisberger, Lauren	£7.99	Paperback	6 Oct 2003	725,899	£4,082,214.24	£5.62
9780552772747	*Undomestic Goddess, The*	Kinsella, Sophie	£7.99	Paperback	2 Jan 2006	664,099	£3,309,240.40	£4.98
9780141019376	*Anybody Out There?*	Keyes, Marian	£7.99	Paperback	8 Feb 2007	661,579	£3,418,117.64	£5.17
9780552771108	*Can You Keep a Secret?*	Kinsella, Sophie	£7.99	Paperback	#######	657,496	£3,751,508.08	£5.71
9780140295993	*Other Side of the Story, The*	Keyes, Marian	£7.99	Paperback	#######	643,309	£3,350,190.46	£5.22
9780330375252	*Bridget Jones's Diary: A Novel*	Fielding, Helen	£7.99	Paperback	#######	572,373	£3,051,445.97	£5.33
9780141026756	*This Charming Man*	Keyes, Marian	£7.99	Paperback	5 Mar 2009	532,007	£2,550,438.98	£4.80
9780552999571	*Shopaholic Ties the Knot*	Kinsella, Sophie	£7.99	Paperback	1 July 2002	511,122	£3,008,450.87	£5.89
9780552772761	*Remember Me?*	Kinsella, Sophie	£7.99	Paperback	4 Dec 2008	483,042	£2,305,351.74	£4.77
9780552998871	*Secret Dreamworld of a Shopaholic, The*	Kinsella, Sophie	£7.99	Paperback	14 Sep 2000	446,790	£2,633,287.07	£5.89

Notes to Chapter 2

1 In a comment posted in *The Guardian Online* as a response to Imogen Russell Williams's (2010) 'Pink book covers make me see red', one blogger ('Blythy') states: 'please don't stop doing it. When I worked in a book store it was far easier to quickly search out the cover style if I knew the author was a chick-lit author, rather than look for authors names' (available online at http://www.guardian.co.uk/discussion/comment-permalink/6859142/, date accessed 18 November 2011). The question of recognizability is, therefore, a well established issue among readers, publishers and those working in the book distribution industry alike.

2 As explained in the introduction, I focus primarily on those novels which are closest to the original formula established in the 1990s and early 2000s, and avoid more recent offshoots such as Sistah Lit or Church Lit.

3 One word of caution is needed at this stage, though. As tends to be the case with most disciplines, there are certain discrepancies in the way scholars employ terminology. I will be highlighting the major commonalities and points of departure in the way the various frameworks that have informed my own analysis use technical terms as and when needed.

4 Some multimodal scholars would, in fact, claim that all kinds of communicative interactions could be catered for by a multimodal take on texts. Because my own analyses are primarily concerned with Chick Lit, I refrain from committing my claims so forcefully here.

5 The paradigms provided by Systemic Functional Linguistics, however, are by no means the only way of approaching multimodal texts. A second, major, branch dealing with multimodal concerns is that informed by cognitivism, as exemplarily illustrated in the work of Forceville (2002, 2006, 2007, 2009 among many other publications). Lack of space, however, prevents me from delving into how cognitivist claims can help a study of Chick Lit book covers.

6 Following Kress and van Leeuwen (1996, 2006) and van Leeuwen (2005a, 2005b, 2006) I am calling this metafunction 'ideational' rather than 'experiential', although other multimodal scholars (for example Nørgaard 2009, 2010a, 2010b, 2010c) prefer to use the latter.

7 As will be discussed below, pink is not a colour that over-features in my selected novels. It is, however, the hue most undeniably associated with the genre because of its many Western-cultural links with femininity.

8 Koller (2008) investigates the functions of the colour pink in multimodal texts. Her research is discussed in detail in relation to Chick Lit later in the chapter.

9 A word of caution in relation to the use of terminology is needed here. Bednarek (2010: 238) appropriately emphasises that the term 'corpus' refers to distinctively different notions in various disciplines. Corpus Linguistics (CL), for instance, employs the term in its technical sense:

> To refer to a collection of electronically stored semiotic data that has been designed according to specific corpus design criteria to be maximally representative of (a particular variety of) language or other semiotic systems [...]. Thus, a corpus is not equivalent to a *database*, a *collection* or *text anthology/archive* [...] as these 'are not necessarily ordered, the selection of material need not be made on linguistic criteria, and there may be no claim that the material is in any sense representative of a language, or one of its varieties' (Butler, 2004: 151).
>
> (Bednarek, 2010: 238)

Strictly speaking, therefore, my own use of the term 'corpus' is in accordance with what Bednarek calls a database, a collection or an archive, as my group of novels is not electronically ordered. However, this does not entail that my selection is unrepresentative of the genre. My corpus is endorsed by the prototypicality criteria earlier defined, according to which these novels are all written by women and for women, generally depict the lives of urbanites who seem to be mainly concerned with appearance issues, jobs and especially (heterosexual) relationships. Furthermore, these criteria have been applied to avoid the dangers of circularity: my choice of novels has not been decided by reference to the semiotic data of the book covers but on the prototypicality criteria I keep referring to. Therefore, any results and conclusions drawn from my analysis are not predetermined by my having opted for those book covers that could have, albeit artificially, backed up my claims. Following the rigour that characterizes stylistics, I am confident that the claims I make based on the semiotic information arising out of the novels are falsifiable because they are verifiable; a wider selection of novels might generate slightly different results to those shown here.

10 There are various editions of some of these novels. The bibliographical references contain the details of the actual version I am using to describe the multimodal features that characterize them. For ease of reference and clarification, visit the following pages which illustrate the versions I describe here (date accessed 18 November 2011):

Alphabet Weekends: http://www.elizabethnoblebooks.com/content/books.asp?loc=uk

Conversations with the Fat Girl: http://www.waterstones.com/waterstonesweb/products/liza+palmer/conversations+with+the+fat+girl/4872924/

Diamonds and Daisies: http://www.guardianbookshop.co.uk/BerteShopWeb/viewProduct.do?ISBN=9780340898048

Game Over: http://www.fantasticfiction.co.uk/p/adele-parks/game-over.htm

Lucy in the Sky: http://www.paigetoon.com/

My Canapé Hell: http://www.amazon.co.uk/My-Canape-Hell-Imogen-

Edwards-Jones/dp/0340767367/ref=as_li_wdgt_js_ex?&camp=2486&linkCode=wey&tag=imogeedwarjon-21&creative=8886
Pants on Fire: http://www.curtisbrown.co.uk/maggie-alderson/pants-on-fire/
The Devil Wears Prada: http://www.guardian.co.uk/books/2003/sep/28/fiction.features
The Last Year of Being Single: http://www.sarahtucker.info/Author/Author/fiction.html
The Undomestic Goddess: http://www.amazon.co.uk/Undomestic-Goddess-Sophie-Kinsella/dp/0552772747

11 Note that, to describe the various distinctive features, I am using Machin's rather than the original definitions by van Leeuwen, as the former seem particularly clear and specifically useful for my purpose here. I will, however, still resort to quoting van Leeuwen in this section when necessary.

12 I purposefully refrain from using the term 'regularity' here to avoid confusion with aspects related to the presence or absence of uniformity in letterforms, defined as *regularity* by van Leeuwen (2006: 150).

13 Van Leeuwen's analogy of typographical features to Jakobson and Halle's (1956) characterization of phonemes could be extended further. It could be argued that viewing these distinctive features in a continuum echoes the same kind of relationship described in phonology between the concept of *phoneme* and that of *allophone*; that is, once one particular value is defined in its most absolute form (in phonological terms, the phoneme), there are plenty of other realizations departing from its 'purest' version (that is, the allophones) which, nonetheless, still retain the basic components of that form. In typography, the variation from, for instance, maximum boldness to maximum lightness, still reflects the fact that weight is a compulsory component, as letters must have 'a certain weight' (van Leeuwen, 2006: 150), whatever that might be.

14 Obviously other multimodal formats such as film posters, product adverts and billboards also project meaning on flat surfaces and via typography and colour, among other semiotic resources. I would still argue that book covers, especially if marketed as popular fiction, as is the case for Chick Lit, are particularly in need of maximizing meaning projection in a comparatively small space, for which the weight of the wording component on the cover, when combined with other resources, becomes an especially effective tool.

15 In this assessment I am not including the film tie-in versions of her book covers which aim to publicize the movie by including a photograph of the leading actress and hence make use of completely different semiotic resources.

16 The original layout of the title places one word per line. Also, the quotation marks in the critical commentary appear in the original.

17 The book covers of Adele Parks's novels are especially prolific as far as variation is concerned. For a comprehensive display of how the book jackets have evolved in the various editions of her novels visit: http://www.adeleparks.com/worldwide.html (date accessed 18 November 2011).

18 Koller (2008: 396) emphasises that her findings are limited to a British context and avoids making unsubstantiated generalizations.

19 Shipley (2008) has written on the damaging effect on general women's fiction caused by the staggering presence of Chick Lit features on fictional accounts that have nothing to do with the genre, sometimes even on fiction written by male authors. Distribution technologies, therefore, are certainly reaping the success of the Chick Lit formula and promulgating certain meanings in contexts not always privy to such significations.

20 I use the British, first edition of the novel (Picador).

Notes to Chapter 3

1 The first part of the chapter mainly uses Culpeper's *Language & Characterisation. People in Plays & Other Texts* (2001), especially his work on social cognition (see also Culpeper, 2000). Culpeper's research, however, has subsequently incorporated a corpus stylistics slant (as I do too in the second part of the chapter), as illustrated in Culpeper (2002b) and (2009).

2 Cognitive stylistics, also known as cognitive poetics, is a sub-branch within stylistics which 'highlights the aspects of reading that literature consumers operate when they process literary texts. Cognitive stylistics, essentially, has emanated from the application to literature of models originally used in disciplines such as cognitive linguistics, cognitive psychology and artificial intelligence' (Nørgaard *et al.*, 2010: 7).

3 The multifarious ways in which scholars working in a variety of disciplines use the term 'corpus' has already been discussed in the previous chapter (see Chapter 2, Note 9). As explained there, Bednarek (2010: 238) highlights that there is no consensus regarding the way the term is used, as some scholars employ it to refer to a collection or database whereas others specifically construct corpora based on rigorously discerned linguistic criteria. Whereas, according to some, my own corpus containing a group of novels might be best defined as a collection or database, I maintain the former term throughout the chapter. Although the novels were not selected according to linguistic criteria, they were, nonetheless, chosen because of their prototypicality and representativeness.

4 A slight clarification is needed here. Wmatrix semantic domains are, as explained later, pre-determined and could therefore be considered top-down categories. To ensure a correct analysis some of the tagging was also checked manually as will be seen below.

5 Culpeper's (2001) work on characterization delves into a wide variety of theoretical positions which are not possible for me to account for fully in

this chapter. Whereas I take advantage of his research on social cognition and concepts such as 'prior knowledge' and 'social schemas', I leave aside other theoretical perspectives which he also incorporates into his characterization model, such as attribution theory, foregrounding theory, schema theory and pragmatics. His analysis of characterization is, thus, far more ample than could be dealt with in this chapter. See also Culpeper (2002a).

6 Schema theory has its origins in last century's Gestalt psychology and essentially describes 'the organization of knowledge as the mental structures that are schemata' (Nørgaard *et al.*, 2010: 147). Cognitive scholars using schema theory 'propose that cognition is based on a series of knowledge structures that determine how mental activity takes place. [...] schemata help us make sense of the world by allowing the retrieval of the exact type of stored information pertaining to each particular situation.' (Nørgaard *et al.*, 2010: 147–8). Social cognition scholars, therefore, borrow the term from schema theory but incorporate a social component that was not the main focus of the original proposal.

7 See also Brooks (1999) and Pelling (2000).

8 For instance, see: http://chicklitwriters.com/; http://chicklitbooks.com/; http://theadventurouswriter.com/blogwriting/chick-lit-writing-tips-how-to-write-chick-lit-for-women/; http://www.ehow.com/how_4500646_write-chick-lit-novel.html (date accessed 22 November 2011).

9 Chapter 1 discusses the famous attack by Beryl Bainbridge (2001). See also Ezard (2001) and Lessing (2001).

10 The relationship between emotion and cognition has not always been a happy one. Recently, scholars have advocated the cognitive side of emotion but these matters are amply discussed in Chapter 5, especially in connection with literary reading.

11 The semantic tags in Wmatrix are composed of the following:

an upper case letter indicating general discourse field;

a digit indicating a first subdivision of the field;

(optionally) a decimal point followed by a further digit to indicate a finer subdivision;

(optionally) one or more 'pluses' or 'minuses' to indicate a positive or negative position on a semantic scale;

(optionally) a slash followed by a second tag to indicate clear double membership of categories;

(optionally) a left square bracket followed by 'i' to indicate a semantic template (multi-word unit) (Archer *et al.*, 2002: 1).

Further annotations of the tags are as follows:

Antonymity of conceptual classifications is indicated by +/– markers on tags;

comparatives and superlatives receive double and triple +/– markers respectively;

certain words and collocational units show a clear double (and in some instances, triple) membership of categories. Such cases are dealt with using slash tags, that is, all tags are indicated and separated by a slash (e.g. anti-royal = E2–/S7.1+, accountant = I2.1/S2mf, bunker = G3/H1 K5.1/W3, Admiral = G3/M4/S2mf S7.1+/S2mf, dowry = S4/I1/A9–) (Archer *et al.*, 2002: 1).

Thanks to this classification of the various semantic domains, the semantic tag-set includes a sophisticated and fine-grained distinction of the various lexical items' signification. See also Chapter 5 for further applications of this tag-set.

12 See also McIntyre and Archer (2010) for further applications of how semantic tagging analysis can help explain stylistic features of literary texts – in their case, a corpus-based approach to the notion of mind style.

13 Needless to say, the approach I take here needs not necessarily translate into a successful methodology for all kinds of analytical objectives. It is up to the researcher to decide how to best exploit the advantages of computerized methods and focusing on semantic domains exclusively might not be sufficient in some cases. For examples of work that investigate key words see Fischer-Starcke (2009, 2010), Hoover (2009), Kirk (2009) and McIntyre (fc 2012); for a combination of keyword and key semantic domains analysis see Archer *et al.* (2009).

14 The fact that this chapter does not take on the challenge of considering the matters I highlight here from a corpus perspective does not mean that this is not an insightful task to undertake. For instance, I neglect assessing the way n-grams and collocates function, on the one hand, and cannot afford to look closely at all the various concordances either. These analyses might reveal whether the evaluative beliefs associated to attitude schemas are, if not clearly encoded in, then, indirectly projected by the linguistic make-up of the novels. Once more, space constraints prevent me from pursuing this aim. For more information on the role of n-grams and collocates see Mahlberg (2007a, 2007b).

Notes to Chapter 4

1 I address the use of the terms romance and romantic fiction below, but a more thorough description is provided in Chapter 1. For the most part, I employ these two terms synonymously in this monograph. As I go on to explain, my own analysis here has found it more advantageous to substitute both terms for the labels 'standalone' and 'series-embedded' romances; in essence, though, romances published as independent novels or as part of a series are still very much close in kind and any differences based on the linguistic analysis I implement in this chapter are discussed below.

2 See also Paizis (1998b).

3 I refrain from repeating the distinction between romances/romantic

fiction, on the one hand, and Chick Lit, on the other, that I explore fully in Chapter 1. In bullet point form, the differences can be summarized as:

- Chick Lit, for the most part, develops in urban settings.
- The Chick Lit protagonist prototypically tends to make light of the situations she is involved in so there is an element of mockery and fun which seems absent from romances.
- The packaging of Chick Lit is, by now, specifically associated with the genre, as book covers tend to make Chick Lit novels immediately recognizable.
- As developed further in this chapter, some linguistic features (first-person narration, for instance) also tend to characterize Chick Lit.

4 The six process types have been reworked from the original proposed in the 1960s, and have also been differently formulated by others (see Berry, 1975).

5 Further examples are Jeffries (2007), Kennedy (1982), Nørgaard (2003), Ryder (1999), Simpson (1993) and Wareing (1994).

6 The log-likelihood (LL) value is the statistical method used by Wmatrix (Rayson, 2009) to measure the statistical probability that the results emerging from the comparison between the target corpus and the reference corpus are not obtained by chance or error. The higher the LL value, the more likely it is that the figures are trustworthy.

7 See also Semino and Culpeper (1997); Semino *et al.* (1999); Short (1988, 2003); Short *et al.* (1996, 1999, 2002).

8 The full scale of categories for the three big groupings (Semino and Short, 2004: 30–1) is:

(NRS = Narrator's Report of Speech [= reporting clause of speech, or non-clausal equivalent])
NV = Narrator's Representation of Voice
NRSA = Narrator's Representation of Speech Acts
IS = Indirect Speech
FIS = Free Indirect Speech
DS = Direct Speech
FDS = Free Direct Speech
(NRT = Narrator's Report of Thought [= reporting clause of thought, or non-clausal equivalent])
NI = Internal Narration
NRTA = Narrator's Representation of Thought Acts
IT = Indirect Thought
FIT = Free Indirect Thought
DT = Direct Thought
FDT = Free Direct Thought
(NRW = Narrator's Report of Writing [= reporting clause of writing or non-clausal equivalent])
NW = Narrator's Representation of Writing
NRWA = Narrator's Representation of Writing Acts

IW = Indirect Writing
FIW = Free Indirect Writing
DW = Direct Writing
FDW = Free Direct Writing.
Besides these, Semino and Short also discuss further sub-categories; for more details see Semino and Short (2004), pp. 52–57.

9 NRS stands for Narrator's Report of Speech, used 'for reporting clauses of speech' (Semino and Short, 2004: 30).

10 Note 8 includes all the categories described by Semino and Short (2004). As a reminder, I only include four speech and thought categories respectively, because the rest only play minor roles.

11 NRSAp stands for Narrator's Representation of Speech Acts with Topic, that is 'cases where the narrator presents the illocutionary force of a particular utterance' with 'an indication of the topic of the utterance' (Semino and Short, 2004: 52).

12 This verbless clause could be considered an ambiguous case, halfway between FDT and FIT. Its being immersed in a paragraph characterized by the use of FIT, however, tips the balance in favour of the latter.

13 Modleski's argument here is vehemently contested by Kinsale (1992) who, by being a romance writer herself, differs as to what effect the use of third-person narration actually has:

> Tania Modleski's [...] analysis of how third person point of view works, supposing it to be merely a sort of convenience – no more than first person narrative with 'schizophrenic' asides to the audience – and claiming that 'hardly any critical distance is established between reader and [heroine],' manages not only to overlook the power of third person narrative in controlling and creating emotion and reader identification but to get everything backwards.
>
> (Kinsale, 1992: 33)

Discussing the actual effect of third-person narration in romances falls outside the remit of this chapter; Kinsale seems to have assessed Modleski's otherwise thorough discussion of romances slightly too harshly. In fact, as quoted earlier, Modleski does emphasize that the use of third-person narrators allows the reader to engage emotionally with the novels, something that Kinsale also appears to endorse. As far as Chick Lit is concerned, readers' responses to the general plot, themes and topics of the genre are amply discussed in Chapter 5.

Notes to Chapter 5

1 Needless to say, I am not claiming that every single novel published under the Chick Lit label does incorporate such an ending. As has been the case

for all my analyses, I am concentrating on the prototypical examples that do pursue a happy resolution at the end.

2 It is impossible to do full justice here to the notion of 'disportation' as elaborated by Burke (2011: 231). Very briefly summarized, Burke defines the concept as follows:

> Tension building toward a sense of release at poetic closure suggests that some kind of change takes place in a reader or some shift from one state to another. Disportation is the label I propose to define this embodied affective-cognitive event. The word has an etymological basis incorporating notions of movement and affect. [...] When I use the term disportation I am referring to a heightened emotive state that occurs in affectively-engaged individuals while reading literature.
>
> (Burke, 2011: 231–2)

The way Burke discusses this notion exemplarily combines frameworks and tools from cognitive stylistics, cognitive and neural empirical data, image schemas as described in cognitive science, as well as some philosophical considerations on what the effects of disportation might actually be. My own work on the reader-response data provided by Chick Lit consumers prioritizes stylistic and linguistic concerns rather than the cognitive-aesthetic slant that permeates the notion of disportation, so I do not engage with it further in this chapter.

3 The empirical basis of the analysis of literature is particularly well illustrated in the work carried out by members of IGEL (International Society for the Empirical Study of Literature and Media), of whose associated journal, *Scientific Study of Literature*, van Peer is the editor.

4 This heightened sense of emotional experience can be likened to Burke's notion of disportation (Burke, 2011: 231–2) discussed in Note 2.

5 Drotner (1991), for instance, also looks into the idiosyncratic characteristics of melodrama as a manifestation of popular fictional forms and its emotional implications for the reader.

6 This term is, obviously, mainly discussed in relation to Appraisal Theory as formulated by Martin and White (2005) and elaborated further below.

7 The 12 categories identified by Biber and Finnegan (1989) are the following:

> (1) affect markers (adverbs, verbs, and adjectives); (2) certainty adverbs; (3) certainty verbs; (4) certainty adjectives; (5) doubt adverbs; (6) doubt verbs; (7) doubt adjectives; (8) hedges; (9) emphatics; (10) possibility modals; (11) necessity modals; and (12) predictive modals.
>
> (Biber and Finnegan, 1989: 93)

8 The capability for weblogs to encode emotionality in modes other than the verbal is giving rise to a myriad of publications emerging out of distinct disciplines, especially as far as the use of emoticons are concerned. Unfortunately there is no space to develop this issue here; see

the following for further information on the matter: Derks *et al.* (2007), Krohn (2004) and Provine *et al.* (2007).

9 A further instance in which password protection comes into operation is when trying to access the personal details of the users. The identity of the people posting is, therefore, not disclosed to the whole cyber-community. Besides, the amount of information that is shared with the rest of the forum users is controlled by the person creating the account and the administrator can discontinue threads and posts if these somehow breach basic netiquette norms.

10 In Chapter 2, Note 9, I clarify my own use of the term 'corpus' which according to Bednarek (2010: 238) should be more appropriately termed 'database', 'collection' or 'archive'. I maintain the former label as my data have been appropriately selected according to a set of criteria; although, admittedly, these are not strictly linguistic in nature they are, nonetheless, representative of the discourse type I analyse here.

11 When data collection took place I was based in Spain, as the email address where informants sent their responses indicated.

12 Although all my informants described themselves as female, there is obviously no way of verifying whether this piece of information is actually true. The conclusions I draw are based on the answers given but, unlike the case of face-to-face experiments in which gender is actually verifiable, they might be erroneous or misrepresented if some informants were deliberately deceitful.

13 Having a smaller than desired number of informants is a problem that is often encountered in the humanities. For instance, although dealing with different matters, Koller (2008) also echoes the sample-size issue: 'Given the small sampling basis, the survey is intended as a pilot investigation that can identify possible tendencies to be tested in a larger-scale study' (Koller, 2008: 401). Similarly here, the claims I make are intended to highlight tendencies and general trends rather than categorically discriminate what the Chick Lit reading experience entails for all readers, as that might be judged an enterprise deemed to fail from the start.

14 As has been the case with some of the manifold strands of emotion research mentioned in this chapter, there is no space here to do justice to the way in which the 'fiction paradox' is discussed by Yanal (1999). He reformulates various thought theories that try to account for the fiction paradox as what he calls *Thought Theory T* which can be summarized as follows:

Thought theory must show how thoughts that are not existentially grounded and that occur along with disbelief can generate emotion. [...]

> *Thought Theory T.* Emotion toward what the emoter takes to be a fiction is brought on by the emoter's focused involvement with vivid and detailed thoughts that may be propositional or nonpropositional. The emoter's disbelief in any real reference of the thoughts is rendered

> relatively inactive. The emotion thus produced is real and typically has the character of being richly generated yet unconsummated.
>
> (Yanal, 1999: 102)

Thought theories work under the premise that thoughts not relying on the actual existence of their referent and that occur alongside the emoter's disbelief are still capable of generating emotion, so those that propound these theories accept the affective side of fiction. Yanal's *Thought Theory T*, however, goes a step further and points at the essential function that the emoter's involvement plays in this process. It is this involvement with the vivid and detailed thoughts generated during the reading process that renders the emoter's disbelief in what he is thinking inactive, hence bringing on rich emotions.

15 Question 1 is formulated as follows:

> Do you think you could provide a definition of what you consider to be a Chick Lit novel?
>
> a. Yes/b. No.
>
> If you answered [a] above, could you elaborate below.

16 The meaning of the label 'women's fiction' is not easy to pin down, nor do all critics use it to refer to the same type of writing. Whereas some authors might employ it as a kind of umbrella term to encompass all forms of writing by women, others prefer to restrict the sense in which the label is employed to specifically describe literary fiction and to distinguish it categorically from the forms of popular writing that Chick Lit is normally associated with. For clarification's sake, I use it in the second sense because the responses in the questionnaire seem to underscore that the separation between highbrow literature and Chick Lit is crucial to an understanding of the latter. As a result of this differing conceptualization of high and popular forms of literature, my informants set clear boundaries regarding *what* constitutes Chick Lit, which is, hence, not treated as a fuzzy or vague term but as a label that specifically embodies certain stylistic and other traits that readers are not only able to recognize but that they also expect and look for.

17 Question 2:

> Approximately how many Chick Lit novels have you read so far?
>
> a. 0–5 b. 5–10 c. 10–15 d. 15–20 e. 20–25 f. more than 25

18 Question 8:

> Were any specific memories triggered by this reading experience?
>
> a. Yes b. No
>
> If you have answered 'yes' to the above question, could you please add some detail. For example, did these memories pertain to a specific time in your life or a specific event, or to specific people or a specific place/location, or even a blend of some or all of these? Please elaborate below.

19 Question 9:

> Once you have finished reading a much-enjoyed novel, do you ever go back and re-read some pages or paragraphs?

a. Yes b. No

If you answered [a], why do you think you do this?

20 Question 12:

When you are reading Chick Lit novels, does it matter to you, and to the quality of your subsequent reading experience, where you actually read them, i.e. where you decided to physically put/position your body for the reading process?

a. Yes b. No

If you have answered [a], could you please say something about the physical nature of these locations here. Do you think there is a difference between the location you choose to read Chick Lit fiction and other types of text (poetry, newspapers, literary fiction, magazines, etc.)?

21 Question 14:

Do you think the way in which a novel is written, i.e. the style (e.g. the lexical choices, syntax, punctuation, use of metaphor, etc.) can affect the way you read?

a. Yes b. No

If you chose answer [a] could you please explain how the actual style of the novel affects how you read.

22 Question 16:

Here I would very much appreciate your full collaboration as ideally you should provide an extract from a Chick Lit novel you have particularly enjoyed. If you could type it up here, that would be great. Otherwise you can just tell me the name of the author, title of the novel and exact pages you are referring to. I realise that I cannot make large scale demands on your time so apologies in advance, but having the extract here would greatly help.

[a] Did any particular words in this piece emote you? Please list them and try to explain why.

[b] Were there any particular linguistic units larger than a word that emoted you? It doesn't matter if you are not an expert on linguistic terminology; just list those units containing more than one word here and try to explain why you felt touched by them.

[c] Did any particular typological aspects do anything to you emotionally? For instance, were you particularly touched by the way punctuation or the general layout of pages was used?

[d] Did this piece do anything to you bodily?

a. Yes b. No

If you answered, 'yes' could you please expand below.

23 Although I previously divide the remaining questions in two groups, those dealing directly with emotionality and those raising other issues, I am keeping the discussion of item 15 in the latter group. This question bridges the two groups, as it asks readers to consider whether linguistic components can act as emotion projectors.

24 Question 4:

Have you got any expectations as to what you would want to find in a typical Chick novel?

a. Yes b. No

If you chose [a] above could you please specify what it is you expect to find. Do you feel disappointed/cheated/dissatisfied/frustrated/not really bothered/all of the above, if you can't recognize those elements you would expect in a Chick Lit novel? Please elaborate and add as many details as you need to describe both the elements you look for in these works and your emotional reaction if they are not there.

25 Question 10:

Is there a specific way in which you expect these novels to end?

a. Yes b. No

If the answer to the above is 'yes', could you please expand on what those expectations entail: resolution of any sort, positive outcome for the heroine, punishment for the villain, etc.

26 The way my respondent differentiates but does not negatively discriminate between high and low literature is reminiscent of what some literary writers have also commented on with regard to popular forms. Although already quoted in Chapter 1, Jeanette Winterson's words merit reprising here:

> 'I am unashamedly high art,' she said. 'There is such a thing and we need it in our lives. But I also like entertainment. Chick lit? No problem. *Bridget Jones's Diary*? Love it, just great. I feel completely easy with all that.'
>
> (Winterson, quoted in Allen, 2001)

Chick Lit readership seems to be highlighting a similar acquiescence in the sense that enjoyment of popular forms for Chick Lit consumers does not involve some kind of exclusivity with regard to their possible interest in other forms, including literary fiction. Furthermore, it is the acknowledgement that each form fulfils a distinct function that seems of relevance here.

27 Question 13:

Prior to starting to read a novel, do you think that your mood has ever affected the actual reading event itself?

a. Yes b. No

If you chose answer [a] could you please elaborate somewhat.

28 Question 5:

Do you think that certain themes that may appear throughout a novel can affect your emotional mood during the actual reading process itself?

a. Yes b. No

If you have answered [a] could you please expand on this below. For instance, which themes are you most affected by?

29 Question 7:

Try to recall the moment when you had just finished reading a/some much-enjoyed novel/s. Can you remember the feeling you had at that moment? If so, can you say something about that feeling? You can name the novel/novels if you want to and elaborate on how each particular book made you feel; otherwise you can simply say something about your impressions, ideas or general sentiment after finishing your Chick Lit books.

30 Question 11:

Can you explain what mood you find yourself in after finishing a Chick Lit novel? Does your mood tend to vary depending on the novel itself? Or are you disappointed if you don't end up being emoted in the way you expected to be? Please expand below.

31 Some further comments from bloggers regarding their emotional reaction to the novels are the following:

Most of the time when i've [sic] just finished a book I'm left thinking – wow I really enjoyed that, I think I'll read another of hers, only a few times I've been left thinking – wow that was good BUT I really hope there's going to be a follow up book because it's left the end wide open and not quite finished. [...]

I don't think I've been disappointed in a book before because if they're not going anywhere then I just stop reading it and move onto a better one.

(Kaz80, http://bookclubforum.co.uk/forum/ [posted 20/04/09])

I always find I am in a good mood when i [sic] have finished a good chick lit book. Like the others say I like it to be finished and be sure how the characters lives are going to pan out. :smile2: Recently read 10 reasons not to fall in love by Linda Green and found i [sic] really got into the book and connected with the characters so well I was really happy with how it ended and felt really pleased for the characters and the way everything turned out :mrgreen:

(cathyd, http://bookclubforum.co.uk/forum/ [posted 23/04/09])

32 Some clarification is needed here. Note that Parkinson is not discussing socio-emotional aspects as they pertain to cyber-communication in the way that I have done. The term 'on-line', therefore, is not to be understood as referring to internet exchanges.

33 In fact, as explained in Chapter 3, this is not the only option offered by Wmatrix. In theory it is possible to input any reference corpus for comparison, although Wmatrix comes pre-loaded with the BNC Sampler and its various sub-corpora which I take advantage of.

34 Space constraints prevent me from discussing all the data in detail. For instance, columns 01 and 02 indicate the observed frequency in the target and reference corpora respectively.

35 The semantic annotation provided by Wmatrix develops into

much more fine-grained subdivisions: 'A5.1 Evaluation: Good/bad', 'A5.2 Evaluation: True/false', 'A5.3 Evaluation: Accuracy' and 'A5.4 Evaluation: Authenticity'; in turn, the 'E category' branches out into the following: 'E1 General', 'E2 Liking', 'E3 Calm/Violent/Angry', 'E4 Happy/sad', 'E4.1 Happy/sad: Happy', 'E4.2 Happy/sad: Contentment', 'E5 Fear/bravery/shock', and 'E6 Worry, concern, confident'. Some of these are further referred to because they are statistically significant in my corpus.

36 Wmatrix does, in fact, allow the addition of terms to the pre-loaded dictionary for comparison. Most of the unmatched items, however, were not pertinent for the analysis of emotion or evaluation (bloggers' names and aliases, for instance) so I refrained from doing so.

37 Myers (2009: 339), for instance, describes how multifarious in nature the data collected in traditional face-to-face book-clubs can be, which might, consequently, present some challenges for the researcher interested in investigating readers' opinions on the linguistic or stylistic aspects of the books:

> People in book groups talk about all sorts of things: what their expectations were, how they liked the characters, the plausibility, or not, of plot events, the mood they were in after reading it, the book's length, font size, cover, and price. [...]
>
> Readers may not, without considerable prompting, talk to each other about foregrounding, reported speech, point of view, or metaphor. That is presumably why researchers who want to study responses to these stylistic features usually set up an experiment.
>
> (Myers, 2009: 339)

For the most part, my informants also abide by the affective and evaluative book-analysis formula described by Myers above, so they tend to skip professional stylistic analyses of novels too.

38 The semantic classification of pronouns includes the following forms:

> Pronouns (standard and colloquial):
>
> Prototypical examples: anything, ego (mfn), he (m), hers (f), it, its, itself, my, meself, one, ones, owt, summat.
>
> All that sort of jazz, anything at all, goodness knows what, such and such, this that and the other, whatever you like, what do you call it.
>
> (Archer *et al.*, 2002: 36)

39 The top five words in this domain are: *like, love, enjoyed, loved* and *enjoyed.*

40 The presence of extra pluses indicates further degrees within any specific semantic domain – in this case, 'liking'.

Appendix 1

Typographic Components of Chick Lit Book Covers

TYPOGRAPHIC FEATURES								
Novel	Weight	Expansion	Slope	Curvature	Connectivity	Orientation	Regularity	Flourishes
Alphabet Weekends. Love Lessons from A-Z	Relative weight. Not the heaviest	Spread out. Title spreads from edge to edge	Script-like. Reminiscent of calligraphy handwriting	Rounded ascenders and descenders: loops	Emphasized	Oriented towards the horizontal	Irregular with respect to the baseline: title is slightly wavy	Loops and knot-shaped flourishes on top of 't'. Long tails for 'a' and 'w'. Sans-serif Flat surface
Conversations with the Fat Girl	The lightest font in the corpus	Narrow letters but not the most economical	Heavily slanted, reminiscent of handwriting	Rounded ascenders and descenders: flicks	Letters connected in title	Horizontality emphasized ⇒ fatness	Irregular with respect to the baseline: it goes slightly upwards	Sans-serif Flat surface

Diamonds and Daisies	Heavy weight; bold font	Pretty spread out	Not particularly upright although not as markedly slanted as others	Particularly rounded: entasis	Not connected; because of curvature letters are particularly close to one another ⇒ entasis	The most horizontality-oriented	Irregular: a) baseline b) size c) capital v. non-capitals	Embossing on title Slab serifs at top and bottom of letters. Engraved-style golden stars ⇒ gold foil stamping Glossy letters for title and author's name. Full of flourishes on the back cover Especially capricious Exaggerated curls on letters
Game Over	Heavy font	Particularly spread out. Title virtually takes over the whole page	Not particularly slanted. Upright typefaces	The most angular	Not connected, nearly self-contained	Elongated	Irregular: letters do not rest on baseline	Very pronounced hairline serifs Embossing

Lucy in the Sky	Heavy, bold font	Appears spread out because of marked curvature. Letters in title itself not as spread out as others	Extremely sloping	Especially curvy: rounded ascenders and descenders, loops and flicks especially prominent. Ascenders and descenders help expansion	All letters connected, including name of the author	Flattened, rather than elongated	Irregularity created by combination of capital/ non-capital letters	Embossed typefaces. Raised lettering. The cover is not smooth to the touch
My Canapé Hell	Heavy weight	The most economical; plenty of space not taken up by letterforms	Upright typeface. Closest to printing	Roundness not a concern here although not excessively angular	Not connected, least like handwriting	Not particularly flattened or elongated	The most regular	Sans serif. Foil stamping on title and author's name. Embossed images of stars, glasses and blinis Engraving on title

Pants on Fire	Heaviest font in the corpus	Title spread out	Not particularly sloping	Angularity emphasized: corners of letters stretched out to mark angles	Not connected, especially separated	No over-exaggerated, significant ascenders or descenders	Rather irregular: a) different size b) different colour c) different orientation: left and right. Title and author's name not fully within the baseline	Sans serif. Flourishes: heart-shaped dot on letter 'i'; very thick lettering with stitch-like design ⇒ pants. Raised full colour: glossy finish for title and author's name on dull cover Embossing
The Devil Wears Prada	Bold font	Title spread out: it virtually goes from side to side	Sloping and script-like	Extremely curved full of ascenders and descenders that curl up as if it was Satan's tail	Connected letters	Long ascenders and descenders so verticality emphasized; some of them are rather thick	Pretty irregular, mainly because of flourishes	Main flourishes: horn-like marks on the initial 'd' and Satan's tail-like descender of final 'a' Embossing

The Last Year of Being Single	Bold font for the title in relation to name of author but lightest font (on a par with CFG) in the corpus	More condensed than other fonts	Particularly sloping ⇒ handwriting style	Curved style: Descender flicks especially prominent	Letters connected: most like handwriting	Flicks and loops being thin make it look more elongated	Different sizes: irregular	Sans serif Exaggerated dot on the ‘i’; looks like an orthographic mark for stress Flat surface
The Undomestic Goddess	Irregularity: from maximally heavy to slightly less heavy	First two words more condensed. Third word in the title far more spread out	Sloping	Curved style: curved hooks at the end of ascenders especially prominent. Descenders not to prominent	Letters not touching, but they have hooked feet and protruding loops which extend towards the next letter	Stays mainly within the base line	Different font sizes and different weight: irregular	Pear-shaped curls at end of ‘s’ and ‘G’; inner curl inside ‘o’. Wedged-shaped serifs. Embossing

Appendix 2

Colour Use in Chick Lit Book Covers

Novels	Brightness/ Value	Saturation	Purity	Modulation	Differentiation	Luminosity	Hue
Alphabet Weekends. Love Lessons from A-Z	Light pink ⇒ Middle of the scale	Diluted – light pink ⇒ pastel	Low purity	Flat background	Polychromatic	N/A	Pink: Blue and red
Conversations with the Fat Girl	Light blue ⇒ Closer to white	Diluted ⇒ pastel	Low purity Not a pure colour	Flat background	Polychromatic	N/A	Blue
Diamonds and Daisies	Light purple: lilac⇒ Middle of the scale	Diluted ⇒ pastel	Low purity Not a pure colour	Flat colours	Polychromatic	N/A	Lilac, pale violet
Game Over	Dark/Bright red ⇒ further away from white	Saturated	The purest of reds	Flat background	Polychromatic	N/A	Red
Lucy in the Sky	Dark blue, black and dark pink ⇒ darker	Diluted	Low purity Not a pure colour	The most modulated	Polychromatic	N/A	Blue, pink (blue and pink)
My Canapé Hell	Dark pink	Diluted background	Low purity Not a pure colour	Flat background	Polychromatic	N/A	Pink: White and red

Pants on Fire	Light purple/ lilac	Diluted ⇒ pastel	Low purity Not a pure colour	Flat colours	Polychromatic	N/A	Lilac (light violet)
The Devil Wears Prada	Dark	Diluted	Low purity	Blocks of flat colours: modulation effect because of combination	Polychromatic	N/A	Red
The Last Year of Being Single	Off-white, closest to white	Diluted ⇒ most diluted, pastel	Low purity	Flat colours	Polychromatic	N/A	Off-White
The Undomestic Goddess	Bright yellow	Saturated	Purer than the rest	Flat background	Polychromatic	N/A	Yellow: Mustard

Appendix 3: Homodiegetic and Heterodiegetic Narrators

Homodiegetic narrators

Adams, J. (2003), *Cool for Cats.* London: Black Swan.

Alderson, M. (2000), *Pants on Fire.* London: Penguin.

Bank, M. (1999), *The Girls' Guide to Hunting and Fishing.* London: Penguin.

Colgan, J. (2000), *Talking to Addison.* London: HarperCollins.

Dunne, H. (2001), *Trixie Truder.* London: Orion.

Fielding, H. (1996), *Bridget Jones's Diary.* London: Picador.

Fielding, H. (1999), *Bridget Jones: The Edge of Reason.* London: Picador.

Green, J. (2004), *The Other Woman.* London: Penguin Books.

Kauffman, J. and Mack, K. (2006), *Book Lover.* London and New York: Harper Perennial.

Kean, L. (2005), *The Perfect 10.* London: HarperCollins Publishers.

Keyes, M. (2002), *Angels.* London: Penguin.

Kinsella, S. (2000), *The Secret Dreamworld of a Shopaholic.* London: Black Swan.

Kinsella, S. (2001), *Shopaholic Abroad.* London: Black Swan.

Kinsella, S. (2002), *Shopaholic Ties the Knot.* London: Black Swan.

Kinsella, S. (2003), *Can you Keep a Secret?* London: Black Swan.

Kinsella, S. (2004), *Shopaholic & Sister.* London: Black Swan.

Kinsella, S. (2005), *The Undomestic Goddess.* London: Black Swan.

Kraus, N and McLaughlin, E. (2005), *Citizen Girl.* London: Penguin Books.

MacKesy, S. (1999), *TheTemp.* London: Arrow Books.

Maxted, A. (2001), *Running in Heels.* London: Arrow Books.

McCrossan, L. (2001), *Serve Cool.* London: Warner Books.

Olson, S. (2000), *Welcome to my Planet.* London: Penguin.

Palmer, L. (2005), *Conversations with the Fat Girl.* London: Hodder.

Parks, A. (2001), *Game Over.* London: Penguin.

Parks, A. (2002), *Larger than Life.* London: Penguin.

Sykes, P. (2004), *Bergdorf Blondes.* London: Penguin Books.

Toon, P. (2007), *Lucy in the Sky.* London and Sydney: Pocket Books.

Walker, F. (2000), *Lucy Talk.* London: Hodder & Stoughton.

Weisberger, L. (2003), *The Devil Wears Prada.* London: HarperCollins.

Weisberger, L. (2005), *Everyone Worth Knowing.* London: HarperCollins.

Heterodiegetic narrators

Colgan, J. (2006), *West End Girls.* London: Sphere.
Edwards Jones, I. (2003), *The Wendy House.* London: Hodder and Stoughton.
Fallon, J. (2007), *Getting rid of Matthew.* London: Penguin Books.
Green, J. (2005), *Life Swap.* London: Penguin Books.
Hill, M. (2005), *Never Say Never.* London: Arrow Books.
Holt, D. (2007), *Annie May's Black Book.* London and New York: Pocket Books.
Keyes, M. (1999), *Last Chance Saloon.* London: Penguin.
Lees, A. (2000), *Selling out.* London: Pan Books.
Strachan, B. (2006), *Diamonds and Daisies.* London: Hodder.
Vandever, J. (2005), *The Brontë Project.* London and New York: Pocket Books.

Bibliography

Works Cited: Chick Lit Fiction and Non-Fiction

* Works are not Chick Lit.
† Series-embedded romance.
‡ Standalone romance.

Adams, J. (2003), *Cool for Cats.* London: Black Swan.
Alderson, M. (2000), *Pants on Fire.* London: Penguin.
*Austen, J. ([1813] 2004), *Pride and Prejudice.* Oxford: O.U.P.
Bank, M. (1999), *The Girls' Guide to Hunting and Fishing.* London: Penguin.
†Blake, A. (2007), *Billionaire on her Doorstep.* Richmond, Surrey: Mills & Boon.
*Brontë's Ch. ([1847] 2006), *Jane Eyre.* London: Penguin Classics.
Clark, M. and Aronson, R. (2006), *The Skinny: How to Fit into your Little Black Dress Forever.* New York: Meredith Corporation.
†Cohen, J. (2007), *All Work and No Play.* Richmond, Surrey: Mills & Boon.
Coleman, A. (2008), *The Bright Side.* Dublin: Poolbeg Press.
Colgan, J. (1999), *Amanda's Wedding.* London: Harper Collins.
—(2000), *Talking to Addison.* London: HarperCollins.
—(2006), *West End Girls.* London: Sphere
Dunn, M. (2008), *Ex-Girlfriends United.* London and New York: Pocket Books.
Dunne, H. (2001), *Trixie Trader.* London: Orion.
Dyer, Ch. (2003), *Wanderlust. A Novel of Sex and Sensibility.* London and New York: Plume.
—(2005), *The Loves of a D-Girl. A Novel of Sex, Lies and Script Development.* London and New York: Plume.
Edwards-Jones, I. (2000), *My Canapé Hell.* London: Flame.
—(2003), *The Wendy House.* London: Hodder and Stoughton.
Fallon, J. (2007), *Getting rid of Matthew.* London: Penguin Books.
Fielding, H. (1996), *Bridget Jones's Diary.* London: Picador.
—(1999), *Bridget Jones: The Edge of Reason.* London: Picador.
*Foster, E. M. ([1908] 2006), *A Room with a View.* London: Penguin Classics.
Freedman, R. and Barnouin, K. (2005), *Skinny Bitch. A No-Nonsense, Tough-Love Guide for Savvy Girls who Want to Stop Eating Crap and Start Looking Fabulous!.* Philadelphia: Running Press.
Gray, K. (2009), *The Denim Diet: 16 Simple Habits to Get you into your Dream Pair of Jeans.* Novato, California: New World Library.
Green, J. (2004), *The Other Woman.* London: Penguin Books.

—(2005), *Life Swap.* London: Penguin Books.
Gulab, R. (2005), *Girl Alone.* New Delhi: Penguin Books.
Hill, C. (2010), *Shoo, Jimmy Choo!: The Modern Girl's Guide to Spending less and Saving more.* New York: Sterling Publishing.
Hill, M. (2005), *Never Say Never.* London: Arrow Books.
Hirsman, S. (2010), *Does this Make my Assets Look Fat?: A Woman's Guide to Finding Financial Empowerment and Success.* New York: St. Martin's Press.
Holt, D. (2007), *Annie May's Black Book.* London and New York: Pocket Books.
Ingemarsson, K. (2004), *Small Yellow Lemons/ Små Citroner Gula.* Sverige: Forum
*Jong, E. ([1973] 1998), *Fear of Flying.* London: Vintage.
Kauffman, J. and Mack, K. (2006), *Book Lover.* London and New York: Harper Perennial.
Kaushal, S. (2004), *Piece of Cake.* New Delhi: Penguin.
Kean, L. (2005), *The Perfect 10.* London: HarperCollins Publishers.
Keto, J. (2008), *Don't Get Caught with your Skirt Down: A Practical Girl's Recession Guide.* New York: Atria Paperback.
Keyes, M. (1996), *Watermelon.* London: Poolbeg Press.
—(1997), *Lucy Sullivan is Getting Married.* London: William Heinemann.
—(1999), *Last Chance Saloon.* London: Penguin.
—(2002), *Angels.* London: Penguin.
—(2004), *The Other Side of the Story.* London: Michael Joseph
—(2006), *Anybody Out There?* London: Penguin.
Kinsella, S. (2000), *The Secret Dreamworld of a Shopaholic.* London: Black Swan.
—(2001), *Shopaholic Abroad.* London: Black Swan.
—(2002), *Shopaholic Ties the Knot.* London: Black Swan.
—(2003), *Can you Keep a Secret?* London: Black Swan.
—(2004), *Shopaholic & Sister.* London: Black Swan.
—(2005), *The Undomestic Goddess.* London: Black Swan.
Kraus, N. and McLaughlin, E. (2005), *Citizen Girl.* London: Penguin Books.
Lees, A. (2000), *Selling out.* London: Pan Books.
Lette, K. (1993), *Foetal Attraction.* London: Picador.
—(1998), *Altar Ego.* London: Picador.
MacKesy, S. (1999), *TheTemp.* London: Arrow books.
Mason, M. (2004), *The Catch.* London: Time Warner Paperbacks.
Maxted, A. (2001), *Running in Heels.* London: Arrow books.
McCrossan, L. (2001), *Serve Cool.* London: Warner books.
*Merrick, E. ed. (2006b), *This is not Chick Lit. Original Stories by America's Best Women Writers.* New York: Random House Trade.
Metelitsa, K. (2008), *Diary of Louise Lozhkin/Dnevnik Luizy Lozhkinoy.* Moscow: Eterna.
Noble, E. (2005), *Alphabet Weekends.* London: Hodder and Stoughton.
Olson, S. (2000), *Welcome to my Planet.* London: Penguin.
Olszewski, M. (2010), *Live it, Love it, Earn it.* New York: Portfolio.
Palmer, L. (2005), *Conversations with the Fat Girl.* London: Hodder.
Parks, A. (2001), *Game Over.* London: Penguin.

—(2002), *Larger than Life.* London: Penguin.
Plaisted, C. (2005), *10 Things to Do before you're 16.* New York: Simon & Schuster Children's.
*Plath, S. ([1963] 2005), *The Bell Jar.* London: Faber and Faber.
*Richardson, S. ([1740] 2001), *Pamela. Or Virtue Rewarded.* Oxford: Oxford University Press.
‡Roberts, N. (1991), *Suzanna's Surrender.* Richmond, Surrey: Silhouette Books.
—‡(1996), *Megan's Mate.* Richmond, Surrey: Silhouette Books.
Sanchez, P. (2001), *Girlfriends.* New York: Kensington Books.
Strachan, B. (2006), *Diamonds and Daisies.* London: Hodder.
Sykes, P. (2004), *Bergdorf Blondes.* London: Penguin Books.
Thakor, M. and Kedar, S. (2007), *On my Own Two Feet: A Modern Girl's Guide to Personal Finance.* Avon, USA: Adams Media.
*Thomas, S. (2002b), *Going Out.* London: Fourth Estate.
Toon, P. (2007), *Lucy in the Sky.* London and Sydney: Pocket Books.
Tuccillo, L. (2008), *Como Ser Solteira.* Lisbon: Record.
Tucker, S. (2003), *The Last Year of Being Single.* Richmond, Surrey: Mira Books.
Vandever, J. (2005), *The Brontë Project.* London and New York: Pocket Books.
Walker, F. (2000), *Lucy Talk.* London: Hodder & Stoughton.
Weisberger, L. (2003), *The Devil Wears Prada.* London: HarperCollins.
—(2005), *Everyone Worth Knowing.* London: HarperCollins.
*Wollstonecraft, M. ([1790]1994), *Political Writings.* (ed. Jane Todd). Oxford: Oxford University Press.

References

Adolphs, S. (2006), *Introducing Electronic Text Analysis: A Practical Guide for Language and Literary Studies.* London: Routledge.
Allen, R. (2001), 'Give "chick-lit" the flick!'. *London Evening Standard,* 23 August. http://www.thisislondon.co.uk/showbiz/article-899914-give-chick-lit-the-flick.do (date accessed 19 March 2011).
Archer, D., Culpeper, J. and Rayson, P. (2009), 'Love – "a familiar or a devil?" An exploration of key domains in Shakespeare's comedies and tragedies', in D. Archer ed., *What's in a Word-List? Investigating Word Frequency and Keyword Extraction.* Farnham, Surrey: Ashgate; pp. 137–57.
Archer, D., Wilson, A. and Rayson, P. (2002), 'Introduction to the USAS category system'. http://ucrel.lancs.ac.uk/usas/ (date accessed 19 May 2009).
Bainbridge, B. (2001), 'Bainbridge denounces chick-lit as "froth"'. *Guardian Online,* 23 August. http://www.guardian.co.uk/books/2001/aug/23/bookerprize2001.bookerprize?INTCMP=SRCH (date accessed 21 January 2011).
Baldry, A. and Thibault, P. (2005), *Multimodal Transcription and Text Analysis.* London: Equinox.
Barney, T. (2008), 'Literary evaluation and poetic form: Poetic form and creative tension', in W. van Peer ed., *The Quality of Literature: Linguistic Studies*

in Literary Evaluation. Amsterdam and Philadelphia: John Benjamins; pp. 71–81.

Bartsch, S., Eckart, R., Holtz, M. and Teich, E. (2005), 'Corpus-based register profiling of texts from mechanical engineering'. *Proceedings of the Corpus Linguistics Conference Series,* 1, (1). http://www.corpus.bham.ac.uk/pclc/#complie (date accessed 15 January 2011).

Beach, R. and Anson, C. M. (1992), 'Stance and intertextuality in written discourse'. *Linguistics and Education,* 4, (3–4), 335–57.

Bednarek, M. (2008), *Emotion Talk across Corpora.* Basingstoke: Palgrave Macmillan.

—(2010), 'Corpus linguistics and Systemic Functional Linguistics: Interpersonal meaning, identity and bonding', in M. Bednarek and J. R. Martin (eds), *New Discourse on Language. Functional Perspectives on Multimodality, Identity, and Affiliation.* London: Continuum; pp. 237–66.

Bernard, S. (1999), 'Success and the single girl', *New York,* 26 April. http://nymag.com/nymetro/arts/features/867/ (date accessed 21 January 2005).

Berry, M. (1975), *An Introduction to Systemic Linguistics.* London and Sydney: B.T. Batsford Ltd.

Biber, D. and Finnegan, E. (1989), 'Styles of stance in English: Lexical and grammatical marking of evidentiality and affect'. *Text,* 9, (1), 93–124.

Blood, R. (2002), 'Weblogs: A history and perspective', in R. Blood ed., *We've got Blog: How Weblogs are Changing our Culture.* Cambridge, MA: Perseus Publishing; pp. 7–16.

Boruah, B. (1988), *Fiction and Emotion. A Study in Aesthetics and the Philosophy of Mind.* Oxford: Clarendon Press.

Brewer, M. B. (1988), 'A dual process model of impression formation', in T. K. Srull and R. S. Wyer (eds), *Advances in Social Cognition, Vol. 1.* Hillsdale, NJ: Lawrence Erlbaum; pp. 1–36.

Brooks, L. (1999), 'The joke's on us girls'. *Red Pepper,* December/January.

Burke, M. (2011), *Literary Reading, Cognition and Emotion.* London and New York: Routledge.

Burton, D. (1982), 'Through glass darkly: Through dark glasses', in R. Carter ed., *Language and Literature. An Introductory Reader in Stylistics.* London: George Allen & Unwin; pp. 195–214.

Butler, C. (2004), 'Corpus studies and functional linguistic theories'. *Functions of Language,* 11, (2), 147–86.

Cantor, N. and Mischel, W. (1977), 'Traits as prototypes: Effects on recognition memory'. *Journal of Personality and Social Psychology,* 35, (1), 38–48.

—(1979), 'Prototypes in person perception', in L. Berkowitz ed., *Advances in Experimental Social Psychology, Vol. 12.* New York: Academic Press; pp. 3–52.

Chambers, L. (2004), *Bridget Jones and The Postfeminist Condition: Towards A Genealogy of Thirtysomething Femininities.* Unpublished PhD thesis. Goldsmiths College, University of London.

Chick Lit Books, http://chicklitbooks.com/ (date accessed 28 February 2009)

Chick Lit Writers, http://chicklitwriters.com/ (date accessed 5 November 2010)

Coddington, L. (1997), 'Wavering between worlds: Feminist influence in the romance genre'. *Paradoxa*, 3, (1–2), 58–77.

Cohn, D. (1978), *Transparent Minds: Narrative Modes for Presenting Consciousness in Fiction*. Princeton, NJ: Princeton University Press.

Colgan, J. (2001) 'We know the difference between foie gras and hula hoops, Beryl, but sometimes we just want hula hoops'. *Guardian*, 24 August, http://www.guardian.co.uk/books/2001/aug/24/fiction.fcatures11 (date accessed 31 August 2011).

Conrad, S. and Biber, D. (2000), 'Adverbial marker of stance in speech and writing', in S. Hunston and G. Thompson (eds), *Evaluation in Text. Authorial Stance and the Construction of Discourse*. Oxford: Oxford University Press; pp. 56–73.

Culpeper, J. (2000), 'An approach to characterisation: The case of Katherina in Shakespeare's *The Taming of the Shrew*'. *Language and Literature*, 9, (4), 291–316.

—(2001), *Language & Characterisation. People in Plays & Other Texts*. Harlow: Longman.

—(2002a), 'A cognitive stylistic approach to characterisation', in E. Semino and J. Culpeper (eds), *Cognitive Stylistics: Language and Cognition in Text Analysis*. Amsterdam and Philadelphia: John Benjamins; pp. 251–77.

—(2002b), 'Computers, language and characterisation: An analysis of six characters in Romeo and Juliet', in U. Melander-Marttala, C. Ostman and M. Kyto (eds), *Conversation in Life and in Literature: Papers from the ASLA Symposium*, Association Suedoise de Linguistique Appliquée (ASLA), 15. Universitetstryckeriet: Uppsala; pp. 11–30.

—(2009), 'Keyness: Words, parts-of-speech and semantic categories in the character-talk of Shakespeare's *Romeo and Juliet*'. *International Journal of Corpus Linguistics*, 14, (1), 29–59.

Currie, G. (1997), 'The paradox of caring. Fiction and the philosophy of mind', in M. Hjort and S. Laver (eds), *Emotion and the Arts*. New York and Oxford: Oxford University Press; pp. 63–77.

Damasio, A. R. (1994), *Descartes' Error: Emotion, Reason and the Human Brain*. New York: Avon Books Inc.

Derks, D., Bos, A. E. R. and von Grumbkow, J. (2007), 'Emoticons and social interaction on the Internet: the importance of social context'. *Computers in Human Behaviour*, 23, (1), 842–9.

—(2008), 'Emoticons and online message interpretation'. *Social Science Computer Review*, 26, (3), 379–88.

Dixon, J. (1999), *The Romance Fiction of Mills & Boon, 1909–1990s*. London: Routledge.

Djikic, M., Oatley, K., Zoeterman, S. and Peterson, J. (2009), 'On being moved by art: How reading fiction transforms the self'. *Creativity Research Journal*, 21, (1), 24–9.

Donadio, R. (2006), 'The chick-lit pandemic'. *New York Times*, 19 March. http://www.nytimes.com/2006/03/19/books/review/19donadio.html?_r=2&pagewanted=print (date accessed 19 May 2008).

Drotner, K. (1991), 'Intensities of feeling: Modernity, melodrama, and adolescence'. *Theory, Culture and Society*, 8, (1), 57–87.

Dutta, S. and Kanungo, R. N. (1975), *Affect and Memory: A Reformulation*. Oxford: Pergamon Press.

Eggins, S. (1994), *An Introduction to Systemic Functional Linguistics*. London: Continuum.

—(2004), *An Introduction to Systemic Functional Linguistics* (2nd edition). London: Continuum.

Ehow, http://www.ehow.com/how_4500646_write-chick-lit-novel.html (date accessed 10 August 2011)

Evans, H. (2009), 'Don't patronise popular fiction by women'. *Guardian Online*, 11 November. http://www.guardian.co.uk/books/booksblog/2009/nov/11/dont-patronise-popular-fiction-women (date accessed 11 March 2011).

Ezard, J. (2001), 'Bainbridge tilts at "chick lit" cult'. *Guardian*, 24 August. http://www.guardian.co.uk/uk/2001/aug/24/books.generalfiction (date accessed 19 December 2010).

Felici, J. (2003), *The Complete Manual of Typography. A Guide to Setting Perfect Type*. Berkeley: Peachpit Press.

Ferriss, S. and Young, M. (eds) (2006), *Chick Lit. The New Woman's Fiction*. New York and London: Routledge.

—(2008), 'Introduction: Chick flicks and chick culture', in. S. Ferriss and M. Young (eds), *Chick Flicks. Contemporary Women at the Movies*. New York and London: Routledge; pp. 1–25.

Fischer-Starcke, B. (2009), 'Keywords and frequent phrases of Jane Austen's *Pride and Prejudice*. A corpus-stylistic analysis'. *International Journal of Corpus Linguistics*, 14, (4), 492–523.

—(2010), *Corpus Linguistics in Literary Analysis. Jane Austen and her Contemporaries*. London: Continuum.

Fiske, S. and Taylor, Sh. E. (1991), *Social Cognition* (2nd edition). New York: McGraw-Hill Inc.

Flesch, J. (2004), *From Australia with Love: A History of Modern Australian Popular Romance Novels*. Fremantle: Curtin University Books.

Forceville, C. (2002), 'The identification of target and source in pictorial metaphors'. *Journal of Pragmatics*, 34, (1), 1–14.

—(2006), 'Non-verbal and multimodal metaphor in a cognitivist framework: Agendas for research', in G. Kristiansen, M. Achard, R. Dirven and F. J. Ruiz de Mendoza Ibáñez (eds), *Cognitive Linguistics: Current Applications and Future Perspective*. Berlin, New York: Mouton de Gruyter; pp. 379–402.

—(2007), 'Multimodal metaphor in ten Dutch TV commercials'. *The Public Journal of Semiotics*, 1, (1), 19–51.

—(2009), 'Metonymy in visual and audiovisual discourse', in J. Moya and E. Ventola (eds), *The World Told and the World Shown: Issues in Multisemiotics*. Basingstoke and New York: Palgrave Macmillan; pp. 56–74.

Francis, G. (1993), 'A corpus-driven approach to grammar: Principles, methods and examples', in M. Baker, G. Francis and E. Tognini-Bonelli (eds), *Text and*

Technology: In honour of John Sinclair. Amsterdam and Philadelphia: John Benjamins; pp. 137–57.

Frijda, N. H. (1986), *The Emotions.* Cambridge: Cambridge University Press.

Gavins, J. (2005), 'The year's work in stylistics 2004. Old dogs, new tricks'. *Language and Literature,* 14, (4), 397–408.

Georgakopoulou, A. and Goutsos, D. (1997), *Discourse Analysis: An Introduction.* Edinburgh: Edinburgh University Press.

Gill, R. and Herdieckerhoff, E. (2006), 'Rewriting the romance'. *Feminist Media Studies,* 6, (4), 487–504.

Gilligan, S. G. and Bower, G. (1984), 'Cognitive consequences of emotional arousal', in C. E. Izard, J. Kagan and R. B. Zajonc (eds), *Emotions, Cognition, and Behavior.* Cambridge: Cambridge University Press; pp. 547–88.

Goade, S. ed. (2007), *Empowerment versus Oppression: Twenty-First Century Views of Popular Romance Novels.* Cambridge: Cambridge Scholars.

Gormley, S. (2009), 'Introduction'. *Working Papers on the Web,* 13. http://extra.shu.ac.uk/wpw/chicklit/gormley.html (date accessed 10 March 2011).

Hakemulder, J. (2000), *The Moral Laboratory: Experiments Examining the Effects of Reading Literature on Social Perception and Moral Self-Knowledge.* Amsterdam: John Benjamins.

—(2007), 'Tracing foregrounding in responses to film'. *Language and Literature,* 16, (2), 125–39.

Halliday, M. A. K. (1966), 'Notes on transitivity and theme in English, Part 1'. *Journal of Linguistics,* 3, 37–81 (reprinted in J. Webster ed. (2005), *Studies in English Language. M. A. K. Halliday.* London, New York: Continuum; pp. 5–54).

—(1967), 'Notes on transitivity and theme in English, Part 2'. *Journal of Linguistics,* 3, 199–244 (reprinted in J. Webster ed. (2005), *Studies in English Language. M. A. K. Halliday.* London, New York: Continuum; pp. 55–109).

—(1968), 'Notes on transitivity and theme in English, Part 3'. *Journal of Linguistics,* 4, 179–215 (reprinted in J. Webster ed. (2005), *Studies in English Language. M. A. K. Halliday.* London, New York: Continuum; pp. 110–53).

—(1971), 'Linguistic function and literary style: An inquiry into the language of William Golding's *The Inheritors*', in D. C. Freeman ed. (1981), *Essays in Modern Stylistics.* London and New York: Methuen; pp. 325–60.

—(1994), *An Introduction to Functional Grammar* (2nd edition). London: Hodder Arnold.

Halliday, M. A. K. and Matthiessen, Ch. M. I. M (2004), *An Introduction to Functional Grammar* (3rd edition). London: Hodder Arnold.

Hanson, C. (2004), 'Fiction, feminism and femininity from the eighties to the noughties', in E. Parker ed., *Contemporary British Women Writers.* Cambridge: D. S. Brewer; pp. 16–27.

Harzewski, S. (2006), 'Tradition and displacement in the new novel of manners', in S. Ferriss and M. Young (eds), *Chick Lit: The New Woman's Fiction.* New York and London: Routledge; pp. 29–46.

Henry, A. (2004), 'Orgasms and empowerment: *Sex and the City* and the third wave feminism', in K. Akass and J. McCabe (eds), *Reading Sex and the City*. London and New York: I. B. Tauris; pp. 65–82.

Hogan, P. C. (2003), *Cognitive Science, Literature and the Arts*. New York and London: Routledge.

Hollows, J. (2000), *Feminism, Femininity and Popular Culture*. Manchester and New York: Manchester University Press.

Hoover, D. (2009), 'Word frequency, statistical stylistics and authorship attribution', in D. Archer ed., *What's in a Word-List? Investigating Word Frequency and Keyword Extraction*. Farnham: Ashgate; pp. 35–52.

Hunston, S. (2011), *Corpus Approaches to Evaluation. Phraseology and Evaluative Language*. London and New York: Routledge.

Jackson, S. (1993), 'Love and romance as objects of feminist knowledge', in M. Kennedy, C. Lubelska and V. Walsh (eds), *Making Connections: Women's Studies, Women's Movements, Women's Lives*. London & Washington: Taylor & Francis; pp. 39–50.

Jakobson, R. and Halle, M. (1956), *Fundamentals of Language*. The Hague: Mouton.

James, W. (1884), 'What is an emotion?'. *Mind*, 9, 188–205.

Jeffries, L. (2007), *Textual Construction of the Female Body. A Critical Discourse Approach*. Basingstoke: Palgrave Macmillan.

Johnson, M. (2007), *The Meaning of the Body. Aesthetics of Human Understanding*. Chicago and London: The University of Chicago Press.

Jones, A. (1986), 'Mills & Boon meets feminism', in J. Radford ed., *The Progress of Romance. The Politics of Popular Fiction*. London and New York: Routledge; pp. 195–218.

Jones, E. (2008), 'Inside the world of chick lit'. *BBC News*, 21 June, http://news.bbc.co.uk/2/hi/entertainment/7463417.stm (date accessed 21 January 2010).

Jones, R. (2001), 'Female fiction dumbs down'. *BBC News*, 23 August, http://news.bbc.co.uk/2/hi/entertainment/1504733.stm (date accessed 31 August 2011).

Kennedy, C. (1982), 'Systemic grammar and its use in literary analysis', in R. Carter ed., *Language and Literature. An Introductory Reader in Stylistics*. London: George Allen & Unwin; pp. 83–99.

Kiernan, A. (2006), 'No satisfaction: *Sex and the City, Run Catch Kiss*, and the conflict of desires in Chick Lit's new heroines', in S. Ferriss and M. Young (eds), *Chick Lit: The New Woman's Fiction*. New York and London: Routledge; pp. 207–18.

Kinsale, L. (1992), 'The androgynous reader: Point of view in romance', in J. A. Krentz ed., *Dangerous Men and Adventurous Women. Romance Writers on the Appeal of the Romance*. Philadelphia: University of Pennsylvania Press; pp. 31–44.

Kirk, J. M. (2009), 'Word frequency use or misuse?', in D. Archer ed., *What's in a Word-List? Investigating Word Frequency and Keyword Extraction*. Farnham: Ashgate; pp. 17–34.

Kleinginna, P. R. Jnr. and Kleinginna, A. M. (1981), 'A categorized list of emotion definitions with suggestions for a consensual definition'. *Motivation and Emotion*, 5, (4), 345–79.

Knowles, J. (2004a), 'Editorial'. *Diegesis: Journal of the Association for Research in Popular Fictions* (Special Issue on Chick Lit), 8, 3–4.

—(2004b), 'Material girls: Location and economics in Chicklit fiction, or, how singletons finance their Jimmy Choo collections'. *Diegesis: Journal of the Association for Research in Popular Fictions* (Special Issue on Chick Lit), 8, 37–42.

—(2008), '"Our foes are almost as many as our readers": Debating the worth of women reading and writing – the case of chick-lit'. *Popular Narrative Media*, 1, (2), 217–31.

Koller, V. (2008) '"Not just a colour": pink as a gender and sexuality marker in visual communication'. *Visual Communication*, 7, (4), 395–423.

Konchar Farr, C. (2009), 'It was chick lit all along. The gendering of a genre', in L. J. Goren ed., *You've Come a Long Way. Politics, Feminism and Popular Culture*. Kentucky: The University of Kentucky Press; pp. 201–14.

Kress, G. (2010), *Multimodality. A Social Semiotic Approach to Contemporary Communication*. London: Routledge.

Kress, G. and van Leeuwen, T. (1996), *Reading Images: The Grammar of Visual Design* (1st edition). London and New York: Routledge.

—(2001), *Multimodal Discourse: The Modes and Media of Contemporary Communication*. London: Arnold.

—(2002), 'Colour as a semiotic order: notes for a grammar of colour'. *Visual Communication*, 1, (3), 343–68.

—(2006), *Reading Images: The Grammar of Visual Design* (2nd edition). London and New York: Routledge.

Krohn, F. B. (2004), 'A generational approach to using emoticons as nonverbal communication'. *Journal of Technical Writing and Communication*, 34, (4), 321–8.

Laird, J., Wagener, J., Halal, M. and Szegda, M. (1982), 'Remembering what you feel: Effects of emotion on memory'. *Journal of Personality and Social Psychology*, 42, (4), 646–57.

Lamarque, P. (1981), 'How can we fear and pity fictions?'. *British Journal of Aesthetics*, 21, (4), 291–304.

Lazar, M. (2006), 'Discover the power of femininity! Analysing global "Power Femininity" in local advertising'. *Feminist Media Studies*, 6, (4), 505–17.

Leech, G. and Short, M. (1981), *Style in Fiction. A Linguistic Introduction to English Fictional Prose*. Harlow: Longman.

—(2007), *Style in Fiction. A Linguistic Introduction to English Fictional Prose* (2nd edition). Harlow: Longman.

Lessing, D. (2001), 'Bainbridge denounces chick-lit as "froth"'. *Guardian Online*, http://www.guardian.co.uk/books/2001/aug/23/bookerprize2001.bookerprize?INTCMP=SRCH (date accessed 21 January 2011).

Levorato, A. (2009), '"Be steady then, my countrymen, be firm, united and determined". Expressions of stance in the 1798–1800 Irish paper war'. *Journal of Historical Pragmatics*, 10, (1), 132–57.

Lindauer, M. S. (2009), *Psyche and the Literary Muses: The Contribution of Literary Content to Scientific Psychology*. Amsterdam and Philadelphia: John Benjamins.

Long, E. (2003), *Book Clubs: Women and the Uses of Reading in Everyday Life*. Chicago: The University of Chicago Press.

Lupton, E. (2004), *Thinking with Type: A Critical Guide for Designers, Writers, Editors and Students*. New York: Princeton Architectural Press.

Lutz, D. (2006), *The Dangerous Lover: Gothic Villains, Byronism, and the Nineteenth-Century Seduction Narrative*. Ohio: Ohio State University Press.

Lynn S. N. (2006), *Romancing God: Evangelical Women and Inspirational Fiction*. Chapel Hill, NC: University of North Carolina Press.

Machin, D. (2010), *Introduction to Multimodal Analysis*. London: Bloomsbury Academic.

Mahlberg, M. (2007a), 'Clusters, key clusters and local textual functions in Dickens'. *Corpora*, 2, (1), 1–31.

—(2007b), 'A corpus stylistic perspective on Dickens' *Great Expectations*', in M. Lambrou and P. Stockwell (eds), *Contemporary Stylistics*. London: Continuum; pp. 19–31.

Mahlberg, M. and Smith, C. (2010), 'Corpus approaches to prose fiction: Civility and body language in *Pride and Prejudice*', in D. McIntyre and B. Busse (eds), *Language and Style*. Basingstoke: Palgrave Macmillan; pp. 449–67.

Mar, R. A., Oatley, K., Hirsh, J., de la Paz, J. and Peterson, J. B. (2006), 'Bookworms versus nerds: Exposure to fiction versus non-fiction, divergent associations with social ability, and the simulation of fictional social worlds'. *Journal of Research in Personality*, 40, (5), 694–712.

Marsh, K. (2004), 'Contextualizing *Bridget Jones*'. *College Literature*, 31, (1), 52–72.

Martin, J. R., Matthiessen, C. M. I. M. and Painter, C. (1997), *Working with Functional Grammar*. London: Arnold.

Martin, J. R. and White, P. R. R. (2005), *The Language of Evaluation: Appraisal in English*. London: Palgrave MacMillan.

Martins, D. (1982), 'Influence of affect on comprehension of a text'. *Text*, 2, (1–3), 141–54.

Mazza, C. (2006), 'Who's laughing now? A short history of chick lit and the perversion of a genre', in S. Ferriss and M. Young (eds), *Chick Lit. The New Woman's Fiction*. New York and Abingdon: Routledge; pp. 17–28.

Mazza, C. and DeShell, J. (eds) (1995), *Chick-Lit: Post-feminist Fiction*. Florida: FC2.

McArthur, T. (1981), *Longman Lexicon of Contemporary English*. London: Longman.

McCann, C. D. and Higgins, T. (1990), 'Social cognition and communication', in H. Giles and W. P. Robinson (eds), *Handbook of Social Psychology*. Chichester: John Wiley & Sons; pp. 13–32.

McIntyre, D. (fc. 2012), 'Prototypical characteristics of blockbuster movie dialogue: a corpus stylistic perspective'. *Texas Studies in Literature and Language*, 54(1).

—(fc. 2013), 'Corpora and literature', in C. Chappelle ed., *Wiley Blackwell Encyclopedia of Applied Linguistics*. Oxford: Wiley Blackwell.

McIntyre, D. and Archer, D. (2010), 'A corpus-based approach to mind style'. *Journal of Literary Semantics*, 39, (2), 167–82.

McIntyre, D., Bellard-Thomson, C., Heywood, J., McEnery, A., Semino, E. and Short, M. (2004), 'Investigating the presentation of speech, writing and thought in spoken British English: a corpus-based approach'. *ICAME Journal*, 28, 49–76.

McKenzie, M. (1987), 'Free indirect speech in a fettered insecure society'. *Language and Communication*, 7, (2), 153–9.

McRobbie, A. (2004), 'Postfeminism and popular culture: *Bridget Jones* and the new gender regime', in A. Harris ed., *All about the Girl: Culture, Power and Identity*. New York and London: Routledge; pp. 3–14.

Merrick, E. (2006a), '*This is not Chick Lit*: What's in a title'. *Huffington Post*, http://www.huffingtonpost.com/elizabeth-merrick/this-is-not-chick-lit-wha_b_26838.html (date accessed 10 August 2007).

—ed. (2006b), *This is not Chick Lit. Original Stories by America's Best Women Writers*. New York: Random House Trade.

Meutsch, D. (1986), 'Mental models in literary discourse: Towards the integration of linguistic and psychological levels of description'. *Poetics*, 15, (3), 307–31.

Miall, D. (2008), '"Too soon transplanted": Coleridge and the forms of dislocation', in W. van Peer ed., *The Quality of Literature: Linguistic Studies in Literary Evaluation*. Amsterdam and Philadelphia: John Benjamins; pp. 95–116.

Miall, D. and Kuiken, D. (1994), 'Beyond text theory: Understanding literary response'. *Discourse Processes*, 17, (3), 337–52.

Miller, L. (2004), Email interview quoted in Mazza, C. (2006), 'Who's laughing now? A short history of chick lit and the perversion of a genre', in S. Ferriss and M. Young (eds), *Chick Lit. The New Woman's Fiction*. New York and Abingdon: Routledge; pp. 17–28.

Mills & Boon, http://www.millsandboon.co.uk/ (date accessed 21 January 2010)

Mlynowski, S. and Jacobs, F. (2006), *See Jane Write: A Girl's Guide to Writing Chick Lit*. Philadelphia: Quirk Books.

Modleski, T. (1984), *Loving with a Vengeance. Mass-Produced Fantasies for Women*. London: Methuen.

—(2008), *Loving with a Vengeance. Mass-Produced Fantasies for Women* (2nd edition). New York and London: Routledge.

Montoro, R. (2003), '"Shall we meet for lunch, darling?" or the evaluation of contemporary fiction from a socio-stylistic perspective', in S. Cşabi and J. Zerkowitz (eds), *Textual Secrets: The Message of the Medium*. Budapest: Eötvös Loránd University; pp. 468–77.

—(2007), 'The stylistics of popular fiction: A socio-cognitive perspective', in M. Lambrou and P. Stockwell (eds), *Contemporary Stylistics*. London: Continuum; pp. 68–80.

Myers, G. (2009), 'Stylistics and "reading-in-talk"'. *Language and Literature*, 18, (3), 338–44.

Nørgaard, N. (2003), *Systemic Functional Linguistics and Literary Analysis. A Hallidayan Approach to Joyce. A Joycean Approach to Halliday*. Odense: University Press of Southern Denmark.

—(2009), 'The semiotics of typography in literary texts. A multimodal approach'. *Orbis Litterarum*, 64, (2), 141–60.

—(2010a), 'Multimodality: extending the stylistic tool-kit', in D. McIntyre and B. Busse (eds), *Language and Style*. Basingstoke: Palgrave Macmillan; pp. 433–48.

—(2010b), 'Modality. Commitment, truth value and reality claims across modes in multimodal novels'. *Journal of Literary Theory*, 4, (1), 63–80.

—(2010c), 'Multimodality and the literary text. Making sense of Safran Foer's *Extremely Loud and Incredibly Close*', in R. Page ed., *New Perspectives on Narrative and Multimodality*. London and New York: Routledge; pp. 115–26.

Nørgaard, N., Busse, B. and Montoro, R. (2010), *Key Terms in Stylistics*. London: Continuum.

O'Halloran, K. (2007), 'Corpus-assisted literary evaluation'. *Corpora*, 2, (1), 33–63.

O'Halloran, K. L. ed. (2004), *Multimodal Discourse Analysis*. London: Continuum.

Oatley, K. (1992), *Best Laid Schemes: The Psychology of Emotions*. Cambridge: Cambridge University Press.

—(1994), 'A taxonomy of the emotions of literary response and a theory of identification in fictional narrative'. *Poetics*, 23, (1–2), 53–74.

—(2003), 'Emotional expression and experience in the visual and narrative arts', in R. J. Davidson, K. R. Scherer and H. H. Goldsmith (eds), *Handbook of the Affective Sciences*. New York: Oxford University Press, pp. 481–502.

—(2011), 'Fiction and its study as gateways to the mind'. *Scientific Study of Literature*, 1, (1), 153–64.

Oatley, K. and Jenkins, J. M. (1996), *Understanding Emotions*. Oxford: Blackwell.

Oatley, K. and Johnson-Laird, P. N. (1987), 'Towards a cognitive theory of emotions'. *Cognition and Emotion*, 1, (1), 29–50.

Oliver, M. B. (1993), 'Exploring the paradox of the enjoyment of the sad films'. *Human Communication Research*, 19, (3), 315–42.

Oliver, M. B., Weaver III, J. B. and Sargent, S. L. (2000), 'An examination of factors related to sex differences in enjoyment of sad films'. *Journal of Broadcasting and Electronic Media*, 44, (2), 282–300.

Opas, L. L. and Tweedie, F. J. (1999), 'The magic carpet ride: Reader involvement in romantic fiction'. *Literary and Linguistic Computing*, 14, (1), 89–101.

Opas-Hänninen, L. L. and Seppänen, T. (2010), '2D and 3D visualization of stance in popular fiction', in. D. McIntyre and B. Busse (eds), *Language and Style.* Basingstoke: Palgrave Macmillan, pp. 272–92.

Paizis, G. (1998a), *Love and the Novel. The Poetics and Politics of Romantic Fiction.* Basingstoke: Macmillan.

—(1998b), 'Category romances. Translation, realism and myth'. *The Translator,* 4, (1), 1–24.

Parkinson, B. (1995), *Ideas and Realities of Emotion.* London: Routledge.

Parkinson, B., Fishcher, A. H. and Manstead, A. S. R. (2005), *Emotion in Social Relations. Cultural, Group, and Interpersonal Processes.* New York and Hove: Psychology Press.

Pearce, L. and Stacey, J. (eds) (1995), *Romance Revisited.* London: Lawrence & Wishart.

Pelling, R. (2000), 'You've only got yourself to blame, Bridget Jones ...'. *Daily Mail,* 6 April.

Pennington, D. C. (2000), *Social Cognition.* London: Routledge.

Pérez Serrano, E. (2009), 'Chick Lit and Marian Keyes: The ideological background of the genre'. *Working Papers on the Web,* 13. http://extra.shu.ac.uk/wpw/chicklit/gormley.html (date accessed 10 March 2011).

Phillips, M. (1989), 'Lexical structure of text'. *Discourse Analysis Monographs 12.* Birmingham: University of Birmingham.

Picard, R. (1997), *Affective Computing.* Cambridge, MA: MIT Press.

Provine, R. R., Spencer, R. J. and Mandell, D. L. (2007), 'Emotional expression online. Emoticons punctuate website text messages'. *Journal of Language and Social Psychology,* 26, (3), 299–307.

Radway, J. (1991), *Reading the Romance. Women, Patriarchy, and Popular Literature* (2nd edition). Chapel Hill, NC, and London: The University of North Carolina Press.

Rayson, P. (2009), *Wmatrix: A Web-based Corpus Processing Environment,* Computing Department, Lancaster University. http://ucrel.lancs.ac.uk/wmatrix/ (date accessed 15 July 2010).

Rayson, P., Archer, D., Piao, S. and McEnery, T. (2004), 'The UCREL semantic analysis system'. *Proceedings of the Workshop on Beyond Named Entity Recognition Semantic Labelling for NLP Tasks,* in association with the 4th International Conference on Language Resources and Evaluation (LREC 2004), Lisbon, Portugal; pp. 7–12.

Regis, P. (2003), *A Natural History of the Romance Novel.* Pennsylvania: University of Pennsylvania Press.

Rimmon-Kenan, Sh. (2002), *Narrative Fiction. Contemporary Poetics* (2nd edition). London and New York: Routledge.

Rochelle Mabry, A. (2006), 'About a girl: Female subjectivity and sexuality in contemporary "chick" culture', in S. Ferriss and M. Young (eds), *Chick Lit. The New Woman's Fiction.* New York and London: Routledge; pp. 191–206.

Roeh, I. and Nir, R. (1990), 'Speech presentation in the Israel radio news: Ideological constraints and rhetorical strategies'. *Text,* 10, (3), 225–44.

Romance Writers of America, http://www.rwanational.org/cs/the_romance_genre (date accessed 24 December 2007).

Romantic Novelists' Association, http://www.rna-uk.org/index.php?page=romanticfiction (date accessed 24 December 2007).

Royle, N. (1996), 'Yarn in the USA'. *Time Out: London*, 3 July.

Rumelhart, D. E. (1984), 'Schemata and the cognitive system', in R. S. Wyer and T. K. Srull (eds), *Handbook of Social Cognition*, Vol. 1. Hillsdale, NJ: Lawrence Erlbaum; pp. 161–88.

Russell Williams, I. (2010), 'Pink books make me see red'. *Guardian Online*, 28 July. http://www.guardian.co.uk/books/booksblog/2010/jul/28/queen-of-teen-award-pink-book-covers#start-of-comments (date accessed 3 August 2010).

Ryder, M. E. (1999) 'Smoke and mirrors. Event patterns in the discourse structure of a romance novel'. *Journal of Pragmatics*, 31, (8), 1067–80.

Schramm, H. and Wirth, W. (2010), 'Exploring the paradox of sad-film enjoyment: The role of multiple appraisals and meta-appraisals'. *Poetics*, 38, (3), 319–35.

Selinger, E. (2007), 'Rereading the romance'. *Contemporary Literature*, 48, (2), 307–24.

Semino, E. and Culpeper, J. (1997), 'Using a computer corpus to test a model of speech and thought presentation'. *Poetics*, 25, (1), 17–43.

Semino, E. and Short, M. (2004), *Corpus Stylistics: Speech, Writing and Thought Presentation in a Corpus of English Writing*. London: Routledge.

Semino, E., Short, M. and Wynne, M. (1999), 'Hypothetical words and thoughts in contemporary British narratives'. *Narrative*, 7, (3), 307–34.

Shipley, D. (2008), 'The great chick lit cover-up'. *Guardian Online*, 29 July. http://www.guardian.co.uk/books/booksblog/2008/jul/29/thegreatchicklitcoverup (date accessed 25 June 2011).

Short, M. (1988), 'Speech presentation, the novel and the press', in W. van Peer ed., *The Taming of the Text*. London: Routledge; pp. 61–81.

—(1996), *Exploring the Language of Poems, Plays and Prose*. Harlow: Longman.

—(2003), 'A corpus-based approach to speech, thought and writing presentation', in A. Wilson, P. Rayson and T. McEnery (eds), *Corpus Linguistics by the Lune: A Festschrift for Geoffrey Leech*. Frankfurt: Peter Lang; pp. 241–71.

Short, M. and Semino, E. (2008), 'Evaluation and stylistic analysis', in W. van Peer ed., *The Quality of Literature: Linguistic Studies in Literary Evaluation*. Amsterdam and Philadelphia: John Benjamins; pp. 117–37.

Short, M., Semino, E. and Culpeper, J. (1996), 'Using a corpus for stylistics research: speech and thought presentation', in J. Thomas and M. Short (eds), *Using Corpora in Language Research*. London: Longman; pp. 110–31.

Short, M., Semino, E. and Wynne, M. (2002), 'Revisiting the notion of faithfulness in discourse presentation using a corpus approach'. *Language and Literature*, 11, (4), 325–55.

Short, M., Wynne, M. and Semino, E. (1999), 'Reading reports: discourse presentation in a corpus of narratives with special reference to news reports', in H. J. Diller, E. Otto, and G. Stratmann (eds), *English via Various Media.* Heidelberg: Universitätsverlag C, Heidelberg; pp. 39–66.

Simon-Vandenbergen, A. M. (2008), '*Almost certainly* and *most definitely*: degree modifiers and epistemic stance'. *Journal of Pragmatics,* 40, (9), 1521–42.

Simpson, P. (1993), *Language, Ideology and Point of View.* London: Routledge.

Smith, C. (2008), *Cosmopolitan Culture and Consumerism in Chick Lit.* New York and London: Routledge.

Snitow, A. B. (1986), 'Mass market romance: pornography for women is different', in A. Snitow, Ch. Stansell and Sh. Thompson (eds), *Desire: The Politics of Sexuality.* London: Virago; pp. 258–75.

Stone, P. (2008), 'Review of 2007: Paperbacks ride high'. *The Bookseller,* 18 January. http://www.thebookseller.com/in-depth/feature/51638-review-of-2007-paperbacks-ride-high.html (date accessed 5 March 2008).

Swann, J. and Allington, D. (2009), 'Reading groups and the language of literary texts: A case study in social reading'. *Language and Literature,* 18, (3), 247–64.

Tan, E. (1996), *Emotion and the Narrative Film: Film as an Emotion Machine.* Hillsdale, NJ: Lawrence Erlbaum Associates.

The Adventurous Writer, http://theadventurouswriter.com/blogwriting/chick-lit-writing-tips-how-to-write-chick-lit-for-women/ (date accessed 10 July 2011)

Thomas, S. (2002a), 'The great chick lit conspiracy'. *Independent. Books,* 4 August. http://www.independent.co.uk/arts-entertainment/books/features/the-great-chick-lit-conspiracy-638935.html (date accessed 30 January 2011).

Thomas, S. (2002b), *Going Out.* London: Forth Estate.

Thompson, G. (2008), 'From process to pattern: methodological considerations in analysing transitivity in text', in C. Jones and E. Ventola (eds), *From Language to Multimodality. New Developments in the Study of Ideational Meaning.* London: Equinox; pp. 17–33.

Thompson, G. and Hunston, S. (2000), 'Evaluation: An introduction', in S. Hunston and G. Thompson (eds), *Evaluation in Text. Authorial Stance and the Construction of Discourse.* Oxford: Oxford University Press; pp. 1–27.

Tognini-Bonelli, E. (2001), *Corpus Linguistics at Work.* Amsterdam and Philadelphia: John Benjamins.

Trachtenberg, J. (2005), 'Chick Lit goes "glam": why novelists are pushing stylish, powerful women'. *Wall Street Journal,* 15 October, http://www.josie-brown.com/josie_brown/about-true-hollywood-lies/ (date accessed 18 March 2011).

Traister, R. (2005), 'Women's studies: Chick lit is often dissed for being trashy and dumb. Back off! These novels of fashion and family are recording women's history'. *Salon.com,* 1 November, http://dir.salon.com/story/books/feature/2005/11/01/chick_lit/index.html (date accessed 10 November 2010).

Tulving, E. (1972), 'Episodic and semantic memory', in E. Tulving and W. Donaldson (eds), *Organization of Memory.* New York: Academic Press; pp. 382–403.

Umminger, A. (2006), 'Supersizing Bridget Jones: What's really eating the women in Chick Lit', in S. Ferriss and M. Young (eds), *Chick Lit: The New Woman's Fiction.* New York and London: Routledge; pp. 239–52.

van Dijk, T.A. (1987), *Communicating Racism: Ethnic Prejudice in Thought and Talk.* Newbury Park: Sage.

—(1988), 'Social cognition, social power and social discourse'. *Text,* 8, (1–2), 129–57.

—(1990), 'Social cognition and discourse', in H. Giles and W. P. Robinson (eds), *Handbook of Language and Social Psychology.* Chichester: Wiley; pp. 163–83.

van Leeuwen, T. (1999), *Speech, Music, Sound.* London: Macmillan.

—(2005a), *Introducing Social Semiotics.* Abingdon and New York: Routledge.

—(2005b), 'Typographic meaning'. *Visual Communication,* 4, (2), 137–43.

—(2006), 'Towards a semiotics of typography'. *Information Design Journal + Document Design,* 14, (2), 139–55.

van Peer, W. (1986), *Stylistics and Psychology: Investigations of Foregrounding.* London: Croom Helm.

—(1992), 'Literary theory and reader response', in E. F. Nardocchio ed., *Reader Response to Literature: The Empirical Dimension.* Berlin and New York: Mouton de Gruyter; pp. 137–52.

—(1994), 'Emotional functions of reading literature', in R. Sell and P. Verdonk (eds), *Literature and the New Interdisciplinarity: Poetics, Linguistics, History.* Amsterdam: Rodopi; pp. 209–20.

—(1997), 'Towards a poetics of emotion', in M. Hjort and S. Laver (eds), *Emotion and the Arts.* Oxford: Oxford University Press; pp. 215–24.

—(2007), 'Introduction to foregrounding: A state of the art'. *Language and Literature,* 16, (2), 99–104.

—(2008), 'The evaluation of literary texts: A new perspective', in W. van Peer ed., *The Quality of Literature: Linguistic Studies in Literary Evaluation.* Amsterdam and Philadelphia: John Benjamins; pp. 1–14.

van Peer, W., Hakemulder, J. and Zyngier, S. (eds) (2007a), *Muses and Measures: Empirical Research Methods for the Humanities.* Cambridge: Cambridge Scholars Press.

—(2007b), 'Lines on feeling: Foregrounding, aesthetics, and meaning'. *Language and Literature,* 16, (2), 197–213.

Walker, B. (2010), 'Wmatrix, key concepts and the narrators in Julian Barnes's *Talking it Over*', in D. McIntyre and B. Busse (eds), *Language and Style.* Basingstoke: Palgrave Macmillan; pp. 364–87.

Walther, J. B. and D'Addario, K. P. (2001), 'The impacts of emoticons on message interpretation in computer-mediated communication'. *Social Science Computer Review,* 19, (3), 324–47.

Wareing, S. (1994), 'And then he kissed her: The reclamation of female characters to submissive roles in contemporary fiction', in K. Wales ed., *Feminist Linguistics in Literary Criticism.* Cambridge: D. S. Brewer; pp. 117–36.

Warhol, R. (2003), *Having a Good Cry. Effeminate Feelings and Pop-Culture Forms.* Columbus: The Ohio State University Press.

Webster, J. ed. (2005), *Studies in English Language. M. A. K. Halliday*. London and New York: Continuum.

Westerman, S. J., Sutherland, E. J., Robinson, L., Powell, H. and Tuck, G. (2007), 'A multi-method approach to the assessment of web page designs', in A. Paiva, R. Prada and R.W. Picard (eds), *Affective Computing and Intelligent Interaction. Lecture Notes in Computer Science, 4738*. Berlin and Heidelberg: Springer-Verlag; pp. 302–13.

Whelehan, I. (2000), *Overloaded. Popular Culture and the Future of Feminism*. London: The Women's Press.

—(2002), *Helen Fielding's Bridget Jones's Diary. A Reader's Guide*. New York and London: Continuum.

—(2004), 'Sex and the single girl: Helen Fielding, Erica Jong and Helen Gurley Brown', in E. Parker ed., *Contemporary British Women Writers*. Cambridge: D. S. Brewer; pp. 28–40.

—(2005), *The Feminist Bestseller*. Basingstoke: Palgrave.

Wolcott, J. (1996), 'Hear me purr: Maureen Dowd and the rise of postfeminist chick lit'. *The New Yorker*, 20 May, 54–9.

Wollheim, R. (1980), 'On persons and their lives', in A. Oksenberg Rorty ed., *Explaining Emotions*. Berkeley: University of California Press; pp. 299–321.

Yanal, R. J. (1994), 'The paradox of emotion and fiction'. *Pacific Philosophical Quarterly*, 75, (1), 54–75.

—(1999), *Paradoxes of Emotion and Fiction*. University Park, Pennsylvania: The Pennsylvania State University Press.

Yang, Ch., Lin, K. H.Y and Chen, H. H. (2007), 'Building emotion lexicon from weblog corpora'. *Proceedings of the Association for Computational Linguistics*, 133–6.

Yardley, C. (2006), *Will Write for Shoes. How to Write a Chick Lit Novel*. New York: St. Martin's Press.

Zyngier, S., Hakemulder, J. and Van Peer, W. (2007), 'Complexity and foregrounding. In the eye of the beholder?'. *Poetics Today*, 28, (4), 653–82.

Index